MAKING BUDGETS

Volume 63, Sage Library of Social Research

Sage Library of Social Research

making budgets

Public Resource Allocation

JAMES N. DANZIGER

Preface by Robert T. Golembiewski

Volume 63
SAGE LIBRARY OF
SOCIAL RESEARCH

 **SAGE PUBLICATIONS**   Beverly Hills   London

For information address:

SAGE PUBLICATIONS, INC.
275 South Beverly Drive
Beverly Hills, California 90212

SAGE PUBLICATIONS LTD
28 Banner Street
London EC1Y 8QE

Printed in the United States of America

Library of Congress Cataloging in Publication Data

Danziger, James N
    Making budgets.

    (Sage library of social research ; v. 63)
    Bibliography: p. 241
    1. Local budgets—Great Britain. I. Title.
HJ9423.D35   352'.12'0941   78-2394
ISBN 0-8039-0999-3
ISBN 0-8039-1010-X pbk.

FIRST PRINTING

CONTENTS

*To My Parents
and to Lesley*

PREFACE

REFLECTIONS ON A TRADITION OF INQUIRY

One of the joys of the research craft lies in seeing a good project grow and develop. Thus some projects will generate results of unexpected depth. And a precious few projects will evolve into a "tradition of inquiry." The feelings may be most pleasant in the case of one's own project, but the pleasure also extends to the work of others.

James Danziger's *Making Budgets* permits such pleasure. Let me review some history. A few years ago, I served on the Leonard D. White Award Committee of the American Political Science Association, which recognized Danziger's dissertation as the year's best in the field of public administration. The Committee's citation minced no words about their choice.

> This dissertation was outstanding in quality of prose style, statistical sophistication and excellence of research design. The design was beautifully, thoroughly, and painstakingly carried out. The work is truly—not just superficially—comparative in execution and the writer is exceedingly careful in the inclusion of all the caveats, alternative hypotheses, and interpretations to which the data and findings are susceptible.

Danziger's *Making Budgets*—a revision of his dissertation—reflects major improvement over what had been a very fine effort. And I now look forward to its development by Danziger into a tradition of research, for the topic can bear that weight, and he provides compelling evidence of the required skills and energy.

Danziger gives refreshing proof that methodological sophistication and obfuscation need not go hand-in-hand, but a few comments may help orient the reader. Danziger focuses his comparative design on British county boroughs, an all-purpose local authority in English and Welsh urban communities, and searches for similarities/differences in the yearly revenue budget. His analysis has three basic emphases, two dealing with output and the third with processes, and uses aggregate statistical analysis as well as interviews to probe in depth. First, Danziger establishes the substantial potential for local discretion in the county borough, basically by surveying applicable statutes and by overviewing external constraints actually exercised. Second, Danziger establishes that major variations in resource allocations exist between county boroughs, and then seeks to test whether those variations can be basically accounted for by explicit local choice or by two categories of explanations —conventional demographics and several versions of the "incremental" approach. Third, Danziger also applies two classes of process explanations to the variation in yearly revenue budgets —at both the organizational and individual levels.

Let me suggest several guides that I believe will help extend Danziger's very real contribution into a tradition of work. What follow are one man's suggestions for moving beyond individual excellence.

(1) *Research Teams and Large Populations.* As Danziger notes at several points, the several explanations of output variation that he evaluates are more complementary than alternative. Hence the real choice typically will not be: perspective X or Y? Alternatively, the issue will often involve X and Y as levels of explanation that must be linked and whose salience will depend on complex sets of conditions.

Perhaps the prime implication of complementarity concerns the scale of research. Despite all attendant problems, the next breakthroughs in research like Danziger's will come from comprehensive designs applied to large populations by research teams with broad-spectrum competencies. This does not necessarily mean social science equivalents of the Manhattan Project, but that thought inspires.

(2) *Dimensionality.* Large research efforts are required because we have only crude maps of the dimensions of reality. The point often evades serious attention in policy analysis, given such exceptions as the "dimensionalities of nations" programs of recent memory. Danziger is careful about conceptualization and is sensitive to the problems of multiple operationalization; but only research enterprises of far larger scale can do the job that now requires doing—refining conceptual definitions and especially comparing the efficacy of numerous alternative operationalizations of the same concept. Technical reasons require large populations, and especially for the second variety of work, which may be called "comparative analysis of operationalizations." The related need to specify numerous intervening variables also implies large populations.

The present point is often neglected in budget-related research, and especially in aggregate analyses of demographic or economic measures, whose availability implies nothing about their dimensionality. So, for example, correlational matrices representing the relationships of demographic or economic measures with budget outputs have no clear interpretations, common notions to the contrary notwithstanding.

The point can be illustrated by a simple contrast. Much relevant work of the past decade with the covariates of public policy outputs has in effect busied itself with demonstrating this point: We can process huge arrays of data relating budget outcomes and available demographic measures. I do not disparage the significance of this demonstration when I note what I see as the basic future question: what constitutes a useful set of dimensions of reality to measure? Guidance exists for approaching such a question, some of it long-standing guidance that only indicates what approaches should be avoided. Factor analysis in psychological research has been one tactic for isolating dimensions of reality, a tactic presenting a mixed bag of opportunities and problems.

(3) *Concepts of "Change."* All research in the analysis of budgetary behavior which I know has assumed an almost-certainly inadequate concept of change—variations in degree of a stable state. Substantial experience* and some analytic work** require a view that distinguishes at least two kinds of change: movement from one state to another, as in transitioning from the water-state to the ice-state; and variations within a state, as in lowering the temperature of a volume of water. Failure to distinguish the two kinds of change can be powerfully mischievous.

(4) *Manipulating vs. Describing Reality.* Future work also will have to make very substantial use of simulation, experimentation, and especially applied or action research. Danziger respects the point, even though his design is "descriptive." The "manipulative" research strategies reflect a unifying theme: that the real test of a perspective or theory is not so much that it seems to describe but far more that it permits intervening in nature in ways that generate predictable effects. Establishing that theories or perspectives "work" is methodologically preferable to, for example, correlational analysis, which permits less robust explanations of results.

Robert T. Golembiewski

---

*Paul Watzlawick, John H. Weakland, and Richard Fisch, *Change: Principles of Problem Formation and Problem Resolution* (New York: W. W. Norton, 1974).

**Robert T. Golembiewski, Keith Billingsley, and Samuel Yeager, "Measuring Change and Persistence in Human Affairs," *Journal of Applied Behavioral Science,* Vol. 12 (June 1976), pp. 133-157.

ACKNOWLEDGMENTS

This research enterprise was manageable for a single person only with more than a little help from my friends and colleagues. The ideas were first generated during my two years at Sussex University as a Marshall Scholar. From this period, I owe thanks to John Dearlove and Bruce Graham for their thoughtful support. During a second research journey, kindly financed by the Foreign Area Fellowship Program, I received counsel and institutional support from Jean Blondel and Jim Alt of Essex University.

The large set of interviews in the county boroughs could not have been accomplished without substantial assistance from members of each county borough. I am especially grateful to the gentlemen who opened many doors and legitimized my enterprise in each local authority: Borough Treasurer R. Morgan, Deputy Borough Treasurer A. Williams, Assistant Borough Treasurer A. Hopkins, and Deputy Borough Treasurer F. Jones. Thanks also to the many patient and even enthusiastic persons who were willing to be "interviewees." Production of the book has benefitted from Kathy Alberti's typing skills and particularly from Helen Wildman's efficient midwifery.

In the development of this analysis, I must credit the thoughtful suggestions of Richard Brody, William Dutton, John Manley, Ken Newton, Anthony King, and Aaron Wildavsky, whose observations were illuminating. And my greatest intellectual debt is to Heinz Eulau, whose gentle but firm guidance and unselfish assistance were exceptional and constructive. The errors that remain must be attributed to my insistence on making my own mistakes. I hope this book adds to the search by social scientists for more adequate modes of explaining complex and important social-political behavior.

This book is dedicated, with much affection, to my parents, who got me started, and to Lesley, who helped me finish this particular enterprise.

James N. Danziger

Chapter 1

THE RESEARCH PROBLEM

Interest in the performance of government—in what comes out of political processes—has always been a central concern of political scientists. In recent years there has been a marked growth in this research, which is sometimes described as "public policy analysis."[1] If we think generally in terms of actors, processes, and outputs, then policy analysis focuses on characterizing and explaining outputs. Given Easton's view that government and politics are the institutions and processes that authoritatively allocate certain public values for society, public policy research takes the allocations as the dependent variable, as what is to be explained.

There are, of course, diverse value-outputs that are relevant for public policy research, ranging from judicial decisions on personal freedoms to the distribution of patronage to regulatory policies regarding ecology. A substantial number of these studies take the government's distribution of financial resources as particularly attractive for research because it is the measure, if an imperfect one, of the government's commitment to provide a large number of goods and services that are important to the life of every citizen. There is also the methodological advantage of dealing with variables that exist as interval data. Problems of measurement are minimized and the data allow for rigorous quantitative analysis.

This study attempts to add to the cumulative understanding of the distribution of financial resources. The study takes the set of expenditure commitments registered in the budget as the dependent variables to be explained. It differs from much of the related research in three ways. (1) It integrates a conceptual framework for comparative analysis of the entire population of object units of analysis and the detailed exploration of a group of case studies selected from the population.[2] (2) By means of the case studies, it explores specific linkages between the outputs and the decision-making systems from which the outputs have emerged. (3) The study takes as its object unit of analysis a government structure particularly well-suited for such comparative treatment, the British county borough.

This research is informed by streams of theory developed in the study of inter-unit expenditure variations and in the analysis of organizational decision-making systems. The research operates at three levels: (1) the revenue budget as an important governmental output (2) that is the consequence of a decision-making process and/or other operating forces (3) at the level of British county boroughs.

THE REVENUE (AND CAPITAL) BUDGET

There are many possible conceptualizations of the notion of allocation of financial resources. Conceivable indicators include the awarding of contracts and licenses, zoning decisions, the relative burden of the taxation structure, the redistributive effect of taxing and spending policies, job and patronage decisions, and so on. Here we shall take the yearly revenue budget as the output which most satisfactorily operationalizes the general concept of financial resource allocation. The revenue budget is the document in which the government lists the expenditures it has authorized for nearly all aspects of the goods and services it has chosen to provide. At some point, every resource allocation involves a cash nexus—the exchange of money or of some good or service that can be given a monetary value. Most of the indicators in this study are measures at this point, based on the amount of money committed to provide a service. However, nonmonetary indicators that measure the intensity or the extensiveness of service provision are also utilized.

An analytic distinction is made in some policy studies between the *output,* which is the subjective and/or objective content of a policy decision, and the *outcome,* which is the consequences produced by the output. Our research is limited to the consideration of outputs. Other analytic approaches are necessary to assess the complex relationship between output and outcome, or to operationalize and measure outcome. Existing research shows that there is at best an imperfect correspondence between the level of expenditure and the quality of service provided;[3] but the level of authorized expenditure remains a valid measure of decisional output. It is meaningful as an objective statement of the financial commitment to each spending category and of the share of the total allocated to each category. And, as is shown below, these figures are basic perceptual indicators of output for most budgetary decision makers.

There are important research advantages to treating the budget as the decisional output: (1) the budget is seen as a single statement of a complex of interdependent resource allocations; (2) the output is recorded clearly and publicly; (3) it is itemized in great detail; (4) its recorded form alters little from year to year; (5) it is serial (the process and output repeat in each budget period); (6) it is expressed in terms of a single measurement dimension (currency); and (7) the indicators are an interval measurement scale. The focus is upon the revenue budget, which records both recurring and nonrecurring expenditure for all services during the fiscal year. The impact on expenditure of the capital budget—the program of planned construction or expansion of fixed assets that are financed mainly by loans—will also be considered where relevant.

AS A DECISION-MAKING PROCESS

In this research the revenue budget will be treated as the final, short-run decisional output from the government. The first task will be to derive, from the existing literature, theoretical and empirical propositions concerning how budgetary allocations are made. A *decision-making process* is defined as any set of behaviors or forces that produce the output of the revenue budget. At one level, the research will involve an explication of this process, which necessarily exists, given this definition.

A related concern will be to assess whether there is a clearly defined *decision-making structure* for budgeting. Such a structure can be characterized in terms of role theory as a relatively stable set of actions and relationships among the participants (in their behavior as budgetary actors) to cope with the recurring demands of budget-making. In terms of decision-making theory, this structure can be analyzed by its procedures of search for information and alternatives and by its criteria for selecting acceptable decisions. In this perspective the revenue budget, as a decision, is not viewed as a single, temporal event; rather the decision is seen as a scenario, as a series of episodes in which various participants have made variously important contributions. Within a delimited time segment prior to this budget decision, the objective is to develop the most plausible explanation of the changes that have occurred.

BRITISH COUNTY BOROUGHS AS THE LEVEL OF RESEARCH

The budgetary process can be studied at many levels of government. The unit of analysis selected for this research is the county borough—the "all-purpose" local authority in English and Welsh urban communities between 1888 and 1974. Like all British local governments, the county boroughs were ultimately creatures of Parliament. In a political decision couched in administrative efficiency rationales, the Conservative Government submerged the county boroughs into areawide governments in the Local Government Reorganization Act, 1974.

Although the county boroughs are no longer operating local

governments, they remain an extraordinarily attractive unit of analysis for the theoretical questions raised in this research. In general, the study of local-level governments in a single nation provides a research context that is manageable and accessible in scope and complexity and that is less subject to the confounding effects of cross-cultural characteristics. More specifically, few contemporary local governments have been so well-suited to comparative analysis as the county boroughs. Some aspects of their analytic attractiveness are these characteristics: (1) they provided an extremely full range of services for their citizens, including inter alia: education (from nursery school to further education), highways, local health services, social services (for children, the aged, and the handicapped), parks, libraries, town planning and development, housing, public health services, and fire services; (2) for most services, there was no overlap of responsibility with special districts, boards, or other subnational governments; (3) they were a meaningful government unit to their citizens, in both areal and psychological terms;[4] (4) they controlled their own tax, "the rate"; (5) they were *relatively* autonomous (the issue of their relationship to the central government is examined in Chapter 2); and (6) county boroughs had a comparable governmental structure, with a governing Council elected from partisan wards and with an extensive professional administration. These, and other factors identified in subsequent chapters, mean that there is little interunit variation either in external effects or in basic government-structure characteristics for these local governments. Consequently, interunit differences tend to be more directly linked with critical process and structure variables that are measurable at the county borough level of analysis and are less subject to confounding effects.[5] In sum, it should be clear that analytic, social scientific generalizations can be derived with at least as much validity from the county boroughs as from comparative analysis of any other subnational governments.

Approaches to the Study of
Resource Allocation

There are several distinct theoretical approaches to the study of budgetary resource allocation in the literature. Although some of the approaches are interrelated, they vary in focus, propositions, and explanatory factors. To provide guidance for developing a conceptual framework, this section examines approaches which view resource allocation as: (1) a rational decision-making process; (2) decision-taking severely bounded by the cognitive limitations of the budgeters; (3) the problem-solving system of an organizational process; (4) a set of expenditure levels predicted by simple econometric models; and (5) a set of outputs determined by forces in the environment.

The choice of a conceptual framework is crucial because it influences the phenomena taken as relevant data, the manner in which data are assembled, and the kinds of explanation presented. The budgeting literature rarely confronts the problem of assessing the relative explanatory adequacy of each approach. Thus a central objective of the present research is to treat the study of resource allocation from a variety of perspectives.

RATIONAL-PROCESS MODELS

The belief in the possibility of a rational decision-making system is seductive. The participants list and evaluate goal priorities, pose the alternative programs for achieving the objectives, and select a mix of programs that optimizes the benefits relative to costs. This strategy seems consonant with a normative view of the budgetary decision-making task: the budget is the optimal solution to the problem of allocating scarce resources.

In general, there are two sorts of rational-choice models: one type prescribes the details of the optimal solution, the second type describes the decision-making techniques for achieving the best solution. The first type is composed primarily of pure theories based on some calculus of needs and resources. The needs might be those of the recipients of allocations, as in V.O. Key's exhortation to balance political goods and services with citizen needs and preferences.[6] Others have assessed the needs of the allocators, examining the dynamic between resource allocations to the citizens and the citizens' continued support of the governmental system. Breton, for example, posited an abstract model that centered on the allocative payoffs necessary for a party to sustain an electoral majority.[7] Many of these models have been inspired by the perspective of welfare economics. There is a growing literature with a commitment to theoretical rigor; but this has not yet led to many empirically testable propositions for budgetary allocations.

In contrast, the second type of rational-choice models is an explicit attempt to apply analytic strategies to actual decision situations. This approach is characterized by PPB (Planning Programming Budgeting) systems, and, more recently, by ZBB ("zero-base budgeting"). Developed from operations research, PPB combines a long-term planning dimension with the desire to assess comprehensively the costs and benefits of expenditure on all program objectives.[8] Variations on this method have been attempted by governmental bodies at all levels, especially in the U.S. Program budgeting is, for our purposes, less a conceptual framework than an account of how budgeters might apply a set of techniques. Evidence that PPB or performance budgeting is in operation includes: (1) organizing expenditure categories in programmatic terms; (2) specifying performance objectives for program elements; (3) establishing priorities for general objectives. This analysis assesses the extent to which county-borough budgeters articulate and/or utilize these strategies.

COGNITIVE-LIMITS APPROACHES

Scholars studying decision-making behavior in organizations (in pre-PPB days) observed that rational and comprehensive problem-solving approaches assume intellectual capacities, sources of information, and quantities of time vastly beyond those possessed by real administrators. March and Simon,[9] and Lindblom,[10] among others, developed conceptual approaches that were contrasted with the rational-process model. These centered on an assessment of the characteristics and behavior of the individual decision maker in a complex situation. This explanation of the decision maker in action is often called incrementalism and is based on the notion of bounded rationality, or cognitive limits. Complex decisions are, particularly according to Lindblom's theory, handled by a continual and marginal series of adjustments from the current situation. Only a few alternatives are considered, and feedback from the impact of decisions guides further adjustments.

The techniques of incremental decision-making are employed to simplify drastically the options which are considered. This effectively limits the amount of information that must be gathered and processed, the permutations of choices that must be evaluated, and the extent to which overall objectives must be analyzed. This style of choice-making has been particularly attributed to budgeters. James Barber's study of Connecticut Boards of Finance,[11] Aaron Wildavsky's studies of federal agencies,[12] and to some extent Richard Fenno's findings on Congressional appropriations committees,[13] are classic examples of research utilizing this conceptual framework.

A series of propositions have been developed from these studies concerning the use of simplifying and uncertainty-reducing techniques by budgeters: (1) the previous year's levels of expenditure, the "base," are taken as prima facie valid; (2) attention focuses horizontally—on changes from the previous year's allocation in a specific item—rather than vertically—on comparing expenditure levels between services; (3) amounts of money are reified and seen as direct indicators of level of activity or performance; (4) analysis centers on concrete detail rather than policy alternatives or value choices; and (5) well-established role relationships among budget participants stabilize and regulate the process.

The description of the incremental budget maker has entered the conventional wisdom. There is debate concerning the quality of decisions reached by this approach; but few dispute that the approach describes the behavior of most budgeters most of the time. On the other hand, it might be argued that the cognitive-limits approach lacks theoretical richness. It characterizes the behavior of the modal budgeter, but it does not seem to explain the budgetary process or its outputs except as incrementalism writ large. The basic inference from the approach is the probabilistic statement that the Y_t (this year's) budget will be a marginal adjustment of the Y_{t-1} (last year's) budget. But neither the reasons for nor the impact on decisions of the differential behavior of individuals are specified. And, apart from an infinite-regress explanation, there is little explanation of why the present levels of expenditure or patterns of allocation exist. Thus Chapter 7 examines the adequacy of the cognitive-limits approach as a systematic explanation, and it also explores other data generated by an individual-level, configurative perspective.

ORGANIZATIONAL PROCESS-APPROACH[14]

The organizational-process approach was developed in a key theoretical work by Cyert and March.[15] The approach is related to the cognitive-limits approach; but it provides an alternative explanation based on the organization, rather than the individual, as the object unit of analysis. As the name implies, the organizational-process approach explains a decision as a function of the organization's problem-solving procedures through which conflict and uncertainty are minimized, simple searches for information and for alternatives are undertaken, and acceptable solutions are selected.

According to this framework, the allocation of resources can be explained in terms of the manner in which the problem is broken into a sequence of decisions, the methods by which potential solutions are identified, defined, and evaluated, and the relationship between the goals and acceptable solutions. Crecine's computer-simulation model (for three American municipalities) is the most important application of this approach to budgeting,[16] and Gerwin has applied a nonquantitative version to several school boards.[17] The preferred test of the approach is to develop and evaluate the predictive power of a simulation model. But the greater complexity of county-borough budgeting and the evidence that there are different analytic processes in the different boroughs makes a simulation inappropriate at this point.[18] Thus the application of the approach in Chapter 6 will involve an evaluation, in the county-borough context, of propositions and findings from the Cyert-March theory and from Crecine. Key analytic tasks will be to establish: (1) the major operational goals; (2) the order of attending to problems; (3) the strategy of search for solutions; (4) primary information sources; (5) the criteria for determining an acceptable decision; and (6) the standard operating procedures.

ECONOMETRIC MODELS

The three approaches discussed above are primarily explanations of output as a function of process. An alternative perspective is a predictive model of output based on mathematical estimations of change patterns. Econometricians have developed formulations of varying complexity that estimate budgetary outputs by means of regression equations and stochastic variables. The work of Davis, Dempster, and Wildavsky has been seminal in this area.[19] Some of these kinds of models have achieved quite substantial predictive success; but occasionally this work has lacked conceptual richness, reflecting more concern for predictive power than for any explicit understanding of the process by which resources are distributed.

This approach holds that allocations can be known with accuracy on the basis of formulations that are not contingent upon either the decision maker's psyche or the organization's structure. Assumptions are made about the continuity of expenditure patterns over time and about the dynamics of change. The "naive models" are particularly intriguing, since they operationalize basic explanatory notions of incrementalism, and they generate predictions about both rates of change in current expenditure and longitudinal expenditure patterns. There are at least three formulations of the change in allocations: (1) strict incremental—constant percentage increase in each budget cycle;

(2) base budget—constant percentage share of total budget; and (3) fair share—constant percentage of the increase in total expenditure.[20] These naive models seem attractive, given their potential capacity to characterize the budgetary process in a simple, analytic manner. Hence versions of these and related mathematical models will be operationalized and applied to county-borough budgetary data in Chapter 5.

THE "DEMOGRAPHIC APPROACH"[21]

The demographic approach has, in the last decade, strongly affected the research analyzing governmental decisions. The development of computer technology facilitated the testing of hypothesized relationships with very large numbers of analytic units and variables. The demographic approach involves the search for systematic relationships between governmental outputs, particularly allocation decisions, and various other explanatory factors. A simple, representative version of the conceptual model is Dye's study of the American states, which posited and tested such relationships[22] (see Figure 1.1). Policy outcomes were operationalized by a variety of allocation measures of output (e.g., expenditure per head on highways) and were viewed as the dependent variables. The independent (explanatory) variables were indicators representing the socioeconomic environment (e.g., median family income, urbanization) and the political system (e.g., party control, voter participation).

By means of various correlation techniques, most early studies (including Dye's) found that in nearly every case the impact of the political system variables on policy outputs (linkage b)

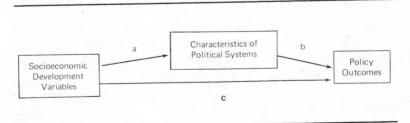

Figure 1.1

was negligible when the socioeconomic variables were controlled. However, when the political system variables were
controlled, the socioeconomic measures continued to display
strong relationships with resource allocations (linkage c).[23]
These findings have been interpreted as a challenge to the traditional assumption regarding the dominance of political factors
relative to social and economic factors as critical determinants
of the allocation of governmental goods and services.

A very large body of literature has developed from the demographic approach.[24] In response to the early studies, some
scholars accepted the basic framework and methodology but
argued for different measures of concepts.[25] Others developed
new dependent variables[26] or amalgamated variables into factor
packages[27] in order to salvage a political component in the
explanation. The mathematics of the model have been attacked,
to be replaced by various treatments using regression coefficients and slopes.[28] Other critiques reject the entire conceptualization, arguing that there is no theory of linkages among the
variables to provide an explanation that is adequate.[29] The
controversy continues as studies emerging from this research
strategy proliferate. Our research must account for the implications of this model.[30] Thus a comprehensive set of political,
social, economic, and demographic indicators for the entire
population of county boroughs are compiled. Correlation and
regression techniques are used to probe linkages between these
explanatory variables and a broad range of indicators that tap
the concept of resource allocation.

SUMMARY

There are several alternative approaches to the study of budgetary decision-making. Different conceptual frameworks evi-
dently yield different explanations. Each approach uses its own
lens to focus on a multilevelled phenomenon. That lens selects
certain data which are treated as relevant evidence. The literature has failed to place these approaches in a single context.
This research attempts to face this problem, and the effort is
to explain financial resource allocations rather than to utilize
a particular analytic approach.

Two substantive interests might yield to different explanatory approaches. The first is an interest in whether distinguishable patterns of allocations have developed in the county boroughs over time. If interborough variations are evident, the analysis seeks to identify the behavior or forces that best explain these variations. The second concern is to characterize the "creation" of the revenue budget—the behaviors, forces, or processes which culminate in the authorization of the individual county borough's budget for the fiscal year. It is not obvious which approach can provide the most satisfactory explanation for either of these research problems.

Thus the research strategy incorporates a variety of perspectives into a single framework—at least in the sense that the various modes of analysis are brought to bear on a common set of outputs. It is difficult to distinguish *competing explanations* from those which Gilbert Ryle terms *"alternative explanations"*—those which are complementary and reinforcing. Initially, the approaches will be treated as if they are competing explanations. The concomitant use of these perspectives should permit an evaluation of their relative validity. Moreover, the use of multiple operationism should provide a more adequate analysis of financial resource allocation than would be obtained with a single conceptual approach or type of data.

Research Design

This research raises three organizing questions. They are: (1) can the county borough make choices on its budgetary allocations; (2) does the county borough appear to exercise this range of discretion; and (3) how are these choices made? The analytic framework entails the testing of various explanations in order to ascertain whether it seems valid to view the local unit as a significant, budgetary decision maker. We must be satisfied that external (to the local government system)[31] constraints are not so powerful as to leave little local discretion on budgetary allocations. And we must determine if the patterns of expenditure show that local actors are exercising choice-making, or whether other sorts of factors seem best to explain allocations. If the evidence affirms the first two organizing questions, it is appropriate to explore those approaches that involve in-depth analysis of selected county boroughs. Thus the progression in the research is to establish that the county boroughs (the object units of analysis) can and do determine their budgetary outputs. The level of the units whose behavior is observed (the subject units of analysis) moves downward from structural properties (the demographic approach) through the budget-making system (the organizational-process approach) to the styles of individual budget makers (the cognitive-limits approach).

QUESTION 1: EXTERNAL CONSTRAINTS

The first concern is with external constraints over the budgetary decisions of the county borough. External constraints can be understood as groups, forces, or decisions that impinge on the potential freedom of the county borough's actors to make choices over resource allocations. The method of assessing external constraints has some kinship to the testing of a null hypothesis, although it is a less rigid approach.[32] The hypothesis to be analyzed is that external constraints over budgetary decisions are of such magnitude that only a trivial scope for potential discretion is left to the local authority. The range of governmental goods and services that the county borough was authorized to provide will be examined and the external constraints will be identified and carefully assessed. If the evidence does not support the notion that external constraints are paramount, the null hypothesis is not disconfirmed. But we shall feel justified in acting on the probabilistic statement that the county borough did appear to have a significant range of potential discretion on its budgetary allocations. This method might be termed the ruling out of plausible rival hypotheses.[33]

The major constraints to be considered in the English context are: (1) the central government, operating through its central departments; (2) the source of monies and other resources affecting budgetary allocations; (3) the fiscal environment, including the impact of the government's fiscal policy, inflation, and externally determined wage settlements; and (4) precepts (autonomous and often supraborough agencies supplying services). The principal types of evidence that will be brought to bear in the examination will be: (1) the legal, statutory powers granted to the county borough; (2) an assessment of the areas and extent to which discretion over spending is limited by the central government and its departments; (3) a determination of the constraints imposed by obligations and shared powers with other service-providing agencies; (4) the sources of monies supporting local expenditure and the restraints upon their use; and (5) local actors' perceptions of their latitude for choice on budgetary allocations.

QUESTION 2: EVIDENCE OF LOCAL CHOICE-MAKING

Having determined that the county borough has, at least potentially, a significant range of discretion, the second question is whether it does appear to make budgetary choices. The organizing (null) hypothesis is that there is little variation in the resource allocations of the county boroughs that cannot be explained by factors independent of the dispositions and actions of the local decision makers.

The question of local choice-making involves several considerations. It must be determined whether significant interborough variations in expenditure exist. Here the concern is the *configuration* of expenditures. A comprehensive set of indicators is developed to measure the allocation of monetary and nonmonetary resources and to measure the intensity and extensiveness of service provision. There are summary measures for groups of related services as well as various indicators for each particular service. Statistics of distribution and dispersion are applied to data for all county boroughs to display variation. If interborough variations were slight, further analysis of allocations would be trivial.

If the data reveal significant variations in levels and patterns of allocations, the major plausible rival hypothesis to local choice-making is that these variations are explained by the demographic approach. To test this, correlation and regression analyses are employed, taking various indicators of resource allocations as the dependent variables, and an extensive selection of political, economic, social, demographic, and "need-demand" indicators as independent variables. By examining and clarifying the relationships between the variables, we can assess the explanatory power of the demographic approach for county-borough resource allocation.

To the extent configurations in expenditure can be explained (in statistical terms) by this mode of analysis, other approaches will be devalued. If the demographic approach fails to explain adequately the variations in budgetary outputs, the commitment to multiple operationism suggests the analysis of the local decision-making system and its actors. This entails approaches which focus on phenomena at the level of the individual county borough.

QUESTION 3: HOW DOES THE COUNTY BOROUGH DO BUDGET-MAKING?

This central issue in the analysis concerns how budgetary decision-making occurs in county boroughs. There are several major research interests related to this organizing question: (1) do the naive models adequately predict the patterns of alterations in expenditure; (2) to what extent do the organizational-process or cognitive-limits approaches explain budgetary outputs; (3) is there a decision-making structure (defined as a set of role relationships and standard operating procedures that are relatively stable over time); (4) what are the linkages between budgetary outputs and the decision-making process; and (5) can we generalize about a process of budgetary decision-making on the basis of the units analyzed?

The naive models suggest that some relatively simple patterns of change characterize the levels of budgetary output. To assess the predictive power of these models, mathematical formulations of these econometric models are applied to budget data from four selected county boroughs for the period 1959-1969. Both the cognitive-limits approach and the organizational-process approach are direct attempts to explain the budgetary process of the county borough. The case studies will test the validity of the theory and propositions of each approach in explaining behavior and process in the four budget-making systems. While the evaluation of these approaches, operationalized in a primarily nonquantitative form, will necessarily be more subjective, a rigorous, analytic assessment of the explanatory adequacy of each approach will be developed.

THE DATA

In examining the naive models, the cognitive-limits approach, and the organizational-process approach, the revenue budget is treated as the final short-run decisional output. For reasons of manageability, the research domain has been delimited with respect to (1) the time-slice studied, and (2) the number of object units of analysis.

(1) Time segment. It is a commonplace in the literature that the most important determining factor in this year's budget is last year's budget.[34] If this is true, a complete study of a county borough's budget ought to trace all spending decisions back to the beginning of the borough's existence. Even if the data were available (which they are not), such a research task would be overwhelming. The historical dimension is treated to some extent in the longitudinal analyses in Chapter 5. In the main, however, we attempt a study of decision and behavior within the defined time-slice of the single budgetary period, the fiscal year. Factors antecedent to this period, including policy decisions and previous budgetary allocations, are taken as given for this study. They are accounted for to the extent they affect the current behavior of the budgeters. This research simplification permits detailed focus on how budgeters operate in creating a budget. The cost is a loss of perspective on how specific patterns of expenditure build over time. This trade-off seems reasonable, assuming that within the time-frame programs will be observable at all stages of development. Further, there is some evidence that the characteristics of the budgetary process may lead actors to think of expenditure primarily in discrete, yearly fashion.[35]

(2) Units of Analysis. The use of case-study analysis rather than an examination of all county boroughs entails certain more-or-less arbitrary choices. The selection of number of units and of particular boroughs is, to some degree, based on research economies, manageability, and the informed judgment of the researcher. Four county boroughs (of the seventy-seven which existed continuously from 1960 to 1970) were selected for intensive examination. The initial subset was defined by population—county boroughs between 100,000 and 250,000 in 1968-1969. Experimentation with various selection procedures failed to produce an especially valid and distinct group of county boroughs. Moreover, there were certain benefits from opting for either a "most dissimilar systems" or a "most similar systems" framework for the analysis.[36] Consequently it was decided to select units for study that seemed interesting and that compromised the similarities-dissimilarities consideration.

The result was the selection of four, English county boroughs of near-equal population from the South and Midlands. They can be viewed as two "relatively matched sets" which are dissimilar to the other set. The selected research sites are Brighton, Dudley, Southend-on-Sea, and West Bromwich. Brighton and Southend, as one set, and Dudley and West Bromwich as the other, have characteristics that make them extremely interesting in terms of our analysis. Brighton and Southend are classified by Moser and Scott[37] as seaside, resort towns, are nearly equidistant from London, have similar class and age composition, including a large elderly population, and both have weak Labour Party representation on the Council. Dudley and West Bromwich are both Black Country industrial towns, satellite boroughs in the West Midlands connurbation, with very high proportions of skilled working class, similar class structures, a young population, Labour strength on the Council, and both were significantly expanded in the West Midlands reorganization of 1966.[38] Appendix A details their statistical characteristics relative to the other county boroughs.

(3) Data Sources. The data base for the four county bor-

oughs is mainly composed of two types of evidence, interviews and budget documents. Other data sources include Council Standing Orders, Council minutes, and relevant statutory documents. Constant cross-checking between these various types of evidence should enhance the quality of the analysis.

(a) Interviews. To establish budget makers' behavior, the most obvious approach is direct observation—watch the participants in action. However, all budgetary deliberations in the county boroughs are strictly private and observation was not possible. The alternative is interviews with relevant actors. These interviews were open-end, structured around a series of questions, and ranged in length from forty-five minutes to three hours. Approximately thirty-five taped, transcribed interviews were conducted in each borough.[39]

(b) Budget Documents. Given that interview data are subject to numerous internal "threats to validity,"[40] the written records are an excellent countersource of evidence, with different inherent errors. For county boroughs there is one publicly available record of spending decisions: the revenue budget. The budget is, in a sense, the prototype of measuring instruments. It records a wide range of allocative decisions in a single measurement dimension that is a ratio scale, is itemized in detail, and is in regularized form. County-borough budget data are highly reliable, coming from either the notarized accounts of the borough or from published documents of the professional body, the Institute of Municipal Treasurers and Accountants. Detailed expenditure data were gathered in the four county boroughs for each year 1959-1960 to 1968-1969, and less detailed data were collected for the period 1925-1959.[41] The analysis begins in Chapter 2 with an assessment of external constraints on the county boroughs' budgetary discretion.

NOTES

1. This perspective underlies such journals as *Policy Analysis* and such books as William and Joyce Mitchell, *Political Analysis and Public Policy* (Chicago: Rand McNally, 1969). See also Charles O. Jones, *An Introduction to the Study of Public Policy* (Belmont, Ca.: Wadsworth, 1970); James E. Anderson, *Public Policy-Making* (New York: Praeger, 1975); *Political Science and Public Policy,* ed. by Austin Ranney (Chicago: Markham, 1968), especially articles by Van Dyke, Salisbury, and Froman; and Joseph La Palombara, "Macrotheories and Microapplications in Comparative Politics," *Comparative Politics,* I, No. 1 (October 1968), pp. 52-91.

2. Object units of analysis are the units whose behavior is to be explained. In this research, the county borough is the object unit and the behavior is its allocative outputs. The research focuses on various subject units of analysis, which are the units whose behavior is observed. For a full treatment of units and levels of analysis, see Heinz Eulau, "Introduction: On Units and Levels of Analysis," in *Micro-Macro Political Analysis* (Chicago: Aldine, 1969).

3. See especially Bleddyn Davies, *Social Needs and Resources in Local Services* (London: Michael Joseph, 1968). Also Ira Sharkansky, "Government Expenditure and Public Service," *APSR* 61, No. 4 (December 1967).

4. Arthur Maass, "Division of Powers: An Areal Analysis," in Maass, ed., *Area and Power: A Theory of Local Government* (Glencoe: Free Press, 1959).

5. Even within-nation comparative studies of local government units tend to ignore rather than confront the confounding effects of interregional differences, such as variations in statutory requirements, in income levels, and in jurisdictional responsibilities and overlaps.

6. V. O. Key, "The Lack of a Budgetary Theory," *APSR,* 34 (1940), pp. 1137-1144. And in response to Key's challenge, Verne Lewis, "Towards a Theory of Budgeting," *Public Administration Review,* XII, No. 1 (Winter 1952), pp. 42-54.

7. Albert Breton, "A Theory of the Demand for Public Goods," *Canadian Journal of Political Science and Economics,* 32, No. 4 (November 1966), pp. 455-467; C. M. Tiebout, "A Pure Theory of Local Expenditure," *Journal of Political Economy,* 27 (October 1, 1956), pp. 416-424; Alan Williams, "The Optimal Provision of Public Goods in a System of Local Governments," *Journal of Political Economy,* 37 (February 1966), pp. 18-33; Anthony Downs, "Why the Government Budget is Too Small in a Democracy," *World Politics,* XII (1960), pp. 541-563; Anthony Downs, *An Economic Theory of Democracy* (New York: Harper, 1957); Paul Samuelson, "The Pure Theory of Public Expenditure," *Review of Economics and Statistics,* 36 (1954), pp. 387-389; James Buchanan and Gordon Tullock, *The Calculus of Consent* (Ann Arbor: Univ. of Michigan Press, 1965); Randall Bartlett, *Economic Foundations of Political Power* (New York: Free Press, 1973).

8. A useful selection of readings on PPB is *Planning Programming Budgeting,* edited by Fremont Lyden and Ernest Miller (Chicago: Markham, 1972). A critique is Leonard Merewitz and Stephen Sosnick, *The Budget's New Clothes* (Chicago: Markham, 1971). On ZBB, see Peter A. Pyhrr, "The Zero-Base Approach to Government Budgeting," *Public Administration Review,* 37 (January/February 1977), pp. 1-8.

9. James March and Herbert Simon, *Organizations* (New York: Wiley, 1958).

10. Charles Lindblom, "The Science of 'Muddling Through'," *Public Administration Review,* 19 (Spring 1959), pp. 79-88. David Braybrooke and Charles Lindblom, *A Strategy of Decision,* (New York: Free Press, 1963).

11. James Barber, *Power in Committees: An Experiment in the Governmental Process* (Chicago: Rand McNally, 1966).

12. Aaron Wildavsky, *The Politics of the Budgetary Process* (Boston: Little, Brown, 1964); see also Aaron Wildavsky, *Budgeting: A Comparative Theory of Budgetary Processes* (Boston: Little, Brown, 1975).

13. Richard Fenno, *The Power of the Purse* (Boston: Little, Brown, 1966).

14. This term, and the general characteristics of the approach, are developed in Graham Allison, "Conceptual Models and the Cuban Missile Crisis," *ASPR*, 58 (September 1969), pp. 689-718. See Allison's larger study, *The Essence of Decision* (Boston: Little, Brown, 1971).

15. Richard Cyert and James March, *A Behavioral Theory of the Firm* (New Jersey: Prentice-Hall, 1963).

16. John P. Crecine, *Governmental Problem-Solving: A Computer Simulation Model of Municipal Budgeting* (Chicago: Rand McNally, 1969).

17. Donald Gerwin, "A Process Model of Budgeting in a Public School System," *Management Science*, 15, No. 7 (March 1969), pp. 338-361; Donald Gerwin, "Towards a Theory of Public Budgetary Decision-Making," *Administrative Science Quarterly*, 14, No. 1 (March 1969), pp. 33-46.

18. Although the process described by Crecine has many commonalities with that of county boroughs, several critical distinctions must be drawn. (1) There is no executive head comparable to the Mayor. His role is the single most important in Crecine's analysis. To some extent a mix of the behavior of some senior Majority Party councillors and/or the Borough Treasurer are a functional equivalent to the Mayor's role. However the different roles involved in the budgeting procedures in the county borough are complex and do not correspond to the "Mayors" submodel (see Chapter 6). (2) In the county borough, the rate (the local property tax) is locally determined and is *set* by the budgetary process in order to balance revenue with expenditure. In Crecine's model, revenue is normally fixed prior to the process and enters it as an independent constraint to be satisfied (see Crecine, pp. 68-69). Hence there is obviously a far greater range of potential solutions for the county borough, since the level-of-expenditure solution is interdependent with the solution for the level-of-the-rate problem. Potentially this problem set is far more difficult than that in Crecine's model. (3) In the three cities there were a few general accounts. Expenditure levels were set for these accounts, leaving detailed allocation to the department. In some county boroughs, accounts are far more detailed and the Council in theory ratifies *each line-item in each account* separately. Standing Orders prohibit more than £X (usually £500) overspending on any "vote" (that is, any line-item allocation). This high degree of detail and the pressure to allocate accurately places far greater stress on county-borough budgeters. For an elaboration of these points, see Chapter 6. For a critique of Crecine's findings, see James N. Danziger, *Budget-Making and Expenditure Variations in the English County Boroughs,* unpublished Ph.D. dissertation, Stanford Univ., 1974, especially Chapters 1 and 8. Due to these kinds of differences and the limited empirical evidence on the county-borough budgeting process, the development of a Crecine-type simulation seems premature.

19. Otto Davis, M.A.H. Dempster, and Aaron Wildavsky, "A Theory of the Budgetary Process," *APSR*, 60, No. 3 (September 1966), pp. 529-547. A more refined version of the theory is Davis, Dempster, and Wildavsky, "Towards a Predictive Theory of Government Expenditure: U.S. Domestic Appropriations," *British Journal of Political Science*, 4 (1975), pp. 419-452.

20. These "naive models" are proposed in Crecine, op. cit.

21. A phrase coined by James Q. Wilson, in his Introduction to *City Politics and Public Policy,* ed. by Wilson (Cambridge: Harvard Univ. Press, 1968).

22. Thomas Dye, *Politics, Economics, and the Public* (Chicago: Rand McNally, 1966), p. 3.

23. The control technique was multiple partial correlations. By means of this technique, the impact of all controlled variables is extracted, according to Dye, from the statistical correlation between the dependent variable and the remaining independent variables. There are numerous criticisms of the attempt to sort out complex relationships by multiple correlation, particularly where the multicollinearity of independent variables is high.

24. Most of this research has been based on cross-sectional data for subnational governments within a single nation-state. A broad overview of the research at the urban-government level, summarizing studies from a variety of countries, is Robert C. Fried, "Comparative Urban Policy and Performance," in *The Handbook of Political Science,* eds. Fred Greenstein and Nelson W. Polsby (Reading, Mass.: Addison-Wesley, 1976), *Volume 6, Policies and Policy Making.* The economists were among the pioneers in analyses of the determinants of expenditure outputs in United States' governments. See, for example, Solomon Fabricant, *The Trend of Government Activity Since 1900* (New York: National Bureau of Economic Research, 1952); Glenn Fisher, "Determinants of State and Local Government Expenditure." *National Tax Journal,* 14 (1969), pp. 349-355. The extensive work by social scientists on U.S. state-government outputs is briefly characterized in John Fenton and Donald Chamberlayne, "The Literature Dealing with the Relationships between Political Processes, Socioeconomic Conditions and Public Policies in the American States: A Bibliographical Essay," *Policy,* 1 (1969), pp. 388-404. Indicative of the extensive work on U.S. local-level political systems are Terry N. Clark, "Community Structure, Decision-Making, Budget Expenditures and Urban Renewal in 51 American Communities," pp. 293-313, and Louis Masotti and Don Bowen, "Communities and Budgets: The Sociology of Municipal Expenditure," pp. 313-324, both in *Community Politics: A Behavioral Approach,* eds. C. Bonjean, T. Clark, and R. Lineberry (New York: Free Press, 1971).

25. Allan Pulsipher and James Weatherby, "Malapportionment, Party Competition, and the Functional Distribution of Governmental Expenditures," *APSR,* 62 (December 1968), pp. 1207-1219.

26. Richard Winters and Brian Fry, "The Politics of Redistribution," *APSR,* 64 (June 1970), pp. 508-522.

27. Richard Hofferbert and Ira Sharkansky, "Dimensions of State Politics, Economics, and Public Policy," *APSR,* 63 (1969), pp. 867-879.

28. Charles Cnudde and Donald McCrone, "Party Competition and Welfare Policies in the American States," *APSR,* 63 (1969), pp. 838-866.

29. Stuart Rakoff and Guenther Schaffer, "Politics, Policy and Political Science: Theoretical Alternatives," *Politics and Society,* 1 (1970), pp. 51-77; Herbert Jacob and Michael Lipsky, "Outputs, Structure and Power: An Assessment of Changes in the Study of State and Local Politics," *Journal of Politics,* 30 (1969), pp. 510-538.

30. Applications of this approach to county-borough spending are discussed fully in Chapter 4. The findings are summarized in K. Newton, "Community Performance in Britain," *Current Sociology,* 22 (1976), pp. 49-86.

31. The local government system in the county borough is defined to include all actors who are either elected or appointed officials of the county borough or are

directly employed by it on a permanent basis. Due to considerations of manageability, research attention is directed almost wholly to members of the Borough Council and the administrative elements (actors concerned with policy advice and organization control) of various spending departments and finance departments.

32. On null hypotheses and falsification of hypotheses, the classic philosophy of science treatment is Sir Karl Popper, *The Logic of Scientific Discovery* (New York: Harper Torchbooks, 1965), pp. 265-281. Dye ably handles this same problem of meta-null hypotheses in testing policy outputs. His approach is extremely similar to the one taken in the present research on this problem. See Dye, (1966), op. cit., pp. 24-25.

33. Eugene Webb, Donald Campbell, Richard Schwartz, and Lee Sachrest, *Unobtrusive Measures: Non-reactive Research in the Social Sciences* (Chicago: Rand McNally, 1966), pp. 8-10.

34. Wildavsky (1964), op. cit., pp. 11-16; Davis et al. (1966), op. cit., p. 537; Crecine (1969), op. cit., p. 219.

35. See Chapter 6 and 7 on this point. With respect to the issue of time-slice, it is perhaps useful to make an explicit point that this research, like other social-scientific analyses that are fundamentally cross-sectional, is time- and context-specific. Hence it should be noted that at the time of both the field research (early 1970s) and of the indicators for most output data (1960-1970), the British economy was in a state that might be characterized as troubled but not traumatized. During this period, development of the public sector of the economy came under increasing scrutiny and financial restraint was generally in a critical phase. Inflation, which was rather moderate during the early 1960s, had become a serious concern by 1970 and was to have substantial impact on the resource-allocation process (both current and capital spending) during the double-digit years of the mid-1970s. Also, the concern for a corporate planning perspective and the use of modern management techniques was less visible in local authorities in 1970 than in the late 1970s. Nonetheless, three of the four authorities studied in this analysis had made significant organizational changes that were inspired by this kind of concern. On corporate planning during this period, see *Corporate Planning in English Local Government: An Analysis with Readings, 1967-72*, eds. R. Greenwood and J. D. Stewart (London: Knight, 1975).

36. See Adam Przeworski and Henry Teune, *The Logic of Comparative Social Inquiry* (New York: Wiley, 1970), pp. 31-39.

37. C. A. Moser, and Wolf Scott, *British Towns: A Statistical Study of their Social and Economic Differences* (London: Oliver and Boyd, 1961), p. 44.

38. Under the West Midlands Act, 1965, West Bromwich was expanded to incorporate parts of the former county borough of Smethwick and all of Aldridge Urban District Council, raising its population from 98,040 to 171,704 and its area from 7,172 to 11,704 acres. Dudley amalgamated with Brierly Hill Urban District, most of Sedgley and Coseley, and parts of Tipton and Amblecote. Its population grew from 63,890 to 181,380 and its area from 4,328 to 14,900 acres. These major and abrupt changes might be seen as threats to the validity of any data analyses. In fact, the evidence in this study suggests that the disruptions were not severe and did not independently alter substantially the budget-making process. They did, of course, alter the magnitude of allocation levels and population served. See Chapters 3, 4, 5, and 6 on these points. Moreover, all county boroughs were amalgamated into new authorities under the Local Government Reorganization Act, 1974. Interesting data

might be derived on the manner in which major reorganization is dealt with, at least in terms of the budgetary process and financial resource allocation.

39. Further details are in Appendix B.

40. Internal "threats to validity" arise from technical shortcomings in the execution of the interview. These include spurious reactions to the interview by the respondent, the interviewer's unintended effects on the respondent or the responses, or sampling error. Webb, et al. (1966), op. cit., argue that the use of multiple data bases with different inherent errors is preferable to any single research technique.

41. A decision was made to use actual expenditure figures. Variations between authorized and actual expenditure in the four county boroughs were found to be minor and unsystematic.

Chapter 2

EXTERNAL CONSTRAINTS

The first concern is whether the range and scope of county-borough choice-making on expenditure was broad enough to merit examination. The analytic question is: can the county borough make choices on its budgetary allocations? The focus is upon the latitude to act and this chapter examines the laws and the structures in the borough's environment that might limit its autonomy on budgetary decision-making. The null hypothesis to be evaluated is that external constraints over budgetary decisions were of such magnitude that only a trivial range of potential discretion was left to the county borough. The method of analysis is to assess plausible rival hypotheses to the position that the county borough did have discretion. The major constraints, external to the county-borough government, that might have limited the nature or extent of the borough's budget-making scope are: (1) the departments of the central government; (2) dependency upon nonlocal revenue resources; (3) the general fiscal environment; and (4) supralocal authorities such as precepts. Initially, however, the chapter examines the range of activity authorized for the county borough.

The Range of County-Borough Activity

The range of the county borough's expenditure options can be established by characterizing the statutory powers of the county borough to provide public goods and services. The county borough, like all local government authorities, was the creation of Parliament.[1] Parliament granted the status of county borough to certain large towns in the Local Government Act, 1888. And, with the Local Government Reorganization Act, 1974, she amalgamated the eighty-three existing county boroughs in England and Wales into areawide governments. These "all-purpose" local authorities levied their own rates (the tax on local property), spent their own money, and had the legal status of corporations. Prior to 1974, they were the only local government authorities that were responsible to and supervised by no other local authority and that had the right to provide virtually all local government services. Other areas had a two-tier system of local government, with a division of powers and service responsibilities between a county government and a more local unit.

Most county-borough activities were based on General Acts of Parliament that either (1) compel the local authority to provide a certain service, or (2) empower it to provide a service if it so desires. This second type is known as "permissive legislation" and comprises a large part of all local government legislation.[2] However, it is the obligatory services which account for most expenditure. Differential use of permissive legislation and of Local Acts resulted in a variation in specific functions performed by each county borough. Most county boroughs provided, at some level, at least these services:[3]

Allotments—provision of
Approved schools and remand homes
Baths, swimming baths, and washhouses

Births, deaths, and marriages—registration of
Building—control of
Cemeteries and crematoria
Civil defense
Education:
   nursery, primary, secondary, special, and further (colleges of education, art, or technology; adult institutes); school meals and milk; and school medical service
Electors—registration of
Entertainments—provision of
Food and drugs—inspection and control
Housing
Infectious diseases—notification and disinfection
Libraries, museums, and art galleries
Local health services:
   midwifery, health visitors, home nursing, maternity and child welfare, ambulance service, prevention of illness, care and aftercare, and health centers
Markets
Mortuaries
Motor vehicles and drivers' licensing
Parks and open spaces
Roads, streets, and bridges—construction, maintenance, cleansing, and lighting
Sanitary services:
   refuse collection and disposal, sewerage, sewage and water drainage, rodent and pest control, and air pollution
Shops inspection
Slum clearance
Social welfare services:
   general social work, domestic helps, and temporary accommodation; children—care, adoption, boarding out, and control of employment; aged—residential accommodation, hostels, and community centers; and mentally ill, handicapped, and blind—homes and training centers
Town planning
Urban redevelopment
Vaccination and immunization
Weights and measures—inspection

Legally, the power of the county boroughs was constrained by the doctrines of *ultra vires,* which required them to base all action on some type of legislative authorization, and of *mandamus,* which required them to perform all duties imposed on them by law.[4] While the application of these legal principles is a complex matter, there is little evidence that they tightly constrained the county borough. A borough was not held to be acting *ultra vires* as long as authority for an action could be reasonably implied from a statute or was reasonably incidental to effecting that statute.[5] A writ of *mandamus* would be upheld only if an obligatory function was not provided at all and other equally effective remedies did not exist.[6] In general, there are almost no cases where either of these principles was applied by the courts to limit the autonomy of county boroughs.[7] Thus they are best understood as setting extremely broad boundaries for the range of permissible activity by the county borough.

Acts of Parliament informed the county borough about which services it was required to provide and which ones it had the discretion to provide. The major expenditure requirements for the county borough were obligatory: education, highways, local health services, and social services. Apart from broadly worded legislation about the nature of the services to be provided, Parliament did not control expenditure allocations. It was the responsibility of the county borough and the central departments, rather than Parliament, to flesh out the statutory skeletons. While Parliament imposed upon the borough the decision to provide most services, decisions about the form and level of provision remained basically the domain of the locality.[8]

With particular reference to county borough finances, Parliament did not interfere to any important extent. She limited neither expenditure nor the rate. She did limit expenditure for a few minor activities and specified the amount that could be accumulated in certain capital funds. Although the preparation of a yearly budget was not a statutory requirement, Parliament compelled the county borough to prepare one by her requirement that a rate be levied each year to cover all estimated needs and contingencies and to liquidate deficiencies.[9] Kitching concludes:

> The *direction* of all local authority expenditure is controlled generally and externally by Parliament. The *volume* of the expenditure is not controlled . . . and the local authority's budget does not need approval by any higher authority.[10]

In sum, the county borough was authorized by Parliament to provide an extremely wide range of public goods and services to its citizens. Within these boundaries, statutory constraints upon the borough's discretion are minimal. As J. H. Warren observes, the local authority "is largely (but not entirely) free to choose the particular manner in which it will do something it has the power to do."[11] Given this range of legitimate authority, it is appropriate to examine those external forces which might constrain the borough's budget-making discretion.

The Scope of Budgetary Choice-Making—External Constraints

It is often contended that the central government controls local-authority expenditure by means of its departments and through fiscal policy. These factors and the dependence of the local government on the central government's financial resources were melded into a "theory of loss" of local power relative to the center. These assertions, characterized by the writings of William Robson, have lost their force in recent years as rich empirical studies have challenged many of their contentions.[12] It is important to examine, if briefly, the apparent effect of the major external constraints on local budgetary autonomy.

CENTRAL DEPARTMENTS

The two undeniable propositions about central department-county borough relations are that they are extremely complex, and that most written work on this subject has been suffused with an ideological bias, characterized by the "democracy versus efficiency" debate. That is, central control has been generally equated with more efficient provision of local services, while greater local autonomy has been linked with increased responsiveness to the local citizenry.

The foundation of the central-local relationship is that each major service which the county borough was required to provide was under the jurisdiction of a specific Ministry, with general coordination under the Department of the Environment. J.A.G. Griffith, in the most authoritative study of central department-local authority relations, observed that three conditions shape the relationship: (1) the providers of the services are the local authorities; (2) the control-influence relationship is two-way; and (3) there is an acceptance (for most services) of a minimum standard which applies to the entire country.[13] According to Griffith, statutory control of most governmental functions was largely local, rather than central, between the seventeenth and twentieth century. A shift toward the center began in this century and has become most notable since the Labour Government of 1945-1951.[14]

The legal powers conferred to ministers over locally executed functions are often vaguely framed in such terms as "general guidance,"[15] "supervision,"[16] or "approval of basic schemes"[17] for administering the service. In only a few cases does the wording give the department clearer responsibility with the local authority as the instrumentality.[18] The county boroughs were autonomous bodies and the department's right to control their activity was contingent upon sufficient statutory justification. The Maud Committee concluded that in most cases, "Ministers are influencing the powers of the local authorities, and have no general statutory responsibility."[19]

Of the formal means of departmental influence examined by Griffith, circulars, inspection, and default power seem the most important.[20] Policy circulars are meant to advise local authorities about how a service ought to be provided. But the local government was obliged only to comply with the spirit of the circulars, which were subjected to an extraordinarily broad range of local interpretation.[21] The inspector's role is to insure that a borough maintain at least a minimum standard for certain services (the schools, the children's service, and the police and fire services). Although a department has the right to take provision of a service away from a local authority, there were virtually no examples of use of this default power against a county borough. Essentially, these formal means constitute a base-level constraint, which assures that a minimum standard is maintained on obligatory services.

Many traditional studies tended to view the existence of ministerial control techniques, rather than evidence of their actual application or effectiveness, as proof of central control. In fact, various empirical analyses reflect that differential levels of control were attempted by various departments and that there was substantial variation in the response of the county boroughs.[22] And a major conclusion of Griffith, a clear advocate of firm central-department control, is that policy tended to be so poorly defined that effective central control of local authorities was not possible.[23] Thus it is clear that the county boroughs, like other local authorities, experienced greater central-department control after 1945. But this relative decline of autonomy does not substantiate the assertion that the county boroughs' choice-making was severely constrained.

DEPENDENCE ON NONLOCAL FINANCIAL RESOURCES

County borough revenue. The most frequently cited constraint upon county-borough spending was its dependence on Exchequer grants. Based on a "he who pays the piper calls the tune" assumption, it was asserted that the increasing importance of Exchequer grants resulted in decreased local autonomy.[24] Evaluation of this contention requires a critical examination of the sources of local revenue and the constraints implied by these sources.

The main source of county-borough revenue was *the rate,* the local tax on the occupation of property.[25] Each county borough was completely free, in legal terms, to set the rate at any level it determined. It was required that the rate produce adequate revenue to balance income with expenditure for the fiscal year. Hence the determination of the rate level was inter-dependent with the decision about total expenditure and with the anticipation of revenue from all other sources.

Exchequer grants were the second major source of borough revenue. Parliament imposed many new functions on county boroughs after 1888. In order to finance services where the benefits were not strictly local, to compensate for interference with local rateable resources, and to subsidize poorer areas with particular need for public services, a system of government grants-in-aid evolved. Generally, the system has alternated over time between block grants (based on formulas measuring local needs for resources) and percentage grants (based on reimburse-ment for actual expenditure on specific services). Since the Local Government Act, 1958, block grants have clearly been the dominant mode of support. As stated in a 1971 Green Paper:

> The Government intend to give greater freedom to local authorities. Specific grants tend to involve the central government in detailed supervision of the particular expenditure to which they relate. This is not so with those block grants whose distribution is not directly related to the expenditure. The Government therefore wish to ex-plore with local government how best to absorb into block grant as many as possible of the remaining specific grants towards both rev-enue and capital expenditure.[26]

The third source of revenue for the county borough was *income*. This income derived from rents and from fees and charges for services and trading undertakings that the borough had chosen to provide. The dependence-on-grants argument normally cited the fact that the ratio of grants to rates was approaching 1:1.[27] However, grants accounted for only 36.9% of total local government income (in 1964). Rates provided 33.3% and rents and income added a "hidden" 29.8%.[28] From this perspective, only about one-third of revenue expenditure was financed by central government grants. Table 2.1 records the sources of all monies financing revenue-budget expenditure

Table 2.1: Sources of Revenue 1969-1970

	Brighton	Dudley	Southend	West Bromwich
1. Rates	£ 6,180,445 35.4%	£ 4,585,695 39.4%	£ 5,119,810 39.6%	£ 5,725,105 47.2%
2. Rents and Income	£ 4,383,185 25.1%	£ 1,427,965 12.3%	£ 3,369,550 26.0%	£ 1,583,840 13.0%
Σ 1 + 2	60.5%	51.7%	65.6%	60.2%
3. Education Pool Reimbursements	£ 2,359,255 13.5%	£ 742,555 6.4%	£ 181,600 1.4%	£ 353,020 2.9%
Σ 1 + 2 + 3	74.0%	58.1%	67.4%	63.1%
4. Rate Support Grant	£ 3,897,385 22.3%	£ 4,746,505 40.8%	£ 3,806,190 29.4%	£ 4,331,915 35.7%
5. Specific Grants	£ 624,385 3.6%	£ 131,235 1.1%	£ 459,310 3.6%	£ 140,235 1.2%
Total Revenue	£17,444,655	£11,633,955	£12,936,460	£12,134,115

in the four county boroughs during 1969-1970. The grants constitute only 26% of total revenue in Brighton and range up to 42% for Dudley. As will be shown in Chapter 6, Dudley's high figure is best explained by a local decision to minimize rate-born expenditure relative to grant-born expenditure. In general, these figures show that locally generated funds are clearly dominant over grants in all four county boroughs.[29] Moreover, only the specific grants, which represent 1% to 4% of the total, are earmarked funds that are directly related to the provision of units of service. These are the only grant monies for which the piper-tune linkage can be powerfully argued.

Loan Sanction.[30] Since most grants are based on generalized distribution formulas, it is central control over loan sanction that operates as a more precise constraint on the expenditure of particular local authorities. Although capital projects can be financed from revenue or capital funds, most are undertaken by loan financing. To borrow, a county borough needed the consent of a "loan-sanctioning authority." For most purposes, this was formally the Department of the Environment; however, each central department had de facto decision power over loan sanction for services under its supervision. Thus the department could offer or withhold loan sanction in the attempt to coerce a borough into modification of plans for a project or to induce or block the development of a particular service area. These decisions might have important implications for the expenditure pattern of a borough, both in terms of its capital budget and, with the completion of a capital project, its revenue budget.

It is not clear that the manipulation of loan sanctions was particularly effective. In Davies' major study of the personal social services, he concluded that loan policies were ineffective.[31] It is an analytic problem to gauge the anticipated reactions that might lead the county-borough actors to alter the borough's service provision in order to gain favor with a Ministry for loan sanction. But local actors in the four boroughs repeatedly expressed mystification about how loan requests were vetted and why one scheme was selected over another. Successes and failures were explained in terms of the fiscal climate or random factors. The general view is typified in the view of a Finance Committee Chairman:

Loan sanction has become an instrument of national fiscal policy. It has not consistently related to (the Borough's) most pressing needs as we see them. A department may be able to stop us for several years from getting what we want; or they can attempt to convince us to do something. But we decide what schemes to submit and we have final choice over both the general conception and even most details of a scheme.

A Borough Engineer observed:

In all the years I have never managed to sort out the vagaries of loan sanction. A few years ago we had done quite well on money from the Ministry (of Transport). Then in February, the DRE (Divisional Road Engineer) rang and asked if I could quietly and quickly spend £95,000 more by April. Of course I had a go. The Minister is competing for money too. He has to spend his total in order to justify more the next year. Why he chose (Borough) I can't really say.

THE FISCAL ENVIRONMENT

The finances of the county boroughs were obviously affected by the unsettled British economic situation in the 1960s. During this period, the "stop-go" policies were characterized primarily by stops—wage and price freezes, periods of restraint, devaluation of the pound, high levels of inflation. The Government's fiscal policies and the macrolevel economic environment had extraordinarily complex impacts on the financial autonomy of the county borough, as one component of those systems. This brief discussion aims only to sensitize the analysis to the fiscal environment rather than to attempt an overlysimplified characterization.

Government fiscal control. The central government consciously aimed to use both loan sanctions and Exchequer grants as means to affect the fiscal environment by manipulating the level of public spending. During the 1960s, the dominant pattern was to limit the rate of expansion in aggregate local capital expenditure. Given such financial stringency, a borough presumably expected lower levels of loan authorization. While these controls had an aggregate impact on borrowing, there is little evidence the particular county borough understood how the situation was affecting it or altered its planning on capital projects.[32]

Similarly, the increases in the major elements of the Rate Support Grant in the late 1960s were calibrated to the level of real growth in local spending that the central government desired. The government felt that controlling grant totals and issuing strongly worded circulars would constrain current expenditure and yet leave each local authority free to determine its own level of spending.[33] Brighton's Chief Accountant characterized the effect of one such provision, Circular 9/68, which called for a restriction in the growth of real expenditure to 3% for 1969-1970:

The Government is not saying we are forced to keep expenditure down to a 3 percent rise after inflation. But if the local authority says: to hell with the Government, then the Government simply says: all right, but pay the extra out of your own resources.

Thus, to the extent a county borough was willing to raise its rate or its income beyond the limits set by the Rate Support Grant and circulars, its expenditure was not tightly constrained by the government's aggregate grant policy.

Inflation. Inflation is among the most pervasive and least controllable external influences on county-borough budgeting. It has a differential impact on different types of expenditure and its interactive effects on costs, prices, and wages are extremely complex.[34] During the decade, budgeters in the four county boroughs reckoned that inflation increased expenditure levels generally at a rate of 4% per year. This rate increased substantially after 1970. While this external constraint is clearly beyond the control of local budgeters, its actual impact on allocation decisions is a function of whether local actors decide to counteract inflated costs. Since this was the typical decision, inflationary pressure must be the explanation, in general terms, for a rise in gross expenditure of about 4% per year during the period under study.

Wage and salary awards. Important groups of county-borough employees received wages whose levels were set by national pay settlements. The association which represents county boroughs was part of the group which negotiated these settlements; but individual county boroughs were powerless over these decisions. A random sample of two years from each county borough revealed that the average yearly impact of wage settlements (but not internally determined scale increases) was an increase of 1.8% of gross expenditure. Although many wage scales were externally set and wages and salaries constituted over 50% of county-borough revenue-budget expenditure, they were by no means uncontrollable. Local decisions about either the quantity of a service provided (e.g., pupil-teacher ratios, case loads, or any measure of intensity of provision), or the quality of a service (filling positions with more or less qualified and thus costly personnel) could have major effects on the aggregate wage and salary figures for a county borough.

Precepts and national pools. Certain services were provided to the county borough by agencies or bodies over which the borough had no direct control. These authorities, called precepts, levied a certain proportion of their costs to the borough, which was obliged to pay. After the police amalgamations in the mid-1960s, the police service became the most costly precept. Table 2.2 displays the precepts in the 1968-1969 budget of the four county boroughs. Southend (.5%) and Dudley 6.65%) were near the extremes on the county-borough spectrum of expenditure for these uncontrollable constraints.

Since teacher training and advanced further education (e.g., colleges of technology) were viewed as national responsibilities, all local authorities were required to contribute toward their provision. These education "pools," like precepts, had costs determined by formula. If the county borough decided to provide teacher training or further education facilities, it was reimbursed for its service provision. Thus the education pools' contributions were not controllable, although the decision to provide these

Table 2.2: Impact of Precepts 1968-1969

	Brighton	Dudley	Southend	West Bromwich
Police[a]	£505,800	£366,285	_[b]	£345,400
Rivers Board	124,000	40,070	£72,000	37,600
Drainage Board	18,070	287,500	—	238,000
Probation Agency[a]	—	11,700	—	12,900
Total	£647,870	£705,555	£72,000	£633,900
Percentage of Gross Expenditure	4.0%	6.65%	0.5%	5.9%

a. Net Cost
b. Police came under a joint, precepted authority from April 1, 1969, in Southend.

services was local. Brighton and, to a lesser extent, Dudley and Southend decided to provide these education services. The pools' contribution, over which there was no control, amounted to 2% to 4% of total spending.

Perceptions of local actors. One important type of evidence on the overall autonomy of local actors on budgeting is the perceptions of the actors themselves. Two general themes emerged repeatedly. The first observation was that there was too much constraint on the county borough, particularly from the central departments. There was an unhappiness with the diminishing autonomy of the local authority relative to the center. On the other hand, the second point was that most Councillors and officers stated plainly that the county borough had a great deal of control over expenditure decisions and budgetary allocations. A few examples are illuminating:

Central government does demand certain standards—as long as we don't fall abysmally below that, there is relatively no interference. We have virtually total discretion over our revenue expenditure provided we keep up a reasonable standard.

[Senior member, Brighton Finance Committee]

Whatever happens, there will always be a proportion of local government expenditures which will come under the direct guidance of the central government. This is more clearly seen on capital than on revenue. On capital we've really got to negotiate to get what we want. On revenue the government does not have very direct control. Their use of the rate support grant works well—but only because the local residents don't want to see a higher rate than is absolutely necessary. We are statutorily responsible to carry out certain expenditure for specified services. But even in the way we carry out those duties we have a large amount of freedom. It is subject to government exhortations. The Ministry exhorts us to do something. But choice is there and it is ours to say yes or no. In education, we decide the types of teaching, the level of additional salaries or allowances to attract teachers, the ratios, and so on. There are surprising areas of freedom available even within the rather rigid educational structure. It is greater in most other services.

[Assistant Borough Treasurer, West Bromwich]

I don't accept the argument that the center controls us to any real degree. The obvious point is that if we let our rate poundage rise, we could spend £100,000 more per year without any government restrictions. Plus there are many capital expenditures that we could charge to revenue. More books, lower pupil-teacher ratios, etc.— there are many examples of possible courses of expenditure that are completely our choice. . . . It is too easy to generalize that we have no freedom. Once you come above their minimum standards, there is very little that they will do to you. There are some areas where we have had our powers curtailed; but it is our choice how much to spend on libraries, parks, local roads and so on. I think in some cases some Chief Officers hide behind the restrictions. In the end, if you are persistent, the Ministry will usually allow you your demands; and if not, there are often ways of going around them. If we were to put our rate in line with some of the higher rating authorities, we could raise about one million more pounds per year— and that represents a lot of local decisions. I think that the central control argument falls on that ground alone.

[A Borough Treasurer]

Conclusion

The range of county-borough activity was quite broad, covering many of the important public goods and services provided to citizens. That range was externally determined in the sense that the county borough could provide only those services authorized by Parliament. Moreover, most expenditure was allocated to services that the borough was obliged to provide. However, Parliament set only broad guidelines for the levels of provisions of various services and did not specify how resources ought to be allocated among services.

The scope of county-borough choice-making was subject to a number of constraints. Each obligatory service was under the general supervision of a central department. The department had formal powers to guarantee that the county borough provided a minimum standard of service. Although the minimum was often ambiguously defined, these base levels of service provisions were a series of vague constraints on the borough's choice-making. Above the minimum, the department could use its resources and controls to encourage or discourage the development of services by the county borough. The degree to which the department attempted to intervene varied, but few departments interfered actively with the borough's service provision. Moreover, most of their powers of sanction were too insensitive to effect desired consequences.

The withholding of loan sanctions by a department was the most precise method of limiting a borough's service expansion. County boroughs usually aspired to undertake major capital projects at a higher rate than government fiscal policy would allow. The department had a veto power; but the county borough made the final decisions on what projects it would propose and what it would undertake. Each department dealt independently with the borough and there is evidence that most departments did not use their powers consistently or even effectively. In general, the county borough's prerogatives on the allocation or reallocation of its financial resources among its services were delimited but not severely constrained by the central departments.

As to the allocative decisions in the budget, precepts and national pool contributions, which constituted about 10% of total gross expenditure, were beyond local control. It is possible that the central departments' specific grant powers significantly influenced the application of another 1% to 4% of the total. But the remaining 85% was allocated by what were primarily local decisions over time, informed by statutory responsibilities and by local circumstances and dispositions. In terms of change from year to year, a general inflationary pressure of about 4% per year and national pay awards of about 2% were beyond local control. Also, budgeters were constrained by their basic staff needs and the fact that most staff were paid on the basis of national wage scales. But, subject to minimum standards, there was significant local discretion on the size and quality of staff, both within a service and relative to other services.

Gross expenditure levels were limited only by the willingness of the Council to tax and of the rate-payers to be taxed. Contrary to the dependence-on-grants argument, over 60% of the revenue financing services was locally generated by rates, rents, and income. And since the Rate Support Grant from the central government arrived as a block allocation, its use could be locally determined. The growth of local expenditure was controlled by the grant total only to the extent that the county borough was unwilling to raise the regressive rate to finance further spending.

In sum, this chapter has undertaken a descriptive analysis of the county borough's financial position in its environment. The evidence presented here does not support the notion that the county borough was a passive agent of the central government in the provision of services, or that it was buffeted so severely by uncontrollable forces in its environment that its budgetary allocation capabilities were trivial. We conclude that the county borough might have quite significant potential discretion over its resource allocations. Chapter 3 is an empirical examination of whether there is actual interborough variation in levels of expenditure.

NOTES

1. In this book, the terms "county borough," "borough," and "local authority" will be used extensively. Unlike the common use of the word "borough" in England, we shall use it as a synonym for county borough, for purposes of style. The term "local authority" applies to all popularly elected local government units in England. It can be understood in that fashion here, although it should be seen as referring particularly to the county boroughs. One difficulty in examining the concerns dealt with in this chapter is that there is very little published work specifically on county boroughs. Most empirical work attempts to deal with all types of local authorities, leading to some imprecision. It is argued in the text that county boroughs are uniquely and broadly empowered "all-purpose" local governments.

2. The Labour Party, *Local Government Handbook* (London: Victoria House, 1960), p. 48.

3. This list is revised from W. Eric Jackson, *Local Government in England and Wales* (London: Penguin, 1966), Appendix to Chapter 4.

4. See the Committee on the Management of Local Government, referred to hereafter as the *"Maud Committee,"* Volume I, Report of the Committee, para. 256.

5. C. A. Cross, *Principles of Local Government Law* (London: Sweet & Maxwell, 1966), p. 8.

6. Ibid., p. 185.

7. One could argue that this indicates the extraordinary power of the statutes as constraints on action. This seems a far less plausible explanation. John Dearlove, in his study of one London borough quotes a Chief Officer: "You can always find some law to enable you to do something, and the officers are to blame if they can't advise the members as to *how* to do something they are keen to do. It's not so much a question of why a thing can't be done, but how a thing can be done." John N. Dearlove, *The Politics of Policy in Local Government,* op. cit., p. 15. Dearlove argues cogently that statutory limitations on local-authority action have been greatly overemphasized in the literature.

8. For example, the National Health Service Act of 1946 made seven services mandatory for county boroughs and empowered them to provide two others. The Act did not set standards for provision; rather each county borough was to submit for ministerial approval a set of proposals based on local need and dispositions. See National Health Service Act, 1946, sections 21-29.

9. A. H. Marshall, *Financial Administration in Local Government* (London: Allen & Unwin, 1961), p. 260.

10. W.A.C. Kitching, *The Finance of Local Government* (London: Allen & Unwin, 1962), p. 75. (His emphasis)

11. J. H. Warren, *The English Local Government System* (London: Allen & Unwin, 1966).

12. William Robson, *Local Government in Crisis* (London: Allen & Unwin, 1966). A more reasoned argument concerning the unintended aspects of central government control is Sir William Hart, "The Increasing Central Control over Local Finance," *County Council Gazette,* 61, No. 12 (December 1968), pp. 339-342. An interesting but dated examination is the West Midland Study Group, *Local Government and Central Control* (London: Routledge, 1956). Among the most complete rebuttals is Dearlove, op. cit., ch. 2. See also Jeffrey Stanyer, *County Government in England and Wales* (London: Routledge & Kegan Paul, 1967), ch. 1.

13. J.A.G. Griffith, *Central Departments and Local Authorities* (London: Allen & Unwin, 1966), pp. 17-18.

14. Ibid., pp. 49-50.

15. The Children's Act, 1948. This, and the following examples are discussed in the Maud Committee, op. cit., para. 258.

16. The Town and Country Planning Act, 1947 and 1962.

17. The welfare services under the National Assistance Act, 1948.

18. The Education Act, 1944. Even in this case there is far more unsaid about the nature of the relationship than is specified. In these areas, the county boroughs have not been passive agents. Among the unstipulated aspects of the service was the lack of ministerial control over the form of secondary education. The Labour Government decided to overcome this problem in 1965 by a strongly worded circular (Circular 10/65) that "requested" all local education authorities to submit within one year plans for comprehensivization of secondary schools. Even under strong political and departmental pressure, many LEAs refused to submit acceptable plans. The Conservative Government later revoked this request.

19. Griffith, op. cit., p. 52.

20. Ibid., op. cit., pp. 54-61.

21. The example of Circular 10/65 on secondary education can be expanded. In the years after the circular, the Labour Government found some local education au-

thorities, especially non-Labour ones, so intransigent to the motives of the circular that the Government was enacting legislation to make comprehensivization mandatory. The victory of the Conservatives in 1970 ended that legislation, and with Circular 10/70 the Department reasserted the right of the local education authority to determine the form of its secondary education. Boaden found that four years after 10/65, only 31 percent of the forty-nine Conservative-controlled county boroughs had reorganized secondary education. Further, many of these had been reorganized while Labour controlled the Council. Boaden claimed that there were only two clear cases of Conservative-controlled Councils reorganizing education. Noel Boaden, "Innovation and Change in English Local Government," *Political Studies,* 19 (December 1971), pp. 416-429. It is hard not to see the history of 10/65 as evidence that, short of Parliamentary statute, the county borough had the autonomy to withstand the concerted pressure of a department.

22. See Davies, op. cit., especially pp. 298-305; Slack, op. cit.; Noel Boaden and Robert Alford, "Sources of Diversity in English Local Government," *Public Administration,* 47 (Summer 1969), pp. 203-224.

23. Griffith concludes, "The refusal or failure or reluctance of government departments to make policy explicit is the most complicating factor in the relationship between government departments and local authorities." Griffith, op. cit., p. 537. Similarly, Davies argues that the policy of many departments "appears to be very unspecific." Davies, op. cit., p. 31. Fuller elaboration of the central department-county borough relationship is Danziger (1974), op. cit., ch. 2.

24. Robson is a very strong advocate of the piper-tune argument. He contends, "The very large increase both in the absolute amount of grants and in the proportion which they bear to rate revenue is both a cause and a consequence of an increase of central control. . . . Can anyone seriously doubt that as the Treasury comes to provide more and more money for the local councils, the voices of Whitehall will speak more often and with greater insistence?" See Robson, op. cit., pp. 53-68, 149-150.

25. For a full discussion of the rating system, see, for example, Kitching, op. cit., Ch. 2.

26. *The Future Shape of Local Government Finance* (Cmnd. 4741, H.M.S.O., July 1971), para. 32.

27. See Robson, op. cit., p. 53.

28. Computed from figures in Maud Committee, op. cit., para. 262.

29. County boroughs treated government payments for their provision of further education and teacher-training facilities as income, since they are not payments for a service that the borough had decided to provide and are not grants.

30. For a discussion of loan sanction, see Kitching, op. cit., ch. 7. We center our discussion on loan procedures that operated during the 1960s, prior to Circular 2/70. This altered the system, dividing expenditure into two general areas, "key sector" and "locally determined schemes" (L.D.S.). To oversimplify vastly, most major capital projects, such as school buildings, social-service homes and facilities, major roads, and so on, became key sector, and loan sanction was handled rather like the process described in the text. Many small or supplementary projects have been classified as L.D.S. Each county borough is set a yearly total of acceptable L.D.S. expenditure and is left free to spend it without loan sanction.

31. Davies, in discussing both grants and loans, concludes with the "fact that local authorities appear not to respond to quite strong social policy and financial

incentives. . . . Some influential theories about how grant systems affect local authorities' behavior depend on the assumption that local authorities respond to price incentives as do firms in a market. If authorities are generally as unresponsive to price incentives as they appear to have been in the fields examined, such theories are invalid." Davies, op. cit., pp. 303-304. More recently, Judge has argued that the central government has been increasingly effective in constraining local authorities' spending by the use of capital-planning mechanisms. See Ken Judge, *Rationing Social Services* (London: Heinemann, 1977).

32. None of the four boroughs reduced their number of loan requests. While local actors noted that the situation was "tight," they persistently claimed that their borough was moderately successful. With respect to the particular local authority, Griffith shows that its total loan debt is not an important consideration in the decision on loan sanction. It is policy and design criteria that predominate decisions on specific sanctions rather than the local financial situation. Griffith, op. cit., p. 552.

33. In the words of the Government: "So far as management of the economy is concerned, the central government are able to influence the decisions of local authorities on current expenditure through the block grant and in other ways, at the same time leaving individual authorities free in the last resort to decide for themselves how much they wish to spend. The Government welcome this. In view of the close working relationship between central and local government, experience shows that the aggregate effect of all these individual decisions can be predicted with some accuracy." *The Future Shape of Local Government Finance,* op. cit., para. 41.

34. A helpful discussion is E. A. Collins, "Inflation and Public Expenditure," *Public Administration* (Winter 1968), pp. 393-410.

Chapter 3

INTERBOROUGH VARIATIONS IN ALLOCATIONS

The county borough, it was argued in the last chapter, appeared to have considerable autonomy over its budgetary allocations. Although the county borough operated in a limiting environment, it is not evident that the potential scope for local choice-making was severely constrained by external forces. But a more compelling case for the existence of local budgetary discretion must be based on evidence that discretion has in fact been exercised. This is the subject of this and the following chapter. The central research question is whether the county borough appears to have made substantial choices on its budgetary allocations.

There is some research which suggests that interborough variations on allocation levels are likely. In Davies' major study of the social-welfare services, the allocation data for the local health services, welfare services, and children's services reflect a substantial degree of expenditure variation among the county boroughs.[1] Other studies of social administration have provided similar conclusions about variability in resource allocation.[2]

J.A.G. Griffith expressed displeasure about the extent of service variability that most central departments allowed the local authorities. And Boaden, to support the contention that county boroughs do make budgetary choices, examined expenditure levels per population for the twenty smallest and the twenty poorest county boroughs. He found that the expenditure levels for each group arrayed throughout the quartile ranges for all county boroughs. This was taken as support that local discretion existed, since neither the very small nor the very grant-dependent boroughs seemed systematically constrained in their expenditure choices.[3]

Hence, we begin the analysis with the question of whether there are *variations in allocation patterns* among the county boroughs. The absence of significant interborough variations would imply either that external constraints did, in fact, severely limit local choice or that the county boroughs opted not to utilize their potential autonomy. While it would be difficult to distinguish between these explanations, the first is the more plausible, given the conventional wisdom about central-local relations. Thus the lack of variations would constitute empirical support for the arguments of central-government dominance.

Conversely, the finding that there are significant variations in allocations would serve two purposes. In the first place, the finding would be important evidence against the central-control thesis. Secondly, the data would be a necessary but not sufficient condition to falsify the null hypothesis that there was no local budgetary choice-making. Even if variations in allocations are present, there is a strong and plausible alternate explanation to local choice-making—the demographic approach. According to the demographic approach, expenditure variations are produced by socioeconomic or demographic factors in the county borough's environment rather than by local choice. In order to approach the hypothesis about budgetary decision-making systematically, the sole focus in this chapter is whether there are variations in the resource allocation of county boroughs. The subsequent chapters will evaluate various explanations for any interborough variation found to exist. Therefore this chapter assesses the null hypothesis: there are no substantial variations in budgetary allocations among the county boroughs.

Types of Indicators of Provision

The operational task is to translate the concept of allocation of governmental goods and services into a series of meaningful indicators that can be compared between county boroughs. Several distinctions characterize the indicators used.

(1) Monetary or nonmonetary measures. Some indicators are expressed in terms of units-of-service-provided; but most are measured as amount-of-money expended. While amount of money does not necessarily correspond to either the quality or quantity of service, it does tap the government's commitment to support a service at a certain level.[4]

(2) Net or gross expenditure. In most instances, a net expenditure (deducting direct income and specific grants) figure is employed for individual services.[5]

(3) Divisible-benefit or indivisible-benefit services. Economists distinguish between those services which have specific recipients of resources (divisible-benefit) and those services which are generally available to the community as a whole (indivisible-benefit).

(4) Taxonomy of local services. While no policy taxonomy is wholly satisfactory, a modification of the Williams and Adrian one will be used.[6] County-borough services are divided into: (a) caretaker services, which regulate and negotiate the community's environment (e.g., police and fire services, streets, sewage); (b) promoter services, which aim to enhance the economic milieu by active manipulation (e.g., town planning, tourist facilities); (c) amenity services, which provide desirable rather than "essential" goods and services (e.g., social-welfare services); and (d) the education services.

(5) Measures of output. Bleddyn Davies' classificatory scheme of output measures will be employed.[7] It includes: (a) measures of resources allocated, as net expenditure on a particular service or on a type of services per head of population,[8] or as the relative percentage of expenditure allocated to a service; (b) measures of intensity of provision, as net expenditure per unit of service provision, or level of service per unit of provision, or level of service per head of population; and (c) measures of extensiveness of provision, as the number of clients benefitting from a service.[9]

Data on Variation in Allocations

The concern with the variation on a measure of allocational output across all the county boroughs suggests the use of statistical measures of dispersion and central tendency. To capture various aspects of this interborough variability, the analysis displays the mean, the standard deviation, the minimum-maximum range, and the coefficient of variation (C.V.). The C.V. is the ratio of the standard deviation on the mean and can be understood as a normalized measure of dispersion around the mean across different variables.[10] None of these measures has a measure of statistical significance; but since the real concern is with *substantive* significance, we suggest (as a rule-of-thumb) that as the C.V. takes values greater than .10, the variation becomes more interesting in a substantive sense.

Tables 3.1 and 3.2 display these descriptive statistics for *measures of resources allocated* to both indivisible-benefit and divisible-benefit services. The most striking overall observation is that the spread on virtually every service is quite high. This might have been expected for the divisible-benefit services, given the interborough differences in client populations. But it is more surprising that the C.V. for expenditure on every service for the community as a whole is at least .14 and most are between .20 and .25. While expenditure on most services doubled during the period from 1960 to 1969, the relative dispersion around the mean remained quite consistent. In Table

Table 3.1: Measures of Resources Allocated: Net rate and grant-born expenditure per population on *indivisible-benefit services*

Service	Year	Mean	Standard Dev.	C.V.	Minimum-Maximum
Highways[a]	60-61	45.7 s.	8.6 s.	.19	26.8— 64.8s.
	64-65	62.4	12.2	.20	35.3— 93.2
	68-69	82.4	17.5	.21	44.5— 138.8
Police[b]	60-61	£1229.9	£189.7	.15	£ 825 —1895
	64-65	1730.7	250.4	.14	1253 —2588
	68-69	95.1 s.	15.9 s.	.17	65.3— 146.1s.
Fire[c]	60-61	£ 640.2	£140.2	.22	£ 396 —1177
	64-65	969.4	208.9	.22	609 —1674
	68-69	1326.1	210.4	.23	851 —2330
Ambulance[c]	60-61	£ 245.4	£ 53.3	.22	£ 136 — 397
	64-65	364.2	80.8	.22	203 — 605
	68-69	511.1	101.2	.20	251 — 787
Sewage and Sewerage[a]	60-61	17.5 s.	9.0 s.	.52	3.5— 45.9s.
	64-65	22.7	11.7	.52	4.3— 54.9
	68-69	33.75	15.8	.47	6.6— 80.8
Refuse[a]	60-61	15.7 s.	3.95s.	.25	6.7— 26.8s.
	64-65	20.75	4.45	.21	11.3— 35.2
	68-69	28.2	5.8	.21	16.3— 49.3
Parks[a]	60-61	16.9 s.	4.3 s.	.25	8.9— 28.0s.
	64-65	23.2	5.5	.24	12.8— 40.3
Libraries[c]	60-61	£ 418.1	£ 84.2	.20	£ 262 — 617
	64-65	576.8	121.2	.21	369 — 857
	68-69	836.4	198.1	.24	561 —1541
Library Books[c]	60-61	£ 140.1	£ 32.0	.23	£ 262 — 616
	68-69	241.1	54.4	.23	561 —1541
Library Staff[c]	60-61	£ 220.4	£ 47.9	.22	£ 133 — 338
	68-69	435.6	84.2	.19	256 — 661
Planning[a]	60-61	3.4 s.	3.5 s.	1.03	0.0— 18.2s.
	68-69	12.65	9.3	.74	0.0— 45.4

a. Expenditure as rates levied per head.
b. Expenditure per 1,000 population for 1960-1961 and 1964-1965, as rates per head 1968-1969.
c. Expenditure per 1,000 population.

Table 3.2: Measures of Resources Allocated: Net rate and grant-born expenditure per population on *divisible-benefit services*[a]

Service	Year	Mean	Standard Dev.	C.V.	Minimum-Maximum
Education:					
Primary	60-61	£ 4,718.1	£ 674.8	.14	£ 2,904– 6,536
	64-65	5,718.9	806.6	.14	3,845– 7,991
	68-69	8,215.4	977.9	.12	5,269–10,387
Secondary	60-61	5,219.8	587.0	.11	4,107– 6,715
	64-65	7,269.4	724.6	.10	5,510– 9,310
	68-69	10,080.0	1148.8	.11	6,786–13,159
Further	60-61	1,951.9	374.9	.19	1,210– 2,917
	64-65	3,369.2	539.1	.16	2,448– 5,062
	68-69	5,666.3	827.5	.15	4,043– 8,339
Special	68-69	869.9	240.7	.28	323– 1,714
Teacher Training	68-69	1,538.0	162.7	.11	1,025– 1,981
Total Education	60-61	£14,929.3	£1423.8	.10	£11,003–18,536
	64-65	20,997.5	1877.7	.09	15,438–25,075
	68-69	30,429.2	2783.7	.09	21,264–35,540
Health:					
Midwifery	60-61	111.7	37.8	.34	37– 195
	64-65	148.2	50.3	.34	45– 237
	68-69	170.0	60.0	.35	53– 309
Domestic Help	60-61	177.6	85.9	.48	28– 420
	64-65	148.2	97.4	.36	60– 532
	68-69	394.1	144.5	.37	155– 820
Home Nursing	60-61	158.7	50.8	.32	75– 313
	64-65	211.6	53.1	.25	102– 378
	68-69	276.8	61.5	.22	154– 474
Health Visiting	60-61	91.6	29.0	.32	33– 178
	64-65	129.2	42.9	.33	48– 261
	68-69	166.1	58.6	.35	50– 319
Mental Health	60-61	115.3	40.8	.35	26– 247
	64-65	242.1	76.8	.32	120– 446
	68-69	451.0	140.9	.31	197– 864
Total Health	60-61	£ 1,366.7	£ 248.5	.18	£ 935– 1,944
	64-65	1,968.9	332.8	.18	1,309– 2,963

Table 3.2 (Continued)

Service	Year	Mean	Standard Dev.	C.V.	Minimum-Maximum	
Welfare:						
Residential	60-61	£ 447.1	£ 132.6	.30	£ 206–	759
Homes	64-65	662.6	176.9	.28	280–	1,168
	68-69	937.2	270.1	.29	415–	1,706
Blind	68-69	119.4	66.6	.56	21–	355
Handicapped	68-69	88.3	51.4	.38	14–	255
Total Welfare	60-61	£ 683.4	£ 158.0	.23	£ 381–	1,082
	64-65	971.3	242.3	.25	501–	1,736
	68-69	1,478.2	277.1	.26	813–	2,351
Children:						
Local Authority	60-61	200.6	82.4	.41	23–	382
Homes	64-65	243.7	110.6	.46	43–	476
	68-69	337.7	158.6	.42	69–	837
Boarded Out	60-61	83.6	28.0	.34	37–	174
Cases	64-65	114.2	38.3	.34	49–	224
	68-69	137.9	52.2	.38	60–	281
Approved Schools	68-69	157.7	70.6	.45	35–	389
Total Children	60-61	£ 463.6	£ 105.1	.23	£ 155–	732
	64-65	667.6	169.5	.25	291–	1,086
	68-69	1,002.7	281.9	.28	514–	1,718
Housing:						
Rate	64-65	45.75s.	18.3s.	.40	11.1–	104.4s.
	68-69	70.5	34.5	.49	14.3–	212.6

a. All services are expenditure per 1,000 population except Housing, which is rates levied per head.

3.2, it is notable that the C.V. is higher for every indicator of a component service within any general service (such as midwifery, domestic helps, and the others within the local health services). It appears that as the data are further disaggregated, the interborough variations become more substantial. It is also clear that the variations on the indicators for the major education services are notably lower than those for other services.

Since these measures do not account for varying size student populations, this is interesting evidence in support of Griffith's contention that the Department of Education and Science has been effective in articulating and promoting a uniform policy of provision among local authorities.[11] The more discretionary education services, such as further education and special education, have variation more in line with that on the personal social services. In sum, the data in Tables 3.1 and 3.2 reveal that there is a substantial amount of interborough variation in resources allocated that must be explained.

Table 3.3 presents indicators which tap the overall levels of expenditure in the county borough. The first measure is the total net expenditure on all rate fund services—the amount financed by rates and all government grants, expressed in terms of rate levied per head of population. The second measure is the rates levied per head when all government grants have been deducted from the first measure. Thus the first figure measures the total commitment of financial resources from *all sources* to provide services. The second expresses the total amount of *local revenue* per head that has been raised to finance the services. Net outstanding debt per head and housing debt per head reflect

Table 3.3: Measures of Resources Allocated: Summary Measures of Expenditure per Head

Service Measure	Year	Mean	Standard Dev.	C.V.	Mimimum-Maximum	
Total Net	60-61	594.4s.	41.3s.	.07	511—	697s.
Rate- and	64-65	825.1	57.7	.07	695—	996
Grant-Born Exp.	68-69	1183.4	97.2	.08	968—	1514
Total Net	60-61	293.8s.	52.6s.	.18	180—	203s.
Rate-Born	64-65	391.4	75.4	.19	249—	589
Exp.	68-69	532.0	95.5	.18	343—	754
Net	60-61	£ 125.1	£30.4	.24	£27.6—	183.3
Outstanding	64-65	162.7	37.8	.23	66.2—	239.1
Debt	68-69	228.1	58.0	.25	82.6—	364.3
Housing Debt	68-69	£ 102	£33.9	.34	£ 28—	178

the magnitude of the borough's long-term investment in capital projects financed by loans.

The relatively low coefficients of variation for total rate- and grant-born expenditure are interesting. They are lower than might have been predicted, given the substantial expenditure variations on individual services. It appears that some force, or set of forces, have produced a level of uniformity across all county boroughs on the total resource commitment per head. The higher variation on rate-born expenditure, viewed in conjunction with the low variation on total net expenditure, suggests that government grants have supplemented a lower rate return in poorer boroughs and assured some uniformity in total available resources. The level of housing debt per head has the greatest C.V. among the measures in the table, with values ranging from £28 to £178 per head. The variation in the net outstanding-debt measure is also quite high. These figures seem to reflect differences in the predispositions to provide major capital projects and/or undertake long-term loan obligations. It might be, however, that other conditions such as local availability of land, endowment of buildings, and so forth, affect these indicators.[12] It will be interesting to test the debt figures against various demographic factors such as density and social class.

Table 3.4 registers measures of intensity of provision across all the county boroughs. While these indicators, particularly the unit-cost measures in Part A, must be interpreted with caution,[13] they are generally consistent with the data in earlier tables. Interborough variation is highest on the measures for personal social services and is lowest on the measures for the basic education services. The pupil-teacher ratios for primary and secondary schools have the lowest C.V. values of any examined. Since these measures are rather more responsive to local circumstances, the interborough variability in Table 3.4 is further persuasive evidence that there are interesting differences in the levels of allocation output to different county boroughs on every type of service. And this conclusion is underlined by the few measures of extensiveness of service

Table 3.4: Measures of Intensity of Provision

Service Measure	Year	Mean	S.D.	C.V.	Minimum-Maximum
A. Resources Expended Per Unit of Service					
Education					
Cost per primary pupil	1960-1961	£ 49.1	£ 4.2	.09	£ 41.8– 63.2
	1964-1965	62.8	4.6	.07	53.2– 76.2
	1968-1969	80.2	5.2	.06	66.1– 94.1
Cost per secondary pupil	1960-1961	£ 81.1	£ 5.8	.07	£ 69.9– 93.0
	1964-1965	116.5	9.4	.08	92.7– 153.8
	1968-1969	156.5	11.6	.08	132.4– 184.7
Health					
Midwifery—cost per case	1968-1969	£ 33.4	£ 11.5	.34	£ 9.0– 68.9
Health visiting—cost per effective visit	1968-1969	13.4s.	4.7	.35	2.4– 30.8s.
Child welfare—cost per attendance	1968-1969	14.3	5.5	.39	3.6– 28.4
Home nursing—cost per visit	1968-1969	9.7	1.8	.18	6.8– 17.3
Domestic help—cost per case	1968-1969	£ 42.9	£ 11.1	.26	£ 25.8– 91.4
Children					
Boarded out—cost per child week	1968-1969	65.4s.	9.1s.	.14	41.6– 88.6s.
Local authority homes—cost per child week	1968-1969	275.6s.	49.4	.17	148.0– 397.0
All homes—cost per child week	1968-1969	245.7s.	44.1	.18	118.6– 378.8
Housing					
Rent as a proportion of housing revenue	1968-1969	76.4%	8.15%	.11	49 – 87%
Repairs—per dwelling	1968-1969	£ 20.0	£ 4.56	.23	£ 12.0– 34.0%

Table 3.4 (Continued)

Service Measure	Year	Mean	S.D.	C.V.	Minimum-Maximum
B. Service Level Per Unit of Population					
Police—population per officer	1960-1961	581.2	74.2	.13	412 — 817
	1964-1965	521.6	58.6	.11	389 — 692
Fire—population per officer	1960-1961	1585.1	380.8	.24	938 —2598
C. Service Level Per Unit of Provision					
Education					
Primary—pupil-teacher ratio	1960-1961	30.2	1.77	.06	25 — 35
	1964-1965	29.6	1.87	.06	24.8— 37.4
	1968-1969	29.3	1.42	.05	25.4— 32.7
Secondary—pupil-teacher ratio	1960-1961	20.8	.96	.05	19 — 23
	1964-1965	18.7	1.00	.05	14.4— 21.1
	1968-1969	18.3	.91	.05	16.0— 20.9
Housing—percentage of all housing that is built by county borough	1960-1965	51.8%	21.0%	.40	10 — 93%
Children					
Percentage in-care children boarded out	1968-1969	49.9%	9.7%	.19	26 — 77%
Percentage in-care children in L.A. homes	1968-1969	28.7	9.1	.32	8 — 52

[67]

Table 3.5: Measures of Extensiveness of Provision

Service Measure	Year	Mean	S.D.	C.V.	Minimum-Maximum
Housing Local authority—built as % of total households	1945-1965	17.1%	5.6%	.33	4 —33%
Children % of children under 18 who are in care	1968-1969	6.24%	2.05%	.33	3.01—11.4%
Welfare Number accommodated per 1,000 population	1960-1961 1968-1969	2.44 2.81	.67 .82	.32 .29	1.11—4.21 1.09—5.06

provision presented in Table 3.5. While these data cannot provide an explanation for why the variations exist or for whether they are a consequence of conscious local choice, they are powerful evidence against the null hypothesis that there are no interborough variations in the level of allocation outputs.

Variation in Allocations in the Four County Boroughs

While descriptive statistics for all the county boroughs capture the broad nature of the variations, it is useful to focus briefly on the particular figures for the four county boroughs which are examined intensively in later chapters. This will provide a richer sense of variation and alterations over time and it will be suggestive of the unique allocation configuration of the four cases. Specifically, this section examines the level of allocation in each borough relative to the average county-borough allocation for that year and, of course, relative to each other. And this section specifies the share of total expenditure which each of the four boroughs has allocated to the various service types.

In Table 3.6, each of the four county borough's allocation is presented with the mean allocation for all the boroughs as an index of 100. For the selected services, it is possible to determine whether the borough is relatively close to the average allocation, to assess the extent to which each borough's allocation is stable over time in relation to the average allocation, and to examine the relative commitment to any particular service among the four county boroughs.

There are two general points which emerge from Table 3.6. First, the patterns of fluctuation in the variation between a county borough's allocation and the mean county-borough allocation defy generalized description. For some services, a county borough has sustained a stable relative allocation during the decade; but for other services, there is a striking level of variability. For example, while expenditure on the fire service has been stable in West Bromwich (relative to the mean expenditure level), it has altered substantially in Dudley. While the more aggregated figures suggest some stability, the more disaggregated figures reflecting the allocations on particular service components tend to alter to a notable extent. The second general point is that the four county boroughs are different from each other in their level of commitment to the various services. It is particularly significant that the expectation that Set I (that is, Brighton and Southend) and Set II (Dudley and West Bromwich) would be systematically distinct on most measures is not strongly supported. There are instances where the two sets are clearly distinguished. These include some of the major services, including highways, police, and primary education. But in many instances where generalized notions that the socioeconomic and political differences between the two sets would lead to allocation differences, the data confound this assumption. On some services, one of the four is clearly different (e.g., West Bromwich on total education spending, Brighton on local health-services spending) and occasionally the four are paired opposite to the expectation (e.g., total rate- and grant-born expenditure).

The general measures of total resources allocated are especially revealing. The figures for total net rate- and grant-born expenditure are in line with the apparent uniformity for this measure across all county boroughs (Table 3.3). Only Dudley's

Table 3.6: Relative Allocation Outputs for the Four County Boroughs[a]

	Year	Bri	Dud	S'end	W Bro
Selected Measures of Resources Allocated					
Indivisible-Benefit Services					
Highways	60-61	105	85	103	70
	64-65	115	103	107	81
	68-69	100	79	122	78
Fire	60-61	111	96	83	90
	64-65	101	103	80	86
	68-69	106	70	84	87
Sewage and Sewerage	60-61	24	95	120	171
	64-65	19	90	99	133
	68-69	20	113	90	122
Libraries	60-61	115	118	99	106
	64-65	139	115	101	85
	68-69	99	99	104	81
Divisible-Benefit Services					
Primary Education	60-61	83	125	88	108
	64-65	85	103	88	115
	68-69	80	102	85	106
Secondary Education	60-61	90	90	106	118
	64-65	89	92	95	115
	68-69	84	91	93	111
Further Education	60-61	75	80	95	114
	64-65	94	73	93	107
	68-69	96	76	94	91
Total Education	60-61	85	98	96	110
	64-65	88	92	90	111
	68-69	87	90	89	105
Health-Midwifery	60-61	69	100	75	122
	68-69	63	125	74	135
Health- Health Visiting	60-61	138	179	51	95
	68-69	184	55	51	101
Health- Mental Health	60-61	51	95	70	96
	68-69	166	89	70	105
Total Local Health Services	60-61	111	89	75	83
	64-65	121	99	73	86
	68-69	139	80	81	80
Total Welfare Services	60-61	157	85	109	75
	64-65	193	85	101	86
	68-69	150	54	115	81
Rate Aid to Housing	68-69	64	89	51	150

Table 3.6 (Continued)

	Year	Bri	Dud	S'end	W Bro
Summary Measures					
Total Rate- and	60-61	93	101	99	105
Grant-Born	64-65	99	99	95	103
Expenditure	68-69	101	88	92	101
Total Rate-Born	60-61	116	92	117	94
Expenditure	64-65	128	106	118	111
	68-69	115	109	71	125
Selected Measures of Intensity and Extensiveness of Provision					
Cost per primary	60-61	104	110	105	96
pupil	64-65	104	108	104	105
	68-69	102	100	103	101
Primary pupils per	60-61	102	99	99	119
teacher	64-65	102	102	90	103
	68-69	99	100	96	94
Midwifery-cost per case	60-61	128	74	106	146
Health visiting-cost per effective visit	68-69	198	75	106	136
Home nursing-cost per visit	68-69	107	111	88	122
All children's homes-cost per child week	68-69	102	106	95	106
Percentage of all housing that is built by the county borough	60-65	48	129	42	118
Housing repairs-cost per dwelling	68-69	145	105	135	113

a. All indicators are indexed to a base 100 for the mean value for all county boroughs.

1968-1969 figure deviates more than 10% from the mean. West Bromwich is the only borough which maintained above average total expenditure per head for all three years. On the evidence of these figures, it appears that Brighton and West Bromwich increased their rate levy, in comparison with their set partner, in order to sustain their higher levels of total expenditure per head. It seems that West Bromwich's revenue effort, in the sense of rate-generated expenditure, is similar to that in Southend. Since West Bromwich received substantially more grants-in-aid per head (in 1968-1969, total grants per head were 504s. in Southend and 605s. in West Bromwich), it can be argued that government grants have not necessarily substituted for locally generated revenue in the finance of services.[14] The very low outstanding debt per head figure in Southend further suggests a broad fiscal conservatism; but it is of a different sort than Dudley, where there seems to have been some reluctance to increase tax levels.

Another perspective on the four county boroughs can be gained by examining the relative proportions of their total spending which are allocated to each service (Table 3.7). In these relative figures, the dominance of the education sector is apparent. In Set II boroughs about 60% of total net expenditure is consumed by the various education services; in Set I the figure is about 50%. This means that the remaining shares that are allocatable among noneducation services are particularly limited in Set II.

Among the policy types, Brighton is substantially higher than the other three in relative spending on the personal services, West Bromwich falls well below the others on the caretaker services, and Southend is high on the promoter services. On individual services, the proportions array in a fashion that varies from one service to the next. The four boroughs' allocative shares are similar on libraries but not on parks, on fire services but not on police services. Dudley's commitment to highways and planning and Brighton's high allocations to the personal services are clear. Across the four boroughs, the ratio of the highest to the lowest proportion allocated is usually greater than 3:2. If the individual services are summed without reference to relative costliness, the comparison of the four county boroughs is:

	Bri	Dud	S'end	W Bro
Allocated highest proportion	18	7	5	8
Allocated lowest proportion	7	8	10	14

Thus there is at least some distribution in the high-low rankings for these allocative proportions. However, it can also be seen in

Table 3.7: Service Net Expenditure as a Percentage of Total Expenditure Financed by Rates and All Grants in the Four County Boroughs, 1968-1969

	Bri	Dud	S'end	W Bro
Caretaker Services				
1. Highways and street cleansing	5.62%	6.85%	6.10%	5.39%
2. Public lighting	1.56	1.26	1.21	.77
3. Sewage, sewerage, rivers	2.36	4.35	3.91	4.60
4. Refuse-collection and disposal	2.60	2.87	3.09	2.20
5. Public health	1.20	1.19	.57	.96
6. Public conveniences	.93	.22	1.15	.20
7. Police service	5.74	4.28	5.51	3.66
8. Fire service	2.65	1.88	2.07	2.17
9. Admin. of Justice	1.91	.76	.68	.45
Σ *Caretaker Services*	24.57	23.66	24.29	20.40
Amenity Services				
1. Parks	4.00	1.50	2.86	1.62
2. Baths	.44	.96	.73	.97
3. Libraries, museums	2.16	1.98	1.77	1.36
4. Housing-rate contrib.	.37	.00	1.26	1.38
Σ *Amenities*	6.97	4.44	6.62	5.33
Promoter Services				
1. Planning	1.30	1.48	.76	.78
2. Development-redevelopment	1.07	1.91	.91	1.02
3. Car parks and traffic control	.63	– –	.94	.24
4. Entertainments and publicity	1.37	.01	1.58	CR .05
Σ *Promoter Services*	2.23	3.40	4.19	1.99
Education				
1. Nursery	.19	.31	.00	.00
2. Primary	12.49	17.51	13.21	16.59
3. Secondary	16.03	18.98	16.52	20.72
4. Further and teacher training	12.34	12.67	12.50	13.29
5. Special	1.24	1.16	1.33	1.61
6. School health	.89	1.07	.45	.70
7. Meals and milk	3.13	3.26	2.95	3.50
8. Youth centres	1.43	1.15	1.70	1.25
Σ *Education*	49.95	58.37	49.66	60.21
Local Health Services				
1. Mother and young child care	.58	.52	.30	.26
2. Midwifery	.22	.54	.29	.48

Table 3.7 (Continued)

	Bri	Dud	S'end	W Bro
Local Health Services (Cont'd.)				
3. Health visiting	.62	.27	.21	.33
4. Home nursing	.90	.52	.52	.41
5. Ambulance service	1.26	1.18	.77	1.07
6. Prevention, care, after-care	.37	.11	.17	.14
7. Domestic helps	1.00	.48	.92	.56
8. Mentally disordered	1.63	.92	.80	.89
9. Handicapped	.26	.42	.19	.56
Σ *Local Health Service*	7.27	4.89	4.15	4.79
Welfare Services				
1. Residential accommodation	2.97	.96	2.93	1.00
Σ *Welfare Services*	4.18	1.70	3.14	2.21
Children's Service				
1. Local authority homes	.80	.55	.60	.42
2. Boarded out children	.24	.13	.38	.26
Σ *Children's Service*	2.38	1.23	1.32	1.37
Σ *Personal Services*	14.83	7.82	8.61	8.37

the table that there are few really dramatic interborough differences in the size of shares. If one knew the proportion allocated to a service in one borough, one could make a reasonable estimate of the proportion on the service in another borough.

Although many variations are not dramatic, two considerations are important. One is that these proportions ought to be compared in relation to one another. Thus while the range on the children's service is only 1.2%, Brighton is spending *twice as much* of its total expenditure as Dudley and nearly double the figures for Southend and West Bromwich. This observation holds particularly for the specific service figures. The second consideration is that small percentage amounts are meaningful in terms of actual expenditure. Each 0.1% difference should be understood as about £9,000 expenditure. If, for example, West Bromwich allocated Brighton's caretaker share, the increase in expenditure would be £400,000, the product of a 10d rate. While many differences appear small individually, it can be argued that they accumulate into configurations (budgets) that are importantly different. The actual expenditure implication of any proportion then, is interdependent with the determination of the total resources to be expended. We conclude that the variations in relative shares allocated in the four boroughs are less pronounced than measures of actual expenditure. But apart from Brighton's higher spending propensity on the personal services, the patterns vary across services and boroughs in a complex fashion. Variation is largest when expenditure categories are most specific; but at all levels there are interesting variations worthy of exploration.

Conclusion

This chapter has presented various types of indicators that measure aspects of the interborough variations in resource allocation. The data were organized to test the hypothesis that there are no significant variations in budgetary allocations among the county boroughs. Indicators for all county boroughs have been analyzed and comparable figures for the four county boroughs have been detailed. With each type of data brought to bear—expenditure per population on both divisible-benefit and indivisible-benefit services, nonmonetary resource allocation, monetary shares allocated to various services, unit costs, ratios of resources to recipients, measures of extensiveness— *there has been substantial interborough variation.*

A ratio of the standard deviation on the mean (the "coefficient of variation") has revealed that interborough variation is generally high across various services and through time. The analysis suggests that variations are even greater when categories are more specific. And these measures for specific services seem to be more appropriate indicators of the concept "resource allocation," since these are the basic components of a particular public good or service. But both aggregate and specific measures display levels of variation that merit explication. Variation has been smallest on the measures for primary and secondary education (except as a proportion of total net expenditure). This includes cost per pupil figures, pupil-teacher ratios, and even measures on which the number of borough school children is uncontrolled. These data support Griffith's observation that the Ministry has operated to effect uniformity of provision on the major education services.

However, on nearly every other service indicator in the analysis, including other education service figures, the variation is quite substantial. There is significant variation on most measures of monetary and nonmonetary resource allocation per unit of population or unit of service. This is particularly interesting because there is some interborough uniformity in total monetary resources allocated per head. Less dramatic than the differences in the absolute levels of expenditure are the differences in the proportions of total expenditure allocated to aggregate categories (other than education) in the four county boroughs. While there is no way to determine whether these cases represent the range of variation among all county boroughs, they display notable and unpatterned variability across individual services. *We conclude that most measures tend to disconfirm the hypothesis that there is no significant interborough variation in resource allocation.*

Thus the data in this chapter powerfully support the position that each county borough has developed, over time, its own "critical policy style." That is, each county borough has a rather unique configuration of resource allocations. Our research, however, holds that interborough variations are a necessary but not sufficient condition to suggest local discretion in budgeting. It is now appropriate to examine the major alternative explanation for these variations, and one that denies a major role for local decision makers, the demographic approach.

NOTES

1. Davies' position is that there is too much variation in expenditure levels which are not correlated highly with measures of local need. Davies, op. cit., especially pp. 16ff., and pp. 289-305.

2. See Ruck, op. cit.; Jean Packman, "Provisions for Deprived Children in England and Wales," unpublished D. Phil. thesis, Univ. of Oxford; and Peter Townsend, *The Last Refuge* (London: Allen & Unwin, 1962).

3. Boaden, op. cit., Chapter 2.

4. See Chapter 1, pp. 14-15. On the other hand, Davies, in the most comprehensive study of the relationships between levels of expenditure, standards of provision, and the needs for certain services in local authorities, argues that expenditure figures "form the most comprehensive index available, since higher expenditures generally imply higher standards." Davies, op. cit., p. 43.

5. The difficult net-versus-gross-expenditure problem has been resolved by taking as the focus the amount of service expenditure that is financed by the collectivity. Basically this means excluding from gross expenditure that portion which the county borough recoups from a direct charge to the recipient for the service rendered. The recipient might be a citizen of the county borough, a visitor, an organization, or another government unit. For the purposes of our analysis, most services are little affected by the choice of net rather than gross expenditure. The measures that are influenced are those with a substantial income, such as further education (reimbursements from the Minister), welfare accommodation (charges to residents), redevelopment areas (rent), parks and baths (charges for facilities). It was decided that resource allocation was more meaningfully operationalized when such direct charges to recipients were not included.

Davies attempted to develop a measure of expenditure during the year directed to the current standard of provision for the service. It was based on an extremely complex formula, and much research energy was expended computing it for a single year (1960-1961). In comparison with the measure that is used here (called by Davies "revenue account net expenditure"), the complex measure distributed slightly more unequally. But the correlation between the two measures was, for most services, above +.96 (for one service it was .91), and Davies used the simpler measure in most of his analyses. See Davies, op. cit., pp. 127-128, 139, 142-145.

Our net expenditure figure also excludes specific grants. Since the county borough has no control over this income or its allocation, it is similarly taken to be beyond our notion of locally determined service expenditure. The bulk of these grants during the 1960s were for school milk, police service, housing, and the administration of justice. Gross expenditure figures are not easily available for all county boroughs but they are used occasionally in our examination of the four case studies.

6. O. Williams and C. Adrian in *Four Cities: A Study of Comparative Policy-Making* (Philadelphia: Univ. of Pennsylvania Press, 1963), see especially pp. 187-270. Our use of the terms is rather different, in order to fit them to the British milieu. For a discussion of policy taxonomies, see James N. Danziger, "Twenty-Six Policies in Search of a Taxonomy," *Policy and Politics*, 5 (December 1976), pp. 201-212.

7. Davies, op. cit., especially pp. 40-56.

8. We have normalized many measures across all the county boroughs by using expenditure per unit of (or per 1,000) population. The emphasis is upon expenditure

rather than benefits received. Even for the indivisible-benefit services we can assume only that the service is potentially available in equal units to all citizens. We cannot assume that every person has equal access to the service or has an equal utility function for it, or that there are no "free riders" (persons who benefit without paying). On most divisible-benefit services, the problem of determining units of benefit is exacerbated by the absence of measures of actual need. Thus we use expenditure per head as the most economic method for standardizing our measures of resource allocation across county boroughs of differing sizes.

9. It is appropriate to note that there are certain limitations in the quality of this comparative data. Interborough costs may be somewhat incomparable due to: (1) differences in accounting conventions; (2) different criteria for determining units-of-service on unit costs; (3) variation in commodity prices between areas; and (4) varying levels of activity by voluntary bodies on the personal services. In general, the impact of these data discrepancies on this research is probably slight. Moreover, the actual expenditure levels reported by each county borough do seem meaningful indices for comparative analysis. As Davies observes in the most thorough analysis of expenditure levels and standards of provision in the social services:

> Irrespective of the degree to which expenditure indices reflect all aspects of standards of provision, they can undoubtedly measure the financial effort made to achieve currently enjoyed services. [Davies, op. cit., p. 47]

10. The formula is:

$$\text{coefficient of variation} = \frac{\sigma}{\mu}.$$

See R.G.D. Allen, *Statistics for Economists* (London: Hutchinson and Co. Ltd., 1968), p. 86. The use of a measure which captures the relative amount of dispersion, particularly between groups, has also gained currency among sociologists. In a recent article, Martin and Gray have argued that the use of the measure of variability (known variously as the "coefficient of variation," "coefficient of variability," and "co-efficient of relative variation") is often misleading, since it does not have a constant range or constant N. They present a series of formulas to standardize this coefficient. Martin and Gray's measure is not necessary in our case since, as they note, the use of σ/μ is appropriate for the kind of data we employ—absolute value, ratio scale data (i.e., non-negative real numbers with a meaningful zero). Also, there is a constant N across all variables in our study. See J. D. Martin and Louis Gray, "Measurement of Relative Variation: Sociological Examples," *American Sociological Review,* 36 (June 1971), pp. 496-502.

11. Griffith, op. cit., pp. 504-505, 522-524; and Chapter 2.

12. Another possible explanation, arising from our discussion of central department-county borough relations, is that there has been a coordinated differential granting of loan sanctions to various boroughs over time.

13. Particular problems are discrepancies in the definition of units served and in the level of volunteer provision on certain personal-social services. Among the unit-cost measures, the least reliable ones are probably health visiting, child welfare, and domestic help. On domestic helps, for example, most cases involve service to the elderly. These cases entail far more time from the staff. Thus the unit-cost measure is strongly affected by the proportion of elderly cases in the borough; but this factor is not accounted for in the values published.

14. This observation is complicated by the fact that West Bromwich has a much lower proportion of rateable value in domestic hereditaments than does Southend. The rates-levied-per-head figures are computed by the I.M.T.A. on the basis of total rate levy on all sources of rateable value. It might be that a better indicator of effort, in the sense of the burden on the domestic ratepayer, is the average rate levied per domestic hereditament. The values for the four boroughs were:

	Bri	Dud	S'end	W Bro
1968-1969	1157.4s.	669.5s.	1097.9s.	697.2s.
1964-1965	962.6	562.1	938.9	583.2
1960-1961	Not available			

This is calculated by

$$\frac{\text{domestic rateable value times rate, minus domestic element R.S.G.}}{\text{number of hereditaments}}$$

Like the rates-levied-per-head measure, this one does not control for the wealth of the area. Thus we cannot say what a burden of 1,100 shillings (£55) to a Southend household means relative to a burden of 700 shillings (£35) to the average West Bromwich household. It does seem that West Bromwich is more willing than Southend to tax in order to raise expenditure per head.

Chapter 4

THE DEMOGRAPHIC EXPLANATION

This chapter extends the evaluation of the hypothesis that the county borough did not make significant choices on its budgetary allocations. Chapter 3 revealed substantial interborough variation in the levels and patterns of resource allocation; but there is a plausible rival explanation to the view that the borough was in fact making choices. The demographic approach explains these variations as the consequence of major forces in the county borough's environment rather than as the product of explicit local choices. Thus this chapter assesses the adequacy of the demographic explanation of county-borough resource allocations.

Theory and Methodology

The demographic approach has been the dominant mode of research on financial resource allocation since 1960.[1] While there has been some variability in the theoretical assumptions, methodology, and findings of the approach, these can be broadly characterized. The demographic explanation, based on a relatively simple input-output conceptualization, holds that the analysis of governmental outputs must locate the political system in the environment within which it operates.

For a comparable set of governmental units, indicators are compiled for policy outputs and for political, social, economic, or other characteristics of the government's environment. Indicators measuring the environment are treated as independent variables and indicators of policy outputs are treated as dependent variables. The basic methodology is to apply statistical techniques of correlation and regression to these sets of variables. The policy output variables are "explained" to the extent they are systematically associated with environmental system variables. Thus the explanation is a statistical one—it measures the percentage of intercase variation in the dependent variable that is accounted for by variation in the independent variable. Various statistical techniques allow the analyst to combine or control for the effect of other variables.[2] If a substantial statistical association is established, there is some (although inadequate) evidence that the policy output has been affected by the environmental factor. The lack of an association is even more telling evidence that there is no systematic relationship between the variables.

The immense outpouring of social-science research applying the demographic approach has been subjected to various criticisms.

(1) Inadequate variables. Some scholars accept the approach and its methodology, but have criticized the variables employed. Typically the variables selected have been suited to measurement as interval measures, have been structural rather than processual, and have measured only a few features of the environment. The basic justification of these simplifications has been the surprisingly high explanatory power of the variables selected, particularly the economic environment ones.

(2) Methodological problems. There are complex methodological issues related to the demographic approach. The common

use of correlation rather than regression coefficients to dis-
criminate among (implicit, but nonetheless) causal models is
extremely questionable.[3] Other serious complications for
evaluating models inferring cause are the result of the high
degree of multicollinearity among many of the independent
variables, making it difficult to sort out their relative effects
on the dependent variable,[4] and the possibility that certain
relationships are not linear and additive, as the analyses normally assume.[5] The more recent applications of the demographic
approach are sensitive to such methodological problems; but
these problems are virtually impossible to overcome completely
when dealing with complex social systems.

(3) Weak Theory. The broadest criticism of the approach has
argued persuasively that it lacks any theory of linkages which
explicates the relationships between policy outputs and characteristics of the environment.[6] There is rarely a fully articulated
theory which informs the analysis; rather, post hoc plausible-
stories-as-explanations are generated for those statistical relationships found to be strongest. There is insufficient explanation of
how environmental characteristics (or in some cases, the changes
in those environmental characteristics) produce particular levels
of policy output.[7] In general, it seems fair to say that demographic-approach studies have been prone to the sins of barefoot
empiricism (that is, of less theory and more method). And the
inconsistent findings of most of the studies have exacerbated
this problem.

Conceptualization

This application of the demographic approach does not avoid
most of these criticisms of theory and method. There are few
empirical findings and no methodological refinements that are
especially relevant in applying the approach to county-borough
resource allocations. Yet this application does seem a reasoned
and valid examination of the demographic approach, in its own
terms. The dependent variables are selected from the allocation

data discussed in Chapter 3 and the units of analysis are all county boroughs which existed throughout the period 1960-1970 (N=77).

Most demographic-approach analyses are presented in more or less causal language. This results in references to social, economic, or political characteristics (e.g., the level of median education, industrialization, or party competition) as "inputs" which "produce" policy outputs. Such conceptualizations are difficult to comprehend. It seems more appropriate to view these socioeconomic and political indicators as measures representing aspects of the environment within which policy outputs are produced. Conceptually, these aspects can be understood as *constraints*—as forces that might limit and shape the nature of a policy output.

Strictly interpreted, the demographic approach holds that resource allocations are externally determined, since neither the behavior of budgeters nor the structure of the budget-making process is treated as important. In this sense, the major constraints can be classified as three types of variables. These types can be called "resources constraints," "need constraints," and "disposition constraints."[8]

Resources constraints are measures which tap the economic characteristics and the wealth of the county borough. *Need constraints* on allocations can be inferred either from the characteristics of the physical environment or from the nature of the county borough's population. *Disposition constraints* are measures which represent characteristics of the local political system, particularly its tendency toward the public provision of goods and services. Given the exploratory nature of this analysis, it is appropriate that the list of operational indicators should be comprehensive rather than overly selective. Thus a broad variety of indicators are displayed in Table 4.1.[9]

The notion of constraint suggests that the boundaries of variation for a dependent variable are influenced by the constraint. As the effect of a constraint becomes stronger, the boundaries of variation narrow. In statistical terms, this means that the intercase variation of a powerful constraint (the inde-

Table 4.1: Indicators of Resources, Need, and Disposition Constraints

Symbol	Measure of:	Operation	Years
RESOURCES			
1. RV/hd	Average Property Wealth	Borough's Total Rateable Value/Population	60,64,68
2. Grant	Inadequate Local Financial Resources	Total Grant from Central Government/ Population	60,64,68
		Private Autos in Borough/Population	66
3. Cars	Affluence	Units of Domestic Rateable Valued over £100/ Total Units of Domestic Rateable Value	64,68
4. Wealthy	Affluence		64,68
5. Dom/Ind	Domestic versus Industrial-Commercial Nature of Borough	Rateable Value in Domestic Property/Total Rateable Value	64,68
NEED	*Socioeconomic class composition:*	*% male population over age 15 in Census groups:*	
6. SES 1	—upper and upper middle class	Groups 12,3,4,13: employers, managers, professionals	61,66
7. SES 2	—skilled working class	Groups 8,9,12,14: foreman, skilled manual workers, own account workers	61,66
8. SES 3	—unskilled laborers	Group 11: unskilled manual workers	61,66
	Age structure:		
9. Elderly	—elderly population	% population aged over 65 years	60,68
10. Pupils	—school population	Primary plus secondary school pupils/1,000 pop.	60,68
	Education Attainment: % males aged 25 or over whose terminal education age was:		
11. Low Ed	—low ed. attainment	under 15 years	61
12. High Ed	—high ed. attainment	over 20 years or continuing	61
13. Nonwhite	Ethnic composition	Number of immigrants with a "New commonwealth country" birthplace/10,000 population	66

[85]

Table 4.1 (Continued)

Symbol	Measure of:	Operation	Years
NEED (Cont'd.)			
14. Pop	Population	Total Borough Population	60,64,68
15. Density	Density of Population	Population Density per acre	64
16. MigBal	Net Population Balance	Net Borough population balance due to births, deaths, and migration/1,000 population	61 (1 yr.) 65 (5 yr.)
17. W/inMig	Internal Population Movement	Total Movements of Households within Borough/1,000	61 (1 yr.)
	Social Conditions:		
18. Amenities	Household amenities	% households with exclusive use of cold and hot water taps, fixed bath, and inside water closet	61,66
19 Crowding	Crowded living space	% of population in dwellings where the room density is greater than 1.0 persons/room	66
DISPOSITION			
20. % Labour	Labour Party Strength	% of Council Seats held by the Labour Party–3 year average	57-59 61-63 64-67
21. Compet	Party competitiveness on Council	$1 \text{ minus} \left(\dfrac{\text{Strongest Pty Seats minus Second Pty Seats}}{\text{Total Council Seats}} \right)$ 3 year average	57-59 61-63 64-67
22. VoPart	Voter Participation	% of registered voters casting vote in Council election (contested seats only)	59,63,67
23. UnoppSts	Competitiveness for Council Seats	% of total Council Seats not contested by two or more candidates	59,67

Table 4.1 (Continued)

Symbol	Measure of:	Operation	Years
DISPOSITION (Cont'd.)			
24. Debt/hd	Tendency to incur loan debt to finance projects	Net Outstanding Debt/population	60,64,68
25. Pub/Priv	Tendency to County Borough versus private activity	% of all housing built in borough 1960-1965 that was built by the county borough rather than privately	60-65

COMMENTS:

2. Grant: Includes all government grants except those for housing and agency services. The great proportion of Grant is composed of figures whose amounts are set by national formulas of local resource base relative to assessed need.

5. Dom/Ind: The industrial-commercial proportion also includes a small amount of Crown property.

13. Nonwhite: "New commonwealth countries" are those other than Canada, Australia, and New Zealand. In the main, the remainder are "Third World" people. There was no direct measure of ethnicity prior to the 1971 Census.

16. MigBal: A constant has been added so that all scores are positive. Higher scores signify more favorable balances.

21. Compet: On this measure, an exactly competitive situation between the two strongest parties would have a score of 1.0. Complete noncompetition (all seats to one party) would have a score of .00.

25. Pub/Priv: A very small percentage of public housing may be from sources other than the county borough.

SOURCES: Data are taken or derived from a variety of published sources. The data can be found as follows:
Variables 3,6,7,8,9,10,11,12,13,16,17,18,19: The General Register Office (1961 and 1966) Census of England and Wales. London: H.M.S.O.
Variables 1,4,5: Ministry of Housing and Local Government (1961, 1964, 1968) Rates and Rateable Values in England and Wales.
Variable 25: Ministry of Housing and Local Government (1960, 1965, 1968) Housing Return for England and Wales. London: H.M.S.O.
Variables 2,10: Institute of Municipal Treasurers and Accountants (yearly) Service Statistics. London: Lowes, Ltd.

pendent variable) will strongly associate with the intercase variation of the allocation measure (the dependent variable). Figure 4.1 suggests broadly how this strict interpretation of the demographic approach can be represented in the classic input-output formulation.

Generally, it might be hypothesized that higher levels of *resources* and wealth will be associated with higher levels of absolute expenditure and more revenue available for discretionary service provision. The *need* constraint is based on the assumption that the direction and magnitude of resource allocation to certain services can be inferred from indicators of the size of particular client populations or from aspects of the physical environment that generate levels of service need. The *disposition* constraint presumes that boroughs which reflect a commitment to the public provision of goods and services and, specifically, those which have a stronger Labour representation on Council, will tend to allocate more resources to the personal social services, to the education services, and to housing. While other factors might partially mitigate the effect of these constraints, the demographic approach leads to the expectation that some of these constraints remain the most powerful influences on the interborough variation in allocations.

Figure 4.1 also reflects the strong probability that the independent variables will be linked to each other. The measures of resources and need are likely to be intercorrelated and both of these might have some impact, as constraints over time, on the disposition indicators. It was expected, primarily on the basis of the research of Moser and Scott,[10] that the independent variables would tend to associate in two contrasting configurations. The correlation matrix in Table 4.2 confirms that the interunit variation on most variable pairs associates systematically. If each indicator is dichotomized in terms of high/low values, one of the two ideal-typical configurations, which will be called the configuration of lower resources, greater need, and stronger disposition (that is, greater inclination toward public provision of goods and services) is characterized by the following:

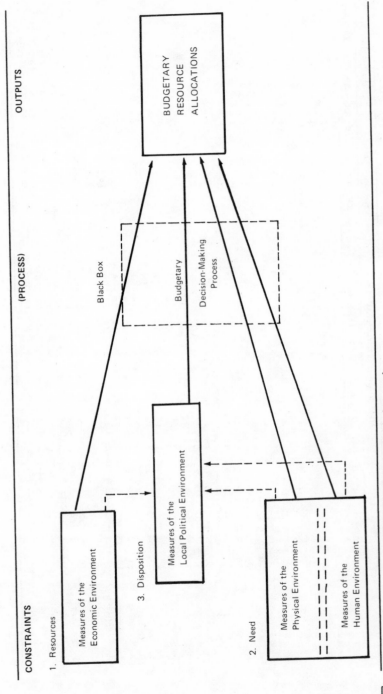

Figure 4.1: A strict interpretation of the Demographic Approach

CONSTRAINTS

(PROCESS)

OUTPUTS

BUDGETARY RESOURCE ALLOCATIONS

Black Box

Budgetary Decision-Making Process

1. Resources

Measures of the Economic Environment

3. Disposition

Measures of the Local Political Environment

2. Need

Measures of the Physical Environment

Measures of the Human Environment

Table 4.2: Mean Correlation Matrix for All Independent Variables

	Resources					Need-Personal Characteristics								Need-Environ. Chars.						Disposition				
	1.	2.	3.	4.	5.	6.	7.	8.	9.	10.	11.	12.	13.	14.	15.	16.	17.	18.	19.	20.	21.	22.	23.	24.
Resources																								
1. RV/hd																								
2. Grant	−86																							
3. Cars	51	−56																						
4. Wealthy	79	−67	48																					
5. Dom/Ind	20	−24	25	64																				
Need-Personal																								
6. SES 1	54	−56	62	76	66																			
7. SES 2	−34	22	12	−58	−54	−54																		
8. SES 3	−45	48	−68	−54	−40	−65	10																	
9. Elderly	49	−48	32	73	66	72	−50	−50																
10. Pupils	−59	63	−44	−74	−50	−65	41	59	−81															
11. LowEd	−53	50	−52	−70	−60	−64	65	48	−52	52														
12. HighEd	55	−48	48	60	25	58	−50	−48	36	−66	−02													
13. Nonwhite	17	−17	09	−02	−26	−02	17	−29	−14	02	02	12												
Need-Environ.																								
14. Pop	10	−08	−10	−03	−22	−12	05	00	−18	08	12	−02	34											
15. Density	−03	06	−46	−14	−14	−34	01	44	−31	27	25	−28	02	43										
16. MigBal	39	−45	58	59	60	66	−30	−52	60	−45	−51	28	−01	−28	−42									
17. W/InMig	11	−12	19	22	29	35	−28	−34	27	−19	−30	20	14	−13	−14	53								
18. Amenities	40	−48	49	42	34	50	−24	−42	18	−29	−44	32	−06	14	−21	40	14							
19. Crowding	−48	58	−69	−52	−41	−60	26	54	−59	59	47	−40	16	27	45	−57	−18	−32						
Disposition																								
20. % Labour	−57	59	−52	−65	−49	−73	47	53	−61	62	60	−47	−11	07	20	−58	−35	−47	54					
21. Compet	21	−34	24	12	04	26	−08	−26	02	−10	−27	21	39	18	11	09	20	18	−16	−44				
22. VoPart	03	−07	22	16	27	30	−26	−30	32	−22	−40	23	−09	−36	−32	32	23	14	−36	−24	27			
23. UnoppSts	−01	08	05	03	−01	−10	12	10	10	−04	04	02	−18	−22	−30	04	−16	−08	03	16	−38	−18		
24. Debt/hd	10	−05	−14	−15	−42	−32	09	16	−41	25	04	09	19	29	25	38	−08	06	35	24	05	−16	−10	
25. Pub/Priv	−29	32	−65	−42	−42	−59	22	50	−49	36	40	−17	00	30	59	−69	−32	−38	58	53	−09	−37	−01	47

	Higher values on:	Lower values on:
Resources:		
	Grant	RV/hd
		Cars
		Wealthy
		Dom/Ind
Need-Personal:		
	SES2	SES1
	SES3	Elderly
	Youth	HighEd
	Pupils	
	LowEd	
	(Ambiguous: Nonwhite)	
Need-Environmental:		
	Density	MigBal (unfavorable)
	Crowding	Amenities
		W/inMig
	(Ambiguous: Population)	
Disposition:		
	%Labour	VoPart
	Debt/hd	UnoppSts
	Pub/Priv	Competition (less competitive)

It is also evident that the indicators taken to represent each type of constraint are related, although the extent of association varies. The indicators of the resources constraint are substantially related, with the exception of the measure of domestic versus industrial wealth. The need-personal constraint measures are consistently associated, except for the nonwhite population measure, which might not accurately tap the borough's "coloured population." It is interesting that the association between the proportions of skilled working class (SES 2) and of unskilled working class (SES 3) is minimal. Among the need-environment constraint measures, density, crowding, and migration balance share some commonality; but population is an important measure that stands somewhat independently. Indicators of the disposition constraint share the least commonality; but the measures of percent Labour Council, debt per head, and public/private activity mix will correspond to our conceptual notion of greater disposition.

In general, the matrix suggests that there are some important instances of multicollinearity to which interpretation of the analytic findings must be sensitive. There might be confounding effects among the age structure, class structure, education, and wealth measures. Factor components could be developed to represent this complex of variables. But the commitment to exploratory research suggests individual treatment of the indicators. It will be possible to utilize partial correlation and regression techniques to estimate relative effects.

Hypothesized Allocation Variable— Constraint Variable Relationships

It is difficult to specify fully the expected linkages between the measures of resource allocation and the constraint variables because of the multiplicity of indicators and methodologies in prior research.[11] The principal demographic-approach findings, summarized in Table 4.3 from work by Alt and Boaden and from Newton's synthesis of research, are far from definitive but can inform hypothesis-generation.[12] If the three types of constraint variables are treated in terms of the ideal-type configurations, it is hypothesized that lower resources, greater need, and stronger disposition will generally associate with:

(1) higher levels of expenditure per head on total, primary, and secondary education;

(2) lower expenditure per pupil and higher pupil-teacher ratios;

(3) lower expenditure per head on most caretaker services;

(4) less intensive provision of the fire and police service;

(5) higher expenditure on the promoter service, planning;

(6) lower expenditure per head on most amenity services (e.g., parks, libraries) but higher expenditure and provision of housing;

(7) lower expenditure per head on welfare services and other services whose primary recipients are the elderly;

Table 4.3: Constraint Variable-Allocation Variable Associations Suggested by Alt, Boaden, and Newton

Associates Significantly[a] with:	Expenditure per 1,000 on:							
	Total Education	Housing[b]	Children's Services	Local Health Services	Welfare Services	Police Service	Fire Service	Highways
Rateable value per head	−	−						
Domestic rateable value in units over £100		−			−			
Percentage of domestic rateable value	−	−	−	−		−	−	
High social class	−	−	−	+		−		
Low social class	+	+					+	
Percentage of population aged 5–14	+	+	+					
Population		−	+			+		
Density		+	+	−				
Amenities		+						
Crowding		+	+	+				
Percentage Labour Party on Council	+	+	+					

a. Blank cells signify the lack of significant association with the independent variable. An association is treated as significant if the Pearson product-moment correlation is equal to or greater than ±.22.

b. Boaden: percentage of local housing that was Council built, 1945-1958; Alt: a housing expenditure figure that is not clearly defined.

(8) higher expenditure per head on the local health services and the children's service; and

(9) lower total expenditure per head.

The method of analysis is to test these as null hypotheses. That is, does analysis falsify the notion that there is no systematic linkage between the variables? In the first instance correlation analysis is utilized. Where patterns of relationship are complex, regression analysis is used to estimate the most powerful constraint variables.[13] While tests of statistical significance are not necessary (given the whole population as units of analsis), these tests are employed as a rule-of-thumb measure of the real interest, substantive significance. Only those associations are reported which are higher than might occur by chance ($r = \pm .22$, at the .05 level of significance).[14]

The Findings

OVERVIEW

As a basic assessment of the adequacy of the demographic explanation, Table 4.4 displays the r̄-values for selected measures of resource allocation with the variables representing the resources, need, and disposition constraints. Prior to exploring the patterns of findings for each type of allocation, several general observations about the data are worthy of attention.

First, it is both striking and surprising that, with few exceptions, there are a limited number of significant associations between allocation measures and constraint measures. For nearly every allocation measure, most of the indicators of resources, need, and disposition constraints do not attain a level of simple correlation greater than chance. Of 650 possible associations (excluding total net expenditure), there are only 145 r̄-values higher than $\pm .22$, an average of 5.8 significant correlations per output.

Second, the magnitudes of significant r̄-values are generally low. Excluding the substantial correlations on the two housing

Table 4.4: Mean Correlation Values for Resource-Allocation Measures with Variables of Resources, Need, and Disposition Constraints[a]

	RV/hd	Grant	Cars	Wealthy	Dom/Ind	SES 1	SES 2	SES 3	Eld	Pupils	LowEd	HighEd	Nonwhite	Pop	Dens	MigBal	W/inMig	Amen	Crowd	% Lab	Comp	VoPart	UnoppSts	Debt/hd	Pub/Priv
Highways	22					28		-30	-30	-33		38	26		-31							28			
Sewerage			23														-24					-29			
Refuse				24							30		26	42	32		29								
Police							-37	45	24					38											
Fire		32	-28									23	-26	-22											
∑ Caretaker	23																								
Pol Pop/Off[b]					-28		44		-30	-22															
Fire Pop/Off[c]					-22		-40						30	36											
Planning	27	-22					-23					22												36	
Libraries							-26																		
Parks	29		54	36		22		-44	35			40													
Hous-Rent	60	-66	27	53	-42	48	26	38	-60	49	-48				-30	44	23	47	-52	-61				63	-46
Hous-Built			-32	-40	-50	-50									27	-46	-37		47	40		-27		37	58
PrimEd[d]					-28	-22			-27	(82)			27	30					-28	37				32	
SecEd[d]					-25				-28	(74)			36	36						30	25			37	
FurtherEd				-30	-29	-35		-22	-34	25	24	27		30	-26	-32								27	
SpecialEd							31				-22			36	28				43					35	
Cost/PrimPupil												25													
Cost/SecPupil																									
PrimPup/Teach																									
SecPup/Teach												30	30											30	
∑ Ed[d]					-37			-24	-22	(74)		30	30												
LocalHealthSrv			-25		-28	-23					27	30	32	32	33		-34	-33	30	29					31
Children'sSrv			-22		-32	-32					22		34	34			-31	-31	31	23					30
WelfareSrv												25	25												
∑ ServicesElderly																									
∑ NetExp	-22	49	-27	-36	-51	-40		27	-36	44	27					-48		-35	44	48				41	33

measures and the total spending on basic education services, there are only 28 cases where any independent variable explains at least 10% of the interborough variation in any resource-allocation measure.[15]

A third important finding is that no single independent variable is highly correlated with a large number of allocation measures. Not one constraint indicator associates significantly with at least half of the allocation measures.

Fourth, there is no apparent configuration of associations in the table. That is, there are no systematic patterns of association between a type of constraint variable and a type of allocation measure. Unlike most demographic-approach analyses in American contexts, this lack of strong associations is evident for social and economic environment variables, as well as local political system ones.

Hence a broad appraisal of these data reflects that for these types of allocation decisions in county boroughs the demographic approach does not seem to provide a powerful, generalized explanation. More detailed analyses of particular allocations might suggest refinements or aspects of the approach that have explanatory appeal. But these ought to be measured against

---

NOTE FOR TABLE 4.4:

a. The table displays all correlations for which the mean Pearson product-moment correlation is greater than ± .21. In most cases, the figure is the mean for two or three r-values. The pairings between independent variables and allocation measures are as follows:

Allocation-Measure Year	Independent-Variable Year
1960-1961	same year data, except: 1957-1959 (party-political) 1964 (density)
1964-1965	same year data, except: 1966 (Five Year Census data, 1961-1965) 1963-1965 (party-political)
1968-1969	same year data, except: 1966 (Five Year Census data, 1961-1965) 1966-1967 (party-politicl)

b. Values for 1960-1961 and 1964-1965 only.
c. Values for 1960-1961 only.
d. These education-constraint variables correlations are first-order partials, controlling the effect of the relevant student population.

the overall findings listed here. The subsequent sections examine more fully the data for each type of resource-allocation measures.

THE CARETAKER SERVICES

It was hypothesized that levels of provision on the caretaker services, which provide essential services for a healthy and safe environment, would associate with the county-borough configuration of higher resources, better social conditions, and weaker disposition. This expectation is derived primarily from American-based findings that wealthier and more politically conservative governments tend to spend more on such services as highways.[16] The relevant analyses did not support any systematic configuration on these services for the county boroughs. In fact, the resource-allocation measures for the caretaker services have only scattered and low correlations with the constraint variables of resources, need, or disposition. Highways spending is associated in the expected direction with lower personal need (that is, with a higher social-class milieu); but these simple correlations are moderately low and there is never more than a single, low correlation of significance with any indicator of resources, environmental need, or disposition. There is one interesting linkage between spending on refuse collection and disposal and a constraint variable: the cost per head of providing the refuse service tends to be higher in county boroughs with a larger population.

Population size seems also to be a factor influencing the cost of provision for both the fire service and the police service. Increased population is related to higher spending levels for police services but to lower spending levels on the fire service. One might suggest post hoc explanations of scale economies on fire services and of the "crimogenic" impact of increased population and density. There actually seems to be a broader contrast between police-service and fire-service allocations. Increases in both spending levels and intensity of provision of police service (measured as population per officer) tend to be associated with indicators of greater population and lower proportions of the skilled working class. For the fire service, increases on these measures of allocation are linked to smaller population and larger proportions of unskilled, as opposed to skilled, working class. This intriguing contrast is not easily explained; morever, it should not be overdrawn, since it involves only a few of the constraint variables.

Given these low correlation levels for the caretaker services, there is minimal need to sort out problems of multicollinearity among independent variables. However, to explore and perhaps to further illuminate the relationships, regression analytic techniques were employed with these and with subsequent allocation measures.[17] This technique can be used in an exploratory fashion to select the set of independent variables which best explain (in the sense of minimizing the residual variance in a regression equation) the interunit variation of the dependent variable. Four independent variables do estimate about 45% of the interborough variation in police-service expenditure (1968-1969). Higher spending on the police is best estimated by a less favorable migration balance, a smaller skilled working class, a greater population, as well as more high-value land parcels (Wealthy).[18] While nearly half of the variation on police spending can be accounted for by the best combination of demographic variables, the inadequacy of the demographic explanation for caretaker services is underscored by other services, where the fractions of explained variance are: highways = 19.5%; fire services = 24.2%; sewerage = 28.7%; and total caretaker services = 27.6%.

THE PROMOTER SERVICES

There are reliable data for only one resource-allocation measure on a promoter service. This is expenditure per head on town and country planning. This figure, which also includes some development-redevelopment expenditure, accounted for 20% to 60% of total net expenditure on promoter services in the four county boroughs. It was hypothesized that planning expenditure would increase with lower resources, greater need, and stronger disposition. In fact, four of the five significant associations in Table 4.4 are opposite this pattern, although all are quite weak. However the highest correlation is with the disposition measure of the willingness to incur loan debt. In multivariate analysis, only this disposition measure and the resource capacity suggested by higher rateable value per head are significantly associated with higher planning expenditure. While each of these linkages can be understood intuitively, it is clear that none of the constraint variables is substantially affecting expenditure decisions on planning.

THE AMENITY SERVICES

The amenity services have been characterized as those governmental goods and services whose provision is generally perceived to be desirable rather than basic and necessary. There is no initial expectation that all amenity services will associate with the constraint variables in the same manner, since some are indivisible-benefit services and others are divisible-benefit services with quite disparate client groups.

The library and parks services. The library service and the parks service are the only indivisible-benefit amenity services for which data are available. Although these services are available to all citizens, it is unlikely that they are used or valued equally by all. They might be considered marginal services in the sense that expenditure is expected to be greater where the pressure on available financial resources is less severe. Thus it is hypothesized that higher levels of allocation to libraries and to parks will associate with greater resources and lower personal need. Actually, the level of library spending has virtually no associations with the constraint variables in Table 4.4. Parks spending is rather more in line with the hypothesis, since there are some correlations in the expected direction with measures of greater resources and lower personal need. However the effect of one resource measure (Wealthy) eliminates the effect of all other

constraint measures and the optimal regression equation explains only 10.8% of the interborough variance in parks expenditure.

The personal social services. The personal social services—the
welfare services for the aged, the children's service, and most of
the local health services—are among the governmental activities
most closely linked to the notion of the welfare state. The
general shape of these services was established by major legislation of the postwar Labour Government, and the nature of
provision has been elaborated over time by means of Parliamentary Acts, ministerial circulars, and local decisions.[19] The
basic demographic-approach hypothesis is that levels of resource allocation will be particularly constrained by patterns
of need for the particular service. An operational problem is
that there are no accurate measures of the magnitude or intensity of client need for most personal social services.[20] Our
indicators for the concept of need can, at best, be viewed as
aggregate-level personal and environmental characteristics from
which client need can be inferred.[21] In general, it is expected
that resource allocation to the children's service and to the local
health services will be higher where need is greater—that is,
where there are less favorable environmental conditions and
lower socioeconomic levels. It is especially difficult to link
welfare-service resource allocation to the constraint variables,
due to the social-class differences in caring for the elderly.[22]
It might be that the proportion of population over 65, while
not measuring specific client need, will have some relationship
to welfare-service spending.[23]

Expenditure levels on the children's service and on the local
health services do have some moderate correlations in the
hypothesized direction with constraint variables. Greater expenditure per head is most closely linked to measures of environmental need, such as lower amenity levels, greater crowding, and population size or mobility. These social services also
have a few low-magnitude correlations with stronger disposition
and lower resource levels. When regression analysis was applied

to ascertain interaction effects among measures of the constraint variables, the patterns of relationships were substantially
simplified. Interborough differences on local health services
expenditure is primarily accounted for by the amenities indicator. It is the only independent variable with a significant beta
weight in a regression in solution, and it accounts for only
11.7% of the total variation. Spending on the children's service
is mainly accounted for by the effect of three indicators of the
environmental-need constraint. The optimal regression solution,
which explains about 32% of the interborough variation, is:

Children's Service Expenditure =

	b	Stnd. error	Par. F
Density	18.246	5.741	10.100
Nonwhite	.650	.228	8.163
Amenities	−8.946	3.277	7.452
(constant)	1250.351		

Mult. R =   .566
R^2 =   .320
F = 11.132 $> .01$

Total expenditure on the welfare services is correlated with
only two personal-need indicators and each of these $\bar{r}$-values is
extremely low. Since there is a broader range of services whose
clients are the elderly, a measure of total expenditure on "services for the elderly" was developed, including net spending on
the welfare services, domestic helps, and home nursing.[24] However, interborough variation on this cumulative measure is not
associated significantly with a single independent variable.

In general, the extent to which resource allocations to the
personal social services can be explained by the demographic
constraints ranges from moderate to none. This generalization
applies to measures of expenditure, of extensiveness, and unit
costs.[25] The weak explanatory power of constraint variables
might be attributed to the absence of sensitive measures of
client need for these services. Allocations to the children's

service and the local health services do associate most strongly with measures which suggest conditions of personal need and particularly of environmental need. These relationships do not hold on allocations to social services for the elderly. Although the Labour Party's ideological commitments might be expected to influence resource allocation on the personal social services, there is only a weak linkage between the recent Labour strength on Council and the allocation levels. Moreover, the resources constraint has almost no significant associations with resource allocations. Thus the limited capacity of the demographic variables to explain variation in personal social service allocation centers primarily in the indicators of need.

Housing. The provision of council houses and flats was one of the major amenity-service options of the county borough. The general shape of the county borough's housing program was, in the short-run, strongly influenced by the housing and loan policies of the central government. There were various Exchequer subsidies for existing housing and most new programs entailed loan sanction.[26] However, the county borough was the housing authority for its area, making the final decisions on building, acquiring, altering, or selling most units of public housing. Over time, it was responsible for the numbers and types of public housing in the borough.

Housing provision is probably the most political county-borough service. The Conservative Party, locally and nationally, has stressed the primary role of private enterprise in meeting housing needs.[27] The Labour Party has expressed a continuing commitment to provide housing as a redistributive service which benefits less advantaged members of the community.[28] The provision of council houses and flats has been viewed as a particular priority under disadvantageous social conditions, such as overcrowding and lack of amenities.[29] Thus it is hypothesized that indicators of housing provision will associate substantially with Labour Party disposition and with need-environment measures.

The primary measure of policy output on housing is a measure of extensiveness—the number of units of postwar housing (1945-1965) built by the county borough as a proportion of the total households in the borough. In addition to this comprehensive measure, the extent to which the Council provides revenue for the Housing Revenue Account by extracting rent from the tenants is examined. It is generally true that to the extent the housing account utilizes nonrent revenue (primarily revenue from tax-payers and rate-payers), the county borough's housing policy is effectively redistributive.[30]

It is evident in Table 4.4 that housing is the first service to have numerous high correlations with the independent variables. On the ratio of borough-built houses to total households, every significant correlation operates in a consistent configuration: higher provision is associated with greater Labour disposition, greater need, and lower resources. Two of the three highest correlations are with measures of disposition, as hypothesized.[31] However, contrary to expectations, the need-personal characteristics associate more strongly with this housing measure than do the need-environment indicators. The social conditions measures such as crowding and amenities provision were recorded in 1961 and 1966. It might be that county boroughs most active in providing postwar housing have improved upon these environmental conditions, while class and age structure indicators continue to reflect the kind of social environment for which housing need was posited.

Given the problem of interdependent effects, multiple-regression analysis is a useful method to identify the most powerful explanatory variables for variation in housing provision. The regression equation is:

Housing Provision =

	b	Stnd. error	Par. F
Elderly	−.759	.165	21.093
Pub/Priv	.115	.034	11.569
MigBal	.063	.019	11.493
Debt/Hd	2.954	.928	10.136

| W/inMig | −.119 | .050 | 5.588 |
| (constant) | 17.094 | | |

Mult. R = .775
R^2 = .600
F = 20.742   > .01

These five variables explain 60% of the interborough variation in provision. The regression equation verifies the importance of the disposition measures, both of which have highly significant regression coefficients. The proportion of the population over 65, which has the most significant beta weight, is probably best interpreted as a general indicator of age structure, given its extremely high and negative correlation with the number of pupils. In this sense, greater housing provision is closely linked to the need represented by a large proportion of children and young families. Both measures of population migration also contribute importantly to the equation. The sign change for migration balance is easily interpreted statistically; but this sign change is perplexing substantively and difficult to explain except as a statistical artifact. In general, then, it is the age structure and stronger disposition to public provision of goods and services that associate most powerfully with the level of housing provision. No resources measures enter the equation.

Although the proportion of housing revenue coming from rent underwent some standardization by central-government policies, it remains an interesting measure of redistribution. Rent burden has even stronger and more numerous correlations with the independent variables than the housing extensiveness measure. Interestingly, the strongest associations are with all four resource measures of wealth and with Labour's Council strength. The relationships suggest that as a borough is wealthier and has weaker Labour representation on Council, it extracts larger amounts of the housing-account revenue from rents. The most important variables in estimating the rent burden, as identified in a multiple-regression equation, are:

Housing Rent 1968 =

	b	Stnd. error	Par. F
Grant	−.044	.007	39.874
Pupils	.157	.047	11.000
Density	−.365	.123	8.777
%Labour	−.114	.044	6.759
Amenities	.200	.085	5.538
(constant)	73.825		

Mult. R = .809
R^2 = .655
F = 26.208 $> .01$

This equation reveals that the level of grants is the most important estimator of the rent burden. Since the grant indicator does
not include housing grants, this linkage suggests that boroughs
with less financial resources relative to needs (as assessed by the
general grant formulas) extract less rent from Council house
tenants. When the effect of grant level is controlled, there is a
sign change suggesting that the revenue pressure resulting from
a large student population becomes competitive with lower rent
in allocation decisions. A greater reliance on rent charges is also
associated with environmental quality (lower densities, more
amenities) and less Labour strength on Council. These variables
explain two-thirds of the interborough variation in rent burden.

Thus each housing allocation measure is powerfully linked to
a small set of constraint variables. Extensiveness of housing provision is most strongly associated with measures of disposition
and with characteristics of the social structure of the population.
The ongoing decisions regarding rent burden are also tied to
the disposition constraint, with the local Labour Party appar-
ently acting to redistribute the burden of housing provision
away from the renters. But the most potent explanatory factor
for rent burden is the measure reflecting limited local resources
relative to needs. It seems that different sets of constraints are
operating on the two housing allocation measures, an observa-

tion supported by the lack of significant correlation between the two measures (−.17 for 1960-1961 and .09 for 1968-1969).

THE EDUCATION SERVICES

The education services dominated the general rate fund expenditure of the county borough and these services typically accounted for between 50% and 60% of total net revenue account spending. As local education authority, the county borough was responsible for providing a wide range of education-related services, including not only compulsory primary and secondary schools, but also further education facilities, and a school health service, among others.[32]

The basic hypothesis is that higher levels of spending on primary, secondary, and total education (per population), lower per-pupil expenditure, and less favorable pupil-teacher ratios will associate with lower resources, greater need, and stronger disposition. It is assumed that absolute expenditure on the compulsory education services will be particularly driven by the need indicator representing the size of the client population (the number of pupils) in the borough. Those boroughs with proportionately less demand to provide the fundamental education services will have marginal resources which might be applied to improve intensity of provision and to allocate more resources to the discretionary education services. Analysis of the data confirms that the relevant number of pupils (per population) is the powerful, dominant constraint on spending (per population). The spending-client group correlations are .82, .74, and .74 for primary, secondary, and total education expenditure per population.[33] Given these strong linkages, the relationships between these three allocation measures and other independent variables are displayed in Table 4.4 as first-order partials in order to clarify the other variables' impact.

With this control, expenditures on both primary and secondary education associate most strongly with the disposition measures of Labour fraction on Council and debt per head. Thus on the basic education services, as with housing, the Labour Party's commitment to resource redistribution seems to receive empirical support in the data. The level of total education expenditure is not, however, significantly correlated with any disposition measure except debt per head when the number of pupils in the borough is controlled. Perhaps the influence of the local Labour Party is to direct financial resources particularly into basic education. The strongest associations between total education spending and constraint indicators, controlling for total number of pupils, are with high educational attainment in the borough and, for some reason, with a larger concentration of industrial-commercial wealth in the borough. A regression estimate which combines the impact of these two constraints and the level of grants along with the number of pupils in the boroughs accounts for fully 70.1% of the interborough variation on total education spending.[34] For secondary education spending, an equation including only the number of secondary pupils and the disposition measure debt per head accounts for 63.5% of the variation.[35]

It might be that the intensity measures of expenditure per pupil are the most appropriate and precise indicators of resource allocation to primary and secondary education. But there are almost no significant correlations between these cost-per-pupil measures and any constraint variable. Greater spending per primary pupil does have one moderate association, with the disposition measure of debt per head. The pupil-teacher ratios, which seem another reasonable indicator of the resource effort in education, do not have a single significant correlation for either primary or secondary education. A partial explanation of this null finding might be that vigorous central-department policies on target pupil-teacher ratios have reduced and made unsystematic the interborough variations on these ratios.[36] Whatever the reason, these fundamental measures of resource allocation to the basic education services are not accounted for by the constraint variables in this analysis.

Although expenditure on further education and on special education can be viewed as discretionary areas of the education service, they are not subject to the same constraints. The borough's commitment to the provision and financing of further education activities has only a few low associations with a mixed set of need characteristics. Expenditure on special education (for handicapped children), however, seems to increase in county boroughs which are more heavily populated and have a working-class character. Thus spending on special education, contrary to the general hypothesis, is not a marginal activity supported more fully in the wealthier boroughs with less basic education expenditure.

In sum, the adequacy of the demographic explanation for resource allocations in the education service is quite varied. A very large proportion of the interborough variation on spending levels for primary, secondary, and total education can be accounted for by an economic set of constraint indicators, dominated by the need represented by the number of pupils. Stronger disposition (for government activity) also associates with primary- and secondary-education expenditure, although not with total education spending. Special education allocations are associated with measures of greater environmental and personal need. But the revealing intensity of provision measures for both pupil-teacher ratios and cost per pupil (for primary and for secondary education) have virtually no significant associations with *any* indicators of the resources, need, or disposition constraint.

TOTAL NET EXPENDITURE

Finally, it is illuminating to examine the allocation measure of total net expenditure per head on all rate fund services. This aggregate measure includes both rate- and general grant-financed spending. In general, one might expect that higher total spending would correlate with greater needs and stronger disposition to governmental provision of goods and services. The data in Table 4.4 are broadly supportive of this expectation. The disposition indicators, particularly the Labour strength on Council, are clearly associated with higher total spending. The linkages with greater environmental-need constraints are also notable. It is also obvious that those county boroughs with less internal financial resources are spending most extensively. The importance of the resource constraint becomes particularly clear in the best regression estimate of total expenditure:

Total Expenditure per head 1968 =

	b	Stnd. error	Par. F
Grant	.689	.069	99.939
Debt/hd	79.497	11.262	49.827
Dom/Ind	−7.401	1.195	38.360
Wealthy	2.847	.717	15.774
Amenities	−2.742	.841	10.635
Cars	6.827	2.696	6.415
Elderly	6.369	2.756	5.342
(constant)	900.034		

Mult. R = .897
R^2 = .804
F = 39.845 $> .01$

Four of the five measures of resources are selected into the regression equation. Further, the level of grants-in-aid is the single most powerful predictor of total expenditure in 1968-1969. The association of grants with total expenditure increased consistently during the 1960s. This finding supports the argument that the county borough became more dependent on government grants, at least in the sense that the grant total was a growing constraint on total expenditure. But this point is balanced by the fact that a disposition measure (debt per head) was the second most powerful predictor of the dependent variable. An equation using *both* the resources and the disposition variable substantially increases the explanatory power (the r^2 rises from .343 to .587) and the statistical significance (the F-level increases from 36.496 to 49.125) for the dependent variable, total expenditure per head. Thus these two measures account for most of the 80% of interborough variation that is explained by the regression equation. Although two measures of need are selected into the regression equation, need seems less important, as determined by regression analysis, than had been hypothesized. Also, the Labour fraction on Council is less important than had been expected. The Labour-fraction indicator is not included in the regression equation because the correlation between Labour fraction and total expenditure is eliminated when both grants and debt per head are controlled (the r-value is reduced from .46 to −.01).[37]

Evaluation of the Demographic Explanation

The demographic approach assumes that an adequate set of indicators for the economic, social, and political environments can explain much of the interunit variation on a measure of policy output. In applying the approach, this chapter has taken a variety of resource-allocation measures in the county boroughs as the outputs. There are at least two broad perspectives from which to assess the adequacy of the demographic explanation. A loose test of adequacy is simply the strength of the statistical "explanation" (for the output) provided by any or all of the constraint variables. A more stringent test is whether there is a distinct set of constraint variables which are systematically associated with related allocation measures. Each of these perspectives is considered briefly.

The stringent test of adequacy for the demographic approach involves the existence of a few constraint variables which seem to have consistently strong relationships with groups of the dependent variables. Ideally, one could explicate these linkages in the sense that the effect of the constraint variable on the allocation measure could be made understandable. It should be recalled that an initial observation about Table 4.4 was that there did not appear to be strong clusters of constraint variables relating to most of the allocation measures. Table 4.5 summarizes the simple correlations between allocation measures and constraint variables. Apart from the three strong, if unremarkable, associations between number of pupils and total school spending, no constraint variable has substantial explanatory power for more than a handful of allocation measures. There is not one independent variable that correlates significantly with

Table 4.5: Level of Correlation for Each Independent Variable of Resources, Need, and Disposition with Indicators of Resource Allocation

Independent Variable	>.60	.60–.51	.50–.41	.40–.31	.30–.22
Resources					
RV/hd		1			5
Grant	1		1	1	1
Cars		1		1	5
Wealthy		1		3	2
Dom/Ind		1	1	2	7
Need-Personal Chars					
SES 1			2	2	4
SES 2			1	3	3
SES 3			2	1	4
Elderly		1		4	7
Pupils	3		2	2	3
LowEd			1		6
HighEd				2	6
Nonwhite				2	5
Need-Environ. Chars					
Pop			1	4	1
Density				3	4
MigBal			3	1	
W/inMig				2	3
Amenities			1	3	
Crowding		1	3	1	2
Disposition					
% Labour	1		1	2	3
Debt/hd	1		1	4	2
Pub/Priv		1	1	2	2
VoPart					3
Compet					1

even one-half of the resource-allocation measures. In fact, no independent variable in Table 4.4 correlates significantly with more than half of the caretaker-service measures, or the education measures, or the personal social-service measures, or the indivisible-benefit amenity-service measures.[38]

The minimal criterion of adequacy for the demographic approach is that the statistical explanation, measured as the fraction of explained variance, is reasonably high. While this assessment of adequacy remains subjective, it might be based either on particular dependent variable-independent variable correlations of high magnitude or on a substantial r^2-statistic from multivariate analysis. For some of the resource-allocation measures examined, the demographic variables have a substantial level of explanatory power. This is particularly true for total net expenditure on all services, for spending per population on total, primary, and secondary education, and for the indicators of housing provision and housing rent burden. In each of these cases, individual constraint variables have quite high correlation coefficients. And in these cases there is a regression equation where an economic set of constraint variables accounts for over one-half of the interborough variation on the allocation measure.

However, most allocation measures for the county boroughs do not clearly meet even this minimal criterion of explanatory adequacy. For most allocation measures, there are few statistically significant correlation coefficients with constraint variables, and there are extremely few instances of correlations with a substantial magnitude. These null findings are generally true for measures of every caretaker service, of parks and libraries, of planning, and of the personal social services. The generalization also holds for primary and secondary cost per pupil, for pupil-teacher ratios, and for other education services. Even the rather mechanical use of stepwise-regression analysis to determine the optimal combination of constraint variables produced only one other instance (net spending on police services) where as much as 35% of the variance could be accounted for.

The absence of significant correlations for some of these constraint variables might be viewed as unexpected. Measures of the economic environment and particularly measures of local financial-resource capacity have often dominated the demographic-approach explanations of resource allocations. Rateable value per head has been viewed as the best available indicator of borough wealth.[39] Apart from a strong relationship with housing rent, however, the level of rateable value is not associated above ±.30 with a single allocation variable and it has only six significant simple correlations. The level of government grants-in-aid is substantially associated with total net spending, but it does not seem to operate specifically as a constraint on any allocation except housing rent burden. This is a surprising finding, given the conventional argument that grants-in-aid are a powerful constraint on a wide range of local allocation decisions.

It is also intriguing that the Labour representation on Council is only moderately related to levels of service provision. Labour fraction has a substantial correlation with housing rent and interesting linkages with expenditure on primary and secondary education. But Labour strength is not generally associated with higher provision levels for either the personal social services or other measures of the education service. And those councils with low Labour representation do not have any clear tendency toward greater provision on the caretaker services, parks, or libraries. Also, the measure of party competitiveness on Council has virtually no systematic relationship with any measure of resource allocation. As in most American studies, the classic Key hypothesis about the influence of party competitiveness suffers another setback.[40]

In sum, each of these modes of evaluation reinforces the basic conclusion that has recurred throughout the chapter: *the demographic approach provides a weak and generally unsatisfactory explanation for the variation in county-borough resource allocations.* What might explain this "failure," given the apparent viability of the approach in studies of American states and municipalities? It could be argued that the indicators employed are unreliable, or invalid, or insufficient. While this cannot be disproven, the indicators seem sound on theoretical grounds, on the basis of prior empirical research, and they are developed from reliable sources. Some policy analysts have argued, on the basis of American findings, that the economic and social environments will necessarily determine the levels of available revenue and, consequently, the levels of spending on most services.[41] But the examination of county-borough data shows that most level-of-allocation measures are not systematically related to levels of environmental development (that is, what we have called resources and need constraints).

It might be that the level of available revenue and the general, areal level of costs (that is, the areal cost-of-living, wage levels, cost of materials, and so on) are general constraints on the level of governmental allocations. If the interunit disparity in available revenue and cost-levels is great (as in an interstate or inter-city American comparison), it is probable that allocation levels for individual services will vary in a somewhat corresponding manner. That is, a unit with high revenue capacity and high cost-levels is expected, ceteris paribus, to have higher spending levels than a unit low on these constraints. Moreover, certain socioeconomic characteristics which would tend to correlate with revenue capacity and areal cost-levels would also tend to correlate with the allocation measures.

Under these conditions, the demographic variable-allocation level correlations could be viewed as spurious, in causal terms. At least, it is unclear what proportion of interunit variation is attributable to cost-levels rather than revenue capacity. Only the latter might be influenced by socioeconomic variables (more specifically, by personal wealth or property wealth measures, to the extent that available resources are dependent on local wealth).

If this argument is valid, a central reason for the failure of the demographic approach in the county-borough context is the effect of two levelers—government grants and uniform wage policies. General grants from the central government are distributed by means of a formula based upon local need and local financial resources. While these unearmarked funds do not produce resource equality, they do close substantially the inter-borough disparity in available financial resources. Uniform wage policies are also an important leveler because wage scales for most county-borough employees are established at the national level. A relatively uniform, national wage structure means that staff-related expenditure becomes a function of local decisions regarding the quantity and quality of staff, rather than a function of gross areal differences in cost-levels. The impact of this on interunit variation in expenditure is evident in the fact that staff-related expenditure accounts for well over half the county borough's spending on many costly services, including education, the personal social services, fire and police.

Therefore, this analysis is a serious challenge to the central conclusions of most demographic-approach studies in the American context. In the British case, the impact of the two levelers seems to reduce substantially the effect of confounding macroeconomic factors on the interunit variation in resource allocations. It is probable that resource capability is an important constraint on total allocation levels. But the county-borough example suggests that, when certain gross economic forces are less varied, there is a great deal of local variation. At least, there is no simple model of socioeconomic determinism which explains resource-allocation decisions. In the county boroughs, the demographic approach has minimal explanatory power for most allocation measures.

NOTES

1. For a listing of representative studies from the immense volume of demographic-approach research, see Chapter 1, footnote 24.

2. There are many explanations of these statistical techniques. For an explication of the basic statistics involved and the methods of manipulating the data, see, for example, Edwards, op. cit., especially chapters 5,6,12. For a discussion of the proper use of correlation and regression techniques in the testing of causal models in nonexperimental research, see Hubert Blalock's classic *Causal Inferences in Non-Experimental Research* (Chapel Hill: Univ. of North Carolina Press, 1964). Dye presents a short, clear explication of his interpretation of the methods, op. cit., pp. 34-42. An alternative methodology, based on Blalock, is well-presented in Cnudde and McCrone, op. cit., especially pp. 860-862.

3. Blalock (op. cit., p. 8 ff) and others argue that such statistics reduce the variations in important variables in the attempt to control background factors. According to Blalock, slopes (beta values) should be used rather than correlation coefficients. But this method involves difficulties in establishing a significance test and it produces results that are not easily compared or grasped. Most studies have continued to use partialling techniques, avoided explicit tests of causal models, and focused on the degrees of association and the amount of variation in the dependent variable that can be explained. Dye (op. cit., pp. 40-41), for example, argues that simple and partial correlations are most appropriate since his research interest is to explain actual policy outputs and to assess the relative importance of environmental and political system variables. He claims that regression coefficients are applicable where the goal is to make predictions about the relationships among

variables. He quotes Blalock's observation: "In most problems in social sciences, attention is rightly focussed on locating the important variables. In explanatory work of this sort, correlational analysis becomes more important than regression analysis." (Blalock, op. cit., p. 51).

4. Blalock (1964), op. cit., pp. 87-93. Also see Blalock, "Correlated Independent Variables: The Problem of Multi-collinearity," *Social Forces*, 42, No. 2 (December 1963), pp. 233-237; D. Farrar and R. Glauber. "Multicollinearity in Regression Analysis," *Review of Economics and Statistics* (February 1967), pp. 92-107; R. Gordon, "Issues in Multiple Regression," *American Journal of Sociology* (March 1968), pp. 562-616. Forbes and Tufte observe: "In complicated multivariate models, there are a number of inherent problems of estimation. These often arise in attempts to distinguish the relative impact of different variables that are themselves highly intercorrelated. The accuracy of the estimates degenerates as the intercorrelation between independent variables approaches unity. Indeed, in the case of perfect correlation between two variables, the variance of the estimates of relative impact is infinite!" (Hugh Forbes and Edward Tufte, "A Note of Caution in Causal Modelling," *APSR*, 62, December 1968, pp. 1263-1264.)

A further technical criticism, relevant to the present study, involves the use of a common denominator for both independent and dependent variables in correlation analysis. Most commonly this occurs when both variables are measured in per population units (e.g., expenditure per head, percent population in a class or age group, and so on). Some scholars argue that this correlation of ratio variables can yield spurious results. There is unresolved debate on this point. It is usually agreed that in cross-sectional studies, the use of ratio variables is generally acceptable if the hypothesis tested is clearly stated in terms of the deflated values. See Edwin Kuh and John Meyer, "Correlation and Regression Estimates when the Data are Ratios," *Econometrica*, 23, No. 4 (October 1955), pp. 400-416; C. Rangarajan and S. Chatterjee, "A Note on Comparison Between Correlation Coefficients of Original and Transformed Variables," *The American Statistician*, 23, No. 4 (October 1969), pp. 28-29.

5. For a discussion of alternate causal models, see Danziger (1974), op. cit., pp. 136-139. Regarding these complex relationships, Blalock explains: "It is very simple to say, 'If X increases, Y increases at a constant rate, other things being equal.' But interaction requires a more complex statement of the form, 'As Z changes, the *relationship* between X and Y changes in a given manner.' " The first case is linear additive; the second case is nonadditive and might be nonlinear. (Blalock, 1964, op. cit., p. 91.) For example, as certain social conditions overlap, they might create a social situation in which needs increase at a curvilinear rate. This type of situation is discussed by Davies: "In education, the relationship between relative 'need' for the service and individual social conditions indices could well be defined as being nonlinear, because interaction might take place between various aspects of bad conditions so that 'need' might be increased by more than the sum of the effects of individual factors on need." (Davies, op. cit., p. 304.)

6. See the powerful critiques by Jacob and Lipsky, op. cit., and by Rakoff and Schaffer, op. cit.

7. In discussing Dye's classic study Jacob and Lipsky assert:

Dye . . . leaves unexplained the nature of the linkages that he asserts exist between economic development and programmatic outputs. We conclude from reading his analysis that by some magic a high level of economic development becomes transformed into high levels of expenditure. The process by which this transformation takes place remains in the shadows. [Jacob and Lipsky, op. cit., pp. 516-517.]

8. This classification of variable types is derived from one used by Boaden, op. cit. This study differs from Boaden's, less in conceptualization than in the formation of dependent variables and particularly in the use and interpretation of methodological treatments. Sharkansky (1971), op. cit., has also been developing the notions of resources and need in some of his demographic approach work.

9. There are jumps of varying lengths between the conceptual variables, the indicators, and the operational measures. The concept to which a measure corresponds is essentially a matter of judgment. Some indicators used in other studies are excluded; for instance, there is no urbanization measure since all county boroughs are urban. There are measures of interest for which there are no available data. For example, there is no measure of personal or family income because this data has never been collected. And some measures have several possible interpretations: density, as well as being an indicator of the physical environment, might also be understood as a rough measure of available land resources; and the ratio of domestic to industrial and commercial rateable value reflects aspects of local social structure as well as its main interpretation as an indicator of local economic structure.

It was not always possible or even desired to have perfect temporal correspondence between the dependent variables and the independent variables in the correlation analysis. Since notions of causality underlie the demographic approach, the independent variable measure precedes or corresponds in time to the dependent variable whenever possible. A set of exceptions to this is that some 1966 Census data (collected in 1965) have been used for the 1964-1965 output measures. Census data are not normally volatile, some measures encompassed a five year period, and the 1965 readings seemed appropriate for the 1964-1965 output data. Also, in those cases where the mean correlation ($\bar{r}$) varies substantially (where two consecutive r values differ by more than ± .25) all values are given.

It is important to note that, unlike the dependent variables, there are a number of independent variables that are not normally distributed. If we assess kurtosis (flat or peaked) and skewness (left or right) for the measures, the five variables are characterized by non-normal distributions: population, High Education, Elderly and Wealthy are peaked, and skewed right; SES 1 is skewed right. The main problem that this non-normal distribution represents for the analysis is that the extreme scores of a skewed distribution will affect the value of the correlation coefficient. Correlations for these variables must be viewed with some caution, and scattergrams were employed to assess the impact of the extreme values. These scattergrams (not displayed in the text) did not seem to threaten the validity of the analyses or interpretations reported here.

10. The main empirical source of evidence on this clustering is Moser and Scott, op. cit., and this clustering is often suggested or inferred in other discussions of the county boroughs. See also Newton (1976), op. cit., pp. 82-84.

11. Alt, for example, uses a random sample of 44 county boroughs, examining them in ten consecutive years (1958-1959 to 1967-1968); Boaden examines all county boroughs in a single-year study (1965-1966). Dependent variables in both studies are primarily measures of expenditure per thousand on major service areas:

education; housing; police; fire; children's service; health service; welfare service. Alt tests the effect of four independent variables: rateable value per head; percent Labour Party on Council; population; and interparty competition. Boaden uses the first three of these variables, plus some variables included in the present study (e.g., distribution by age group and by social class; amenities; crowding; density; education levels; domestic rateable value in units over £100; and domestic property as a proportion of total rateable value). Boaden uses a further set of variables that concern Council behavior (e.g., length of council meetings; number of ad hoc committees; whether there is a tenure limit for committee chairmen, and whether the press is admitted to committee meetings).

Alt records simple correlations, multiple correlations, and some partial correlations. Boaden presents simple correlations and a confusing, unsystematic set of partial correlations which control for one or two independent variables.

12. The most useful single summarization of the demographic-approach findings for the county boroughs is Newton (1976), op. cit. After the classic, early analysis in this mode by Hicks and Hicks, op. cit., the most general applications have been reported by Alt (1971), op. cit., Boaden (1971), op. cit., and James N. Danziger, "Comparing Approaches to the Study of Financial Resource Allocation," in *Comparative Public Policy: Issues, Theories, and Methods,* eds. C. Liske, W. Loehr, and J. McCamant (New York: Wiley-Halsted, 1975). See also F. R. Oliver and J. Stanyer, "Some Aspects of the Financial Behavior of the County Boroughs," *Public Administration,* 47 (Summer 1969), pp. 169-184; Douglas E. Ashford, "The Effects of Central Finance on the British Local Government System," *British Journal of Political Science,* 4 (July 1974), pp. 305-322; Douglas Ashford, "Resources, Spending, and Party Politics in British Local Government," *Administration and Society,* 6 (November 1975), pp. 286-311; and Douglas Ashford, Robert Berne, and Richard Schramm, "The Expenditure-Financing Decision in British Local Government," *Policy and Politics,* 5 (September 1976), pp. 5-24. Somewhat broader perspectives on the questions underlying these kinds of analyses are found in Kenneth Newton and L. J. Sharpe, "Local Outputs Research: Some Reflections and Proposals," *Policy and Politics,* 5 (March 1977), pp. 61-82; Bleddyn Davies, "Social Service Studies and the Explanation of Policy Outcomes," *Policy and Politics,* 5 (March 1977), pp. 41-59; and James E. Alt, "Politics and Expenditure Models," *Policy and Politics,* 5 (March 1977), pp. 83-92.

In general, the analyses have been cross-sectional and have often measured dependent variables and/or independent variables at only a single point in time. Although the studies by Alt and Boaden continue to be treated as benchmark findings, there are important threats to the validity of those works. One of Alt's four independent variables, for instance, is a competition index that is invalid because it fails to account for the possibility of an important third-party representation on Council. Yet during the period studied, there was a substantial third party on about one-third of the Councils and one-sixth of them had clear three-party systems. In Boaden's book-length study, independent variables are strangely operationized. For example, Boaden's education-level variable is taken from the 1951 Census (why not 1961 for 1965-1966 dependent variables?) and includes only a small percentage of adult males (those aged 15-25). More importantly, Boaden's independent variables for particular correlation and partial-correlation analyses are selected in an unsystematic and often puzzling manner. And many data analyses and explanations seem problemmatical and ad hoc, with rather strong inferences being made on the basis of quite weak and inconclusive statistical relationships.

While some of Boaden's empirical findings are questionable, his conceptual framework is a useful departure from the Dye model since it incorporates a more direct set of need indicators into the analysis and since it tests a set of variables (taken from the Maud Committee evidence) that do seem to tap aspects of Council behavior and process. These include: (1) average length of Council meetings; (2) number of main committees and (3) of subcommittees; (4) total ad hoc committees; (5) number of committee recommendations referred back (from Council to committee) in a twelve month period; (6) percent of deputy chairmanships not held by majority party; (7) whether there is a limit on tenure of committee chairmen; and (8) number of sheets of paper circulated to Councillors per month. From this set of Council behavioral measures, *not one* has independent association with Boaden's output measures and there are only scattered cases where a simple correlation reaches $\pm$ .20. Although little attention is devoted to this finding, it is extremely interesting. It seems to support the assumption of the demographic approach that behavioral process does not systematically relate to budgetary outputs. There are, of course, other process variables that could be compiled; but those gathered by the Maud Committee are significant in terms of Council operation. Given the lack of any correlations, we have not retested these variables in this study.

13. The procedure in the selection of independent variables and in the determination of the multiple R^2 (fraction of explained variance), and so on is to utilize a combination of stepwise and simultaneous multiple-regression analysis. For a full statistical treatment of these methods, the reader is referred to J. Johnson, *Econometric Methods* (New York: McGraw Hill, 1963). For a discussion of its specific use in these chapters, see Draper and Smith, *Applied Regression Analysis* (New York: Wiley, 1966).

Basically, the stepwise mode selects, at each reiteration, the independent variable which explains the largest amount of the remaining variance in the dependent variable. At each step, the estimating capacity of all previously selected independent variables is accounted for. Hence the independent variable selected into the equation at that step provides the largest reduction in the residual variation of the dependent variable.

The inclusion level for independent variables is based on the statistical significance of the regression coefficient (unstandardized) for each variable. The test of significance is an F statistic whose formula is:

$$\left(\frac{b}{\text{standard error of } b} \right)^2$$

The F is interpreted in the normal fashion from a table for the distribution of F, given the relevant degrees of freedom. The .05 confidence level has been used. Since this is a relatively stiff test, independent variables below this level (to about .10 confidence level) that might reduce the residual a reasonable amount were reexamined in multiple regression equations. In the very few instances where such details were substantively interesting, the details are noted. For the best discussion of this F statistic, which Draper and Smith call the "partial F," see Draper and Smith, op. cit.

It must be stressed that the regression equations cited are only estimations of the most powerful variables. Given the substantial multicollinearity among the independent variables, the outcomes of such regression analyses are rather volatile. However, careful analysis and data exploration were employed to select the most accurate and reasonable set of variables for each equation. In no case was there an alternative equation with any notable improvement on either the F statistic or the r^2. At this point, the focus is upon estimating equations rather than causal laws. On these matters, see Blalock (1964), op. cit., pp. 43-44, 46-55.

The form of statistics presented in the text is based on a simultaneous (as opposed to stepwise mode of) multiple-regression solution. Information includes:

b	=	unstandardized regression coefficient
Stnd. error	=	standard error of b
Par. F	=	partial F (significance of b)
Mult. R	=	multiple R (for the regression equation)
R^2	=	proportion of explained variance (of the dependent variable by the regression equation)
F	=	F statistic (significance of the regression equation)

14. This assumes a two-tailed significance test for N = 77 cases. This decision is similar to that made by Dye (1966: chapter 1). Moreover, one could argue that while the analysis covers all cases, it is cross-sectional—it is a sample, in time, of the cases.

15. As noted above, the fraction of explained variance (also called the coefficient of determination) is equal to the value of r^2. Thus a simple r value of just over $\pm .33$ yields an r^2 of .10, which can be understood as an explanation of 10% of the variance in the variable defined as the dependent variable. To explain 20% of the variance, a simple r of $\pm .45$ is necessary. These figures do not account for confounding effects. It should be recalled that this explanation is really a measure of how much of the value of the dependent variable can be estimated by its relationship to the independent variable. See Edwards, op. cit., p. 110; also Blalock, op. cit., pp. 35-44.

16. In Dye's American state study, for example, it was found that highways expenditure was strongly correlated with the conservative (Republican) party. It was one of the few outputs for which a political variable had a substantial, independent effect. (Dye, op. cit., pp. 171-172.) Dye also found (pp. 286-287) that both his economic-development and his political-system variable sets had independent, significant relationships with both highways and with a police measure (employees in police protection per population). Highways spending in English local authorities is explored in R. J. Nicholson and N. Topham, "Urban Road Provision in England and Wales, 1962-68," *Policy and Politics,* 4 (September 1974), pp. 3-29.

17. The more extensive research from which these data are drawn also made substantial use of first-order partial-correlation techniques. The results of those analyses are incorporated in the text. For the actual data, see Danziger (1974), op. cit., pp. 132-246.

18. The optimal regression equation for estimating police-service net expenditure (1968-1969) is:

Police Spending (1968-1969) =

	b	Stnd. error	Par. F
MigBal	−.218	.051	17.986
SES 2	−1.273	.388	10.781
Pop	.003	.001	6.229
Wealthy	.305	.136	5.052
(constant)	155.677		

Mult. R = .671
R^2 = .450
F = 11.844 $> .01$

19. The key legislation was: the National Health Service Act, 1946; the National Assistance Act, 1948; the Children's Act, 1948. There are a number of excellent scholarly treatments of provision on the personal social services. Davies' major study has been noted, op. cit., as well as those by Slack, op. cit., and Townsend, op. cit. The literature is vast; but helpful orientation can be found in M. Jeffreys, *An Anatomy of Social Welfare Services* (London: Joseph, 1965); M. P. Hall, *The Social Services of Modern England* (London: Routledge & Kegan, 1966); J. Parker, *Local Health and Welfare Services* (London: Allen & Unwin, 1968).

20. This problem is fully explored by Davies, op. cit., especially pp. 161-185, 248-156, 298-300. For one attempt, see his "Family Care Index," pp. 161-171. A completely different, subjective approach is suggested in *Social Welfare for the Elderly* (London: HMSO, 1968).

21. It should be noted that throughout this analysis, the indicators of personal and environmental needs are aggregate measures. In analyzing divisible-benefit services, need-allocation linkages are discussed. Need-personal indicators should be understood as variables which characterize a type of environment. Chastened by the ecological fallacy, we cannot assume that individuals of a group (e.g., nonwhites, those with low education, and so on) are those who actually receive a service, even if there is a significant correlation between the allocation variable and the need-personal measure.

22. In general, working-class tradition is to care for the elderly within the family structure; but wealthier old people are less likely to use public welfare homes. See Davies, op. cit., pp. 162-164; Peter Willmott, *The Evolution of a Community* (London: Routledge & Kegan Paul, 1963); Peter Townsend, op. cit.

23. Davies, op. cit., pp. 185-186.

24. The rationale to include these local health services is in Davies, op. cit., pp. 71-77.

25. Fuller elaboration of the findings is Danziger (1974), op. cit., pp. 182-223.

26. See The Labour Party, op. cit., especially pp. 82-84. A helpful general study of housing is D. V. Donnison, *The Government of Housing* (London: Penguin, 1967).

27. See, for example, "Housing" (Cmd. 2050, London: HMSO, 1963) for an explication while in office of the Conservative position on housing.

28. For the Labour position while the party was in power, see "The Housing Programme—1965-1970 for England and Wales" (Cmnd. 2838, London: HMSO, 1965).

29. The Labour Party's model point system for selection of tenants is detailed in The Labour Party, op. cit., pp. 89-94.

30. This position is based on the reasoning that the two main alternative revenue sources to rents for the Housing Revenue Account were, throughout the 1960s, rate contributions and Exchequer subsidies. Although Council house tenants pay rates, rate constributions to housing are clearly redistributive in favor of the tenants. Exchequer subsidies are calculated on the basis of certain formulas advantaging Councils which have provided more recent housing, and housing which meets certain desired specifications. The interpretation of this rent measure is not unambiguous and it became a less valid measure as the central government standardized rent and rent rebate schemes. Thus it is afforded less attention in the analysis.

Boaden took rates contribution to the Housing Revenue Account as a major indicator of policy output. This measure is not included in the analysis because it is a deceptive measure. Its mean value was only about £3.10.0 in 1968-1969. And more importantly, about 75% of this total was accounted for by specific Exchequer grants and subsidies. Thus the county borough's own resource commitment, in terms of this measure, was less than £1.0.0 per head.

31. It should be noted that this disposition measure, which we have interpreted as an indicator of the public/private activity mix, is in fact a housing measure. It is the proportion of all housing built 1945-1965 that is built by the county borough rather than privately. Thus part of the high correlation with the housing measures might be due to this underlying correspondence. The difference between the variables is that the independent variable is a proportion whose denominator is the total number of units of housing built by any source, while the dependent variable is a proportion whose denominator is the number of family units within the borough. Thus the first is a measure of the local authority's relative activity in housing and the second is a measure of the county borough's absolute level of provision.

32. This array of services included the statutory requirement to provide compulsory primary and secondary schools, a school health service, nursery schools, special schools for handicapped children, funds or facilities for teacher training and further education, scholarships for local students admitted to universities, as well as others. For a fuller discussion of the education service, see Harold Dent, *The Education System of England and Wales* (London: London Univ. Press, 1961); also see *Half Our Future: Report of the Central Advisory Council for Education in England–The Newsome Report* (London: HMSO, 1963).

33. Due to a major restructuring of secondary education in the 1960s, the figures for 1960-1961 are rather inconsistent with those for 1964-1965 and 1968-1969. It seems most accurate, given our conceptual interests, to deal here solely with the latter two fiscal years. Hence the analysis in this chapter excludes the 1960-1961 figures for secondary education.

34. Total Education Expenditure (1968-1969) =

	b	Stnd. error	Par. F
Pupils	108.757	16.804	41.888
Dom/Ind	−101.828	29.496	11.918
High Ed	508.108	172.130	11.358
Grant	5.944	1.945	9.341
(constant)	11,958.834		

Mult. R = .837
R^2 = .701
F = 40.966

$> .01$

35. Secondary Education Expenditure (1968-1969) =

	b	Stnd. error	Par. F
Pupils	132.625	14.853	79.735
Debt/hd	539.410	147.445	13.384
(constant)	415.409		

Mult. R = .797
R^2 = .635
F = 57.345 $> .01$

36. See Griffith, op. cit., pp. 522-524.

37. The Labour fraction on Council (average, 1965-1967) is the eighth variable brought into a stepwise-regression equation. It adds only .0009 to the multiple R, and its partial F is not significant at the .50 level. Oliver and Stanyer conclude that total gross expenditure per head is not related to Labour strength on Council. (Oliver and Stanyer, op. cit., p. 179.)

38. Population size does correlate significantly with four of the eight caretaker-service measures. Recall that greater population is associated with higher allocation levels on the police service and the refuse service and with lower levels of allocation on the fire service.

39. See, for example, Alt (1971), op. cit., p. 50; Boaden (1971), op. cit., p. 34.

40. For a discussion of the Key hypothesis on the effect of party competition on resource allocations, see Cnudde and McCrone, op. cit., especially pp. 858-860.

41. A good example is the observation of Fry and Winters: "In sum, though one would expect that environmental conditions would largely determine at what level revenues and expenditures will be set, politics is likely to be pivotal in establishing the allocations of rewards and benefits at that level." (Fry and Winters, op. cit., p. 511.) See also Clarke, op. cit.

Chapter 5

INCREMENTAL BUDGETING MODELS

One observation about government budgets has passed into the conventional wisdom: the best predictor of this year's allocation is last year's allocation. In this chapter, the usefulness of this statement is assessed in terms of the allocation data for the county boroughs. The axiom is normally attributed to the logic of incremental decision-making theory. While such derivation is generally correct, it is useful to distinguish two streams of reasoning which are often fused into a single explanation. The first concerns the nature of the budget and the limits of cognitive capacity; the second deals with the content of budgetary allocations relative to matters of realpolitik.

Incremental Theory

March and Simon[1] and Lindblom,[2] among others, developed a theory of decision-making based on the limitations facing a decison maker with a complex problem. The basic argument is that the decision maker, in such a situation, is limited by his

---

AUTHOR'S NOTE: Chapter 5 is a revised version of Danziger: "Assessing Incrementalism in British Municipal Budgeting," *British Journal of Political Science* 6 (July 1976) and is used with the permission of Cambridge University Press.

own intellectual capacities, by time pressures, by available sources of information, and by the costs of analysis. According to Lindblom, the burden of handling a complex decision-problem is minimized by employing incremental problem-solving strategies. The technique is to simplify the decision by structuring alternatives which are concrete, marginal alterations of the status quo.

In a complex decision, it is likely that critical values will be in conflict and that the decision maker may be unable to rank these values. Lindblom asserts that values are adequately grasped and assessed only by comparing them at the margin, as alternatives to the existing situation.[3] Moreover, marginal-value alternatives can be disclosed only by stating and evaluating them in terms of particular policies.[4] Under these constraints, choice-making occurs by ranking preferences among policies that are marginal alterations of the status quo.[5] The feedback mechanism is a corrective guidance system, providing relevant information for evaluating the most recent adjustments and selecting the next one.

A government budget is a classic example of the type of complex decision cited in incremental theory. Each item in the budget is a microindicator, expressed in units of money, of resource-allocation decisions which can be traced back into increasingly abstract judgments about social needs and demands and basic values. There is a near-infinite number of potential solutions (budgets) to the problem of resource allocation. The costs of reassessing basic value choices in each year ("comprehensive budgeting") are staggering.[6] This would entail ranking values, negotiating value disagreements among relevant participants, translating these into program alternatives, and allocating resources among selected programs. Incremental theory contends that budgeters do not have the cognitive capacities to act in this manner. The theory provides both a prescription for and a description of budget-making behavior. The budgeters take the existing budget, the "base," as the starting point. It is transformed into a new budget by selecting a mix of marginal changes in the existing levels of allocations. This process of slow alteration is repeated in each budgeting period, taking the impact of changes into account.

There is a second, political, dimension to the incremental content of a government's budget. Intertwined with the need to simplify a complex task is the fact that political feasibility severely constrains the range of relevant alternatives. This political constraint is quite different from the constraints imposed by cognitive limitations. Regardless of their capacity to devise and evaluate new programs, budgeters attend only to that narrow range of allocative changes that are viewed as politically acceptable. Wildavsky and Hammond stress this point:

> Whatever else they may be, budgets are manifestly political documents. . . . Participants in budgeting use its political components as aids to calculation. They drastically simplify their task by concentrating on the relatively small portion of the budget that is politically feasible to change. The previous year's budget, the largest part of which is composed of continuing programs and prior commitments, is usually taken as a base needing little justification beyond that offered in the past. Attention is normally focused on a small number of incremental changes, increases or decreases, calling for significant departures from the established historical base of the agency concerned. . . . Heavy reliance is placed on receiving feedback from interested parties, if a decision turns out to have adverse consequences for others.[7]

Incrementalism is basically a theory about change. It identifies two general constraints—one dealing with the budgeter's limited resources for analysis, and the second based on political feasibility—which limit solutions to a range of marginal alterations of existing decisions. It assumes that decisions are serial—that the decision situation is repeated at certain intervals. Thus it should be possible, by employing a longitudinal framework of analysis, to evaluate the extent to which county-borough budgetary allocations correspond to expectations derived from incremental theory.[8] It seems useful to distinguish the descriptive, behavioral aspects of incremental theory as a style of budget-making from the predictive, quantitative aspects of the theory as an estimator of the content of budgetary allocations. Chapter 7 assesses incrementalism as a behavioral approach based on cognitive limits. This chapter examines incrementalism as an estimator of the configurations of output.

The Incremental Approach Conceptualized

The approach of the incrementalists is directed primarily to the question of how the creation of the new budget in a particular year ("the budgetary process") is to be explained.[9] The approach seeks to characterize how budgeters respond to the problem of allocating resources, and to develop explanatory models of budgetary outputs. But, despite the volume of research that now exists on budgetary incrementalism, the operationalization of the concept remains an issue, and many of the empirical studies have the limited perspective of a single budget-making system—that is, of one set of resource allocators who employ the same standard operating procedures, rules of search, and so on.[10] Hence this chapter has two objectives: (1) to explicate some simple operational models of budgetary incrementalism; and (2) to examine the adequacy of these models by means of an empirical test in four comparable budget-making systems.

While incrementalism is fundamentally a description of a process of problem-solving behavior by individuals, most recent empirical work on budget-making has been quantitative, focusing upon the content of the decisions produced by the budgetary system. This work has addressed itself to at least three related questions about budgetary outputs: (1) is the magnitude of changes in allocations "incremental?" (2) is there a high level of stability in the allocations? and (3) is there a relatively systematic pattern of year-to-year change in allocations (that can be characterized by a quantitative model)?

(1) The magnitude of change. Since incremetalism predicts marginal alterations, early analyses often assessed the magnitude of budgetary change. Wildavsky set the parameter by asserting that any change is "incremental" if it is within the range ± .3 $ALLO_{t-1}$ (that is, the allocation level in year t−1).[11] While some writers continue to worry over a clear definition of "marginal,"[12] the issue seems subjective and hence unresolvable. At the very least, any figure given must be time- and environment-specific.

(2) Stability of allocations. The incremental approach suggests that outputs will be quite stable over time.[13] Applied to budgeting, the output might be understood as either the absolute allocation level for a service or the service category's proportion of total expenditure. In either case, stability would be confirmed to the extent that the level or proportion allocated was relatively unchanged over time.

(3) Pattern of change. A most intriguing question is whether there is a systematic pattern of allocative changes. The mainstream of recent research has this perspective, attempting to provide predictive models for the configuration of year-to-year changes in allocation decisions.[14] These studies derive equations that would produce allocations consistent with the assumptions of the incremental approach. The equations are then evaluated by examining (usually by means of linear-regression analysis) their predictive/explanatory adequacy for actual budget data.

There is an important output-process inference in all such studies. It is generally accepted that there ought to be some correspondence between a quantitative model of budgeting and the behavioral process that it seeks to explain.[15] In fitting regression equations to budgetary outputs, this behavioral dimension is often submerged. The goal of the model ought to be to specify patterns of marginal change that would result from certain decision rules or standard operating procedures of budgeters and then to establish whether the actual decisions correspond systematically to the predicted configurations of change. One would still, of course, be limited to making inferences about the actual process of budget creation and about the behavior of budgeters.

The Incremental Approach Operationalized

This section suggests operational measures by which to test the predictions of incrementalism about magnitude, stability, and change in budgetary allocations. These measures are discussed below and are summarized in Table 5.1.

MAGNITUDE

If change magnitudes must be categorized, the budgeters' subjectivity might be preferable to the analyst's subjectivity. Interviews with many county-borough budget actors verified that they do distinguish levels of change, based on the *impact* of funding levels on service provision. Essentially, they distinguish among: (1) a "normal" budget, which allows moderate development of service provision; (2) a "development" budget, which provides substantial new funding to increase service provision; (3) a "maintenance" budget, which adjusts for cost increases but does not increase service levels; and (4) a budget cut, requiring some reduction in service. The "normal" budget seems most closely aligned to the notion of an incremental budget, and the other three are relatively incremental. Alterations outside this range can be understood as nonincremental. Using these critieria as guidelines, Table 5.1 operationalizes categories of incrementalism that seem reasonable for the county boroughs during the 1960s.

STABILITY

The incremental-trend model. The most general notion of budgetary incrementalism simply holds that, for any service, $ALLO_t$ will be a marginal alteration of $ALLO_{t-1}$. This model focuses upon the absolute allocation level, rather than upon the configuration of longitudinal change or upon any decision

Table 5.1: Operationalization of the Incremental Models

Where:

$$\text{ALLO}_t = \text{Net budgetary allocation in financial year t}$$

$$\Delta\,\text{ALLO}_t = \frac{\text{ALLO}_t}{\text{ALLO}_{t-1}}$$

$$\text{Base ALLO}_1 = \frac{\text{ALLO}_t\ \text{Service}_i}{\text{ALLO}_t\ \text{Total Expenditure}}$$

$$\text{Prog Base}_t = \frac{\text{ALLO}_t\ \text{Program}_h}{\text{ALLO}_t\ \text{Service}_i}$$

(A) Magnitude of Change in Allocations

"Incremental" $= 1.05\ \text{ALLO}_{t-1}$ to $1.15\ \text{ALLO}_{t-1}$

"Relatively incremental" $= 1.16\ \text{ALLO}_{t-1}$ to $1.30\ \text{ALLO}_{t-1}$

$.90\ \text{ALLO}_{t-1}$ to $1.04\ \text{ALLO}_{t-1}$

"Nonincremental" $= <\ .90\ \text{ALLO}_{t-1}$

$>1.30\ \text{ALLO}_{t-1}$

(B) Stability of Allocation

(B1) Incremental-Trend Model:

$$\text{ALLO}_t = \beta\,(\text{ALLO}_{t-1}) + a$$

(B2) Prosperity-Change Score:

$$P = \frac{\sum_1^n (\text{Prog Base}_t)\ /\ (\overline{\text{Prog Base}})}{n}$$

(C) Change Dynamic in Allocations

(C1) Strict-Incremental Model:

$$\Delta\,\text{ALLO}_t = \beta\,(\Delta\,\text{ALLO}_{t-1}) + a$$

(C2) Fair-Share Model:

$$\Delta\,\text{ALLO}_t\ \text{Service}_i = \beta\,(\text{ALLO}_t\ \text{Total Expenditure}) + a$$

(C3) Base-Budget Model:

$$\text{Base ALLO}_t = \beta\,(\text{Base ALLO}_{t-1}) + a$$

rule underlying process. It is thus a *marginal alteration of total* model and estimates, by means of linear regression, the general trend in allocation changes.

The prosperity-change score. Natchez and Bupp argue that the "apparent massive stability" of the base might hide differential rates of growth or decay for component programs *within* a service department.[16] To achieve comparability with Natchez and Bupp's work, their "prosperity change score" will be computed for programs within two major county-borough services.[17] Table 5.1 displays the equation for this score, which is the average yearly difference between the ratio of program to total service expenditure and the mean of that ratio. The significance of the score must be interpreted subjectively.

CHANGE

There are simple quantitative models that are particularly useful for examining the patterns of incremental change in county-borough budgeting. They are grounded in behavioral notions of how the budgetary process operates, they focus on the marginal change pattern and the configuration of yearly change, and they take the final budgetary output as the primary data. These econometric models have been termed "naive models" by Crecine.[18] The fundamental research question is whether these models adequately predict allocation levels for various spending categories within each county borough and whether these models generate comparable findings across the four budgetary systems.

The strict-incremental model. The strict-incremental model isolates the change dynamic itself, predicting that allocation changes are characterized by about the same proportionate increase or decrease from year to year. Hence, it is a (relatively) *constant percentage change* model. The regression equation in Table 5.1 estimates each $\Delta ALLO_t$ as a function of $\Delta ALLO_{t-1}$.

The fair-share model. This model is derived from Wildavsky's notion of "fair share"—the expectation among budgeters that a spending unit will receive some equitable proportion of the increase (or decrease) in aggregate expenditure.[19] Thus, the fair-share model is based on a *constant percentage of change in total expenditure,* and estimates the change in service expenditure as a function of the change in total expenditure.

The base-budget model. Operationalizing the base as the proportion of total-expenditure allocated to Service$_i$, this model assumes that the change pattern will maintain an allocation as a *constant percentage of total expenditure.* Thus the base-budget model is not strictly a dynamic model; rather it predicts *no* change.[20] The regression equation estimates Base ALLO$_t$ as a function of Base ALLO$_{t-1}$.

The effect of exogeneous variables on the change-of-allocations patterns is a serious conceptual problem for these simple models.[21] This analysis is exploratory and is limited to assessing the adequacy of the incremental models without specifying the impact of exogeneous variables. The models are "naive" in the sense that there is an assumption that, in the shorter run, they are generally accurate regardless of such factors as the national political system, particular organizational procedures, minor economic variations, or demographic characteristics. If one of these models of displays high predictive power, its parsimony makes it attractive relative to alternative explanations. And, by examining the variations in accuracy of model predictions across services or between the four independent budgeting systems, it may be possible to infer the points where other variables seem to have an impact. At least it seems valid and useful to determine whether simple, operational models of incrementalism do in fact predict/explain allocation change.

The units of analysis for this assessment are the four county boroughs.[22] The array of the resource-allocation measures which have been selected for analysis are total net expenditure, for financial years 1958-1969, on:

all rate- and grant-born services,

total education services,

primary education,

local health services,

home nursing,

highways and streets, and

parks.

To assess the models, data are analyzed by linear-regression techniques. The regression coefficients, F-scores, and fraction of explained variance (R^2) provide evidence for evaluating the adequacy, through time and across spending categories, of the various models.[23] Magnitudes of change are summed by category, and "prosperity-change scores" are computed.

Findings From The Incremental Approach

MAGNITUDE

Allocation levels in the four county boroughs for the selected service categories (financial years 1958-1969) are displayed in Table 5.2. If the suggested categories of incrementalism are ap-

Table 5.2: Magnitude of Change in Allocations

	Brighton		Dudley		Southend		West Bromwich	
	%	(n)	%	(n)	%	(n)	%	(n)
Incremental								
$1.05-1.15ALLO_{t-1}$	77	(54)	59	(36)	66	(46)	76	(48)
Relatively Incremental								
$.90-1.04ALLO_{t-1}$	14	(10)	16	(10)	21	(15)	13	(8)
$1.16-1.30ALLO_{t-1}$	9	(6)	23	(14)	11	(8)	10	(6)
Nonincremental								
$<.90$ or >1.30 $ALLO_{t-1}$	0	(0)	2	(1)	1	(1)	2	(1)

plied, 60% to 75% of the changes in each county borough are within the clearly "incremental" range. There are only four examples of "nonincremental" change. As many as 40% of the yearly changes in each borough were not merely slight increases; but the common view that most changes are marginal alterations from the base seems to be supported.[24]

STABILITY

The incremental-trend model. It is obvious from Table 5.3 that the linear-regression estimations of $ALLO_t$ are powerful. *Every* regression coefficient is extremely significant across all four county boroughs and all spending categories. At least 90% of the variance is explained in all but three cases, and there are ten cases in which the R^2 is 99%. Only Southend's allocations are slightly divergent from the model, with R^2 values ranging from 96% to 83%.

These findings seem compelling evidence that absolute allocation levels are characterized by a high degree of stability. However, these figures may be less illuminating than they appear. John Wanat has argued persuasively that the "success" of such models usually reflects the mathematical domination of the new figure over the old figure and that they provide little information about the actual nature of the incremental process. Wanat shows that even randomly generated change levels over an extremely wide range provide very high levels of predictive adequacy.[25] Generally, it seems appropriate to conclude that there is substantial stability; but the moderate differences in the regression coefficients between boroughs and between services within boroughs suggest that there is a variety of stabilities.

Prosperity-change score. Table 5.4 displays the prosperity-change scores for selected education and local health services between financial years 1960 and 1969. Six of the eight services have, on average, suffered a decline during the decade. While Natchez and Bupp found scores ranging from +9.0 to −24.6 in

Table 5.3: Stability of Allocation: Incremental-Trend Model[a]

County Borough's Net Expenditure on:		β [b]	R^2
Total education	Brighton	1.10	.98
	Dudley	1.14	.99
	Southend	1.17	.95
	West Bromwich	1.06	.99
Primary education	Brighton	1.10	.98
	Dudley	1.11	.99
	Southend	1.05	.94
	West Bromwich	1.06	.99
Local health services	Brighton	1.04	.98
	Dudley	1.10	.99
	Southend	.93	.96
	West Bromwich	1.15	.99
Home nursing	Brighton	1.10	.98
	Dudley	1.13	.99
	Southend	.95	.91
	West Bromwich	1.14	.99
Highways	Brighton	.77	.79
	Dudley	1.18	.99
	Southend	.97	.84
	West Bromwich	1.07	.99
Parks	Brighton	.96	.92
	Dudley	.98	.97
	Southend	.92	.83
	West Bromwich	1.02	.98

a. There are eleven or ten observations in each case.
b. $p < .001$ in each case.

programs of the American Atomic Energy Commision,[26] the county-borough scores range only from +5.9 to −5.2. These scores are less dramatic, but they do suggest programmatic shifts—that some services do prosper and decay over time within the "apparent massive stability" of the service-area allocation.

CHANGE

The strict-incremental model. This model, which stresses the configuration of the marginal increments, predicts that the size

Table 5.4: Stability of Allocation: "Prosperity-Change Score" for
Selected Services

"Prosperity-change score" between:	Bri	Dud	S'end	W Bro
(A) Total net education and:				
(1) Primary education	−2.9	−1.0	−2.6	−1.6
(2) Secondary education	−2.8	−1.9	−1.0	−1.4
(3) Further education	+5.1	+5.4	+5.9	+3.0
(B) Total local health services and:				
(1) Care of mothers and young children	+1.1	−3.0	+ .1	+ .7
(2) Health visiting	−2.5	+2.1	−4.5	−3.4
(3) Home nursing	−2.7	−3.8	+5.0	− .8
(4) Ambulance service	−1.3	− .8	− .9	+2.7
(5) Prevention, care, and after-care	+2.3	−3.9	−5.2	−2.2

of the percentage change will be relatively constant from year
to year. In Table 5.5 the regression coefficients are significant
in only four of twenty-eight cases; but the equations explain at
least 20% of the variance in about half the cases.[27]

A most intriguing finding is the pervasiveness of *negative* coefficients. This suggests a change configuration in which years
of expansion are often followed by years of stability or even
decline in allocation level. This inference was further supported
by examining scattergrams of these data. The alternating pattern of changes is particularly evident for such major service
categories as total net expenditure in West Bromwich, total
education spending in Southend, and highways spending in
West Bromwich and Dudley. In total, twenty-one of the regression coefficients (out of twenty-eight cases) are negative,
and many of these are large enough to be interesting.[28]

What might explain this oscillating configuration of allocation changes? One plausible explanation, in political terms, is
that chief officers are less satisfied by continual marginal increases than by larger increases, even when these are granted
less often. These larger increments might provide sufficient
extra financial resources in a single year to undertake a new or

Table 5.5: Change Dynamic in Allocations: The Naive Models[a]

County Borough's Net Expenditure on:	Strict-Incremental Model		Fair-Share Model		Base-Budget Model	
	β	R^2	β	R^2	β	R^2
Total education						
Brighton	−.43	.18	.71	.30	.68*	.53
Dudley	−.48	.15	.54	.29	.85***	.91
Southend	−.77*	.55	−.19	.02	.32	.23
West Bromwich	−.12	.01	.24	.15	.56	.36
Primary education						
Brighton	−.48	.26	.92***	.72	1.09***	.94
Dudley	−.33	.11	.29	.10	1.04*	.63
Southend	−.51*	.24	.18	.01	.13	.02
West Bromwich	−.19	.02	.58*	.56	.88*	.58
Local health services						
Brighton	−.35	.29	.09	.00	.75*	.41
Dudley	−.93*	.55	.26	.04	.82	.38
Southend	−.01	.00	−.37	.01	.31	.36
West Bromwich	.60	.29	.46	.31	1.05***	.77
Home nursing						
Brighton	−.19	.01	.16	.01	−.20	.02
Dudley	1.65	.28	1.10	.19	.92**	.75
Southend	.17	.03	−.59	.10	.73	.30
West Bromwich	−.33	.17	.61	.27	.52*	.46
Highways						
Brighton	.08	.01	1.89	.33	.68**	.64
Dudley	−.93	.50	−.61	.05	.56	.25
Southend	.44	.14	−.02	.00	.63	.27
West Bromwich	−.70	.48	.36	.03	−.19	.02
Parks						
Brighton	−.22	.05	.68	.12	.72**	.66
Dudley	−.39*	.55	.48	.21	.87***	.97
Southend	−.58	.35	.90	.21	.98***	.79
West Bromwich	−.69	.09	.99**	.70	1.07***	.97
Total services						
Brighton	−.52	.25				
Dudley	.45	.06	n.a.		n.a.	
Southend	.07	.01				
West Bromwich	−1.93*	.59				

a. There are eleven or ten observations in each case. The naive model with the highest R^2 value for each county-borough spending category is in bold face.
*** = p < .001
** = p < .01
* = p < .05

substantially expanded service. An alternative explanation, given the apparent two-year cycle, is that pruners find it easier to control the general level of increase in any given year by arguing (to some set of departments) that "you were just given a large increase last year," or that "the increase should be consolidated and its effect assessed prior to further expansion."

Broadly, the strict-incremental model, which focuses upon the dynamic of marginal change rather than the stability of the total allocation level, is moderately successful, in terms of statistical significance. The negative coefficients, suggesting a "fat-lean" pattern of allocation changes, are surprising both in their existence and in their occurrence across all four county boroughs and all spending categories. These findings reveal that there is not a simple consistency to the change dynamic within or between the county-borough budgeting systems.

The fair-share model. The fair-share model predicts that the change in spending on a service will be a relatively constant proportion of the change in total expenditure. The fair-share model is not generally supported in Table 5.5. There are a few cases where the outputs correspond to those predicted by the model; the clearest examples are primary-education spending in Brighton and West Bromwich and parks expenditure in West Bromwich. But in general there is little evidence in the Table that a fair-share constraint is a decision rule in either Dudley or Southend, and the findings for Brighton are mixed. In West Bromwich, however, four of the six services display some support for the model. The occurrence of fair-share outputs might be explained by the existence of a fair-share principle among the decision rules utilized by important budgeters in West Bromwich. In fact, intensive case-study analysis of decision rules in the different county-borough budgeting systems substantiated this finding. The West Bromwich finance officer who had a dominant role in establishing allocation levels during the period studied expressed an unambiguous commitment to a fair-share decision principle. No such principle was mentioned by any budget maker in any of the other three county boroughs.

The base-budget model. As operationalized above, this model predicts that a spending category will maintain a relatively constant proportion of total expenditure. The findings are interesting and mixed. In terms of services, parks spending fits the model's predictions very well for all four county boroughs. Primary education has significant regression coefficients in three of the four county boroughs, and the remaining services have two or one significant beta values. The fraction of explained variance differs markedly (e.g., from 91% to 23% on education, and from 75% to 2% on home nursing).

If one examines the model results for each of the four different budgeting systems, it seems that there is quite strong confirmation for the base-budget model in Brighton, where all but one service (home nursing) have high R^2 values. In contrast to Brighton, only parks spending has a significant regression coefficient in Southend, and the fraction of explained variance is less than 40% for every other service.

Thus there is differential support for the base-budget model across boroughs and across services. It is difficult to generate systematic explanations for why one service or one budgeting system should more or less strongly support the model. On the basis of these data, model adequacy does not seem related to the absolute size of the expenditure category or the labor-intensiveness of the service. One might speculate that the most stable budgeting system would produce outputs more consistent with the base-budget-model predictions. The case-study analyses revealed that Brighton, whose outputs correspond most closely to the model, was the only county borough that maintained a highly stable system of budgeting during the decade. But Dudley and West Bromwich, which implemented fundamental alterations in their budgetary processes midway through the decade, also provided rather strong support for the model. In sum, more adequate analytic variables are necessary to account for the varied findings from the base-budget model.

Concluding Observations

The central concern of this chapter has been to evaluate the adequacy of certain derivations of the incremental explanation of budgetary allocations. The analysis has been comparative both in the sense of using multiple contexts (as units of analysis) and in the sense of examining alternative explanatory approaches. These alternative approaches address themselves to three sorts of issues regarding budgetary allocation levels: (1) the magnitude of change; (2) the stability of allocations; and (3) the systematic configurations of change. All three approaches take budgetary *outputs* as the primary data. The *process* of budget-making can be inferred from the analysis to the extent that the conceptual models are specified in terms of behavioral variables.

The magnitude of change, measured as the percentage change in allocation levels for services in the four county boroughs, is, as incrementalism implies, characterized by marginal alteration. In the pooled data, 60% to 75% of the changes were in the 1.05 to 1.15 $ALLO_{t-1}$ range and there were very few examples of nonincremental change. The stability in allocations is addressed by the incremental-trend model and by the prosperity-change score. The incremental-trend model, whose regression estimates are primarily responsive to stability in the base, has the highest predictive power of any conceptualization of incrementalism. Broadly, existing expenditure clearly dominates the new level of allocation. The prosperity-change scores reveal that programs do prosper and decay within general service categories; but the range of variation is less dramatic than in the American test of this measure. In sum, the most fundamental axiom of incrementalism, stability in the outputs, is again confirmed.

The most interesting models assessed here are those that examine whether there are systematic patterns of change. They are richer models because they probe the nature of the change dynamic itself, because they provide explicit and quantitative predictions, and because they are grounded in decision rules that might explain the process of budgetary incrementalism.

For these naive models—the strict-incremental model, the fair-share model, and the base-budget model—the method of assessing explanatory adequacy is the yardstick of predictive accuracy.

If we employ the loose test that a model ought to predict at least 50% of the year-to-year variation in service categories, none of the three naive models has an exceptional level of adequacy. In these terms, the strict-incremental model, in its positive form, does not explain half the variation in a single case. In its negative (that is, up-down) form, it is successful in only 18% of the cases. The fair-share model explains half the variation in only 12.5% of the cases. Only the base-budget model is moderately adequate, meeting the criterion in exactly 50% of the cases. One of the three models explains at least half of the variance in 62% (fifteen of twenty-four) of the cases.[29] In this sense, the models are most adequate for parks spending and are least adequate for spending on home nursing, highways, and local health services; and they are most adequate in Dudley, least adequate in Southend.

For comparative analysis among the naive models, Table 5.5 identifies the most adequate model for each spending category in each budgeting system in terms of the highest fraction of explained variance. The base-budget model is most adequate in nineteen cases. The strict-incremental model is best in the remaining five cases; and the fair-share model fails to have the highest predictive accuracy in a single case.

The base-budget model so dominates the table that there are few notable interborough or interservice differences between the models. However, while the base-budget model provides a powerful explanation in some instances, including parks spending, it is unsatisfactory in others, such as highways spending. The strict-incremental model does moderately well for highways spending, and some support for the fair-share model in West Bromwich has been noted.

In a broader sense, any assessment of the adequacy of the naive models ought to take into account what they fail to provide. They deal only with the shape of change. They have no capacity to explain what is—why primary education receives

12% or 18% of total expenditure, why spending on parks is in a general decline, why highways allocations change erratically. Moreover, these models, like most quantitative models of budgetary incrementalism, can claim only a loose correspondence to process. They attempt to establish a change dynamic that is consistent from year to year. But they cannot determine whether the incremental constraint on change is a function of cognitive limits, political feasibility, the sum of standard operating procedures, limited revenue, or some other phenomenon. The models do focus attention on deviations from inertial patterns of allocations; but none have theoretical content that accounts for these anomalies.

There is an obvious need for more extensive research using comparable but independent budgeting systems. Many existing studies of budgetary incrementalism generalize on the basis of a single system. Yet a striking characteristic of the comparative research reported here is the variability of model support across budgeting systems and expenditure categories.

The specification of critical macro- or micro-level variables might help; but there is some evidence in this study that, in institutionalized local governments, the changes in budgetary allocations are somewhat unresponsive to such factors in the shorter run. For example, a most perplexing finding is the lack of differentiation between the two sets of budgeting systems. Brighton and Southend on the one hand and Dudley and West Bromwich on the other differ from each other on important social, economic, and political characteristics, and they also differ on the stability and style of their budgetary processes. Yet this broad array of (potentially) discriminating variables, which are reinforcing rather than crosscutting in the four municipalities, do not produce model results that distinguish between the two sets. Perhaps these local governments are "overly determined systems," in which allocation changes will necessarily be best explained in the shorter run by the most rigid no-change model available. Thus the incremental-trend model and, among the naive models, the base-budget model provide the most accurate estimates of budgetary outputs. The incremental approach seems better able to predict how allocations remain the same than to explain the conditions under which they change.

NOTES

1. March and Simon, op. cit.
2. Charles Lindblom (1964), op. cit.; Braybrooke and Lindblom, op. cit.; Charles Lindblom, *The Policy-Making Process* (New Jersey: Prentice-Hall, 1968).
3. Braybrooke and Lindblom, op. cit., p. 84.
4. Ibid., p. 85; Lindblom (1964), op. cit., pp. 158-160.
5. Braybrooke and Lindblom, op. cit., p. 86.
6. See Wildavsky and Hammond, op. cit., for a case study of the attempt by one department of the federal government to do comprehensive budgeting. The participants verified all the arguments of incremental theorists concerning the enormous costs of this strategy in terms of intellectual and psychic resources and time.
7. Ibid., pp. 322-323. Wildavsky is a major advocate of the political constraint on budgetary change. See also Aaron Wildavsky, "Political Implications of Budgetary Reform," *Public Administration Review* (Autumn 1961), pp. 183-190, and Wildavsky, (1964), op. cit. At a broader level, Braybrooke and Lindblom argue: "nonincremental alternatives, even if desirable in some sense, are often politically irrelevant" (p. 89). More dramatically, they declare: "Nonincremental alternatives usually do not lie within the range of choice possible in the society or body politic. ... Political democracy is often greatly endangered by nonincremental change which it can accommodate only in certain limited circumstances" (p. 73).
8. There has been substantial interest in comparing requests and appropriations in the American state and national context. A major contribution to this topic was the development by Davis, et al. of three simple equations which predicted an agency's appropriation on this basis of some combination of the previous year's request and appropriation and a circumstantial variable. See Davis, et al. (1966), op. cit. The request-appropriation framework is not applicable in the county-borough context. The final allocations are the only publicly available set of spending unit requests in the county boroughs which correspond to the agency requests to an appropriations body. Thus it is necessary to deal with actual allocations as the sole data-point.
9. The literature on this question has become quite extensive. Seminal pieces include: Aaron Wildavsky (1964), op. cit.; John P. Crecine, op. cit.; Davis, Dempster, and Wildavsky (1966), op. cit.; John Wanat, "Bases of Budgetary Incrementalism," *American Political Science Review*, 68 (1974), pp. 1221-1228; Barber, op. cit. A second common question in the research is: how is this particular level of allocations to be explained?
10. These concepts are developed in Richard Cyert and James March, *A Behavioral Theory of the Firm* (Englewood Cliffs, N.J.: Prentice-Hall, 1963). There are exceptions to the use of only one budget-making system, particularly Crecine, op. cit.

11. Wildavsky (1964), op. cit., p. 14.

12. John Bailey and Robert O'Connor, "Operationalizing Incrementalism: Measuring the Muddles," *Public Administration Review,* 35 (1975), pp. 60-66.

13. One might also examine directly whether there is stability in the *process* of budget creation. While one could infer process stability from the outputs, stronger confirmation requires case-study analysis. In fact, only one of the four county boroughs maintained a highly stable budget-making process during the 1960s. The problem-solving routines for the budgetary process were altered very substantially in two of the boroughs and some restructuring occurred in the fourth. See Chapter 7.

14. Examples include Davis, et al. (1966), op. cit.; Crecine, op. cit.; and Andrew Cowart, Tore Hansen, and Karl-Erik Brofoss, "Budgetary Strategies and Success at Multiple Decision Levels in the Norwegian Urban Setting," *American Political Science Review,* 69 (1975), pp. 543-558.

15. Crecine, op. cit., pp. 111-112 and Wanat, op. cit., pp. 1222-1223.

16. Peter Natchez and Irvin Bupp, "Policy and Priority in the Budgetary Process," *American Political Science Review,* 67 (1973), pp. 951-963.

17. Ibid., pp. 959-961. The score could also be calculated in terms of Base ALLO–that is, the ratio of service category to total expenditure. For comparability, Natchez and Bupp's focus at the program level has been retained.

18. The strict-incremental model, the fair-share model, and the base-budget model are explicated in Crecine, op. cit., pp. 119-120.

19. Wildavsky (1964), op. cit., p. 18.

20. It should be noted that in the case where an allocation category received a "parity" fair share, the base-budget model would also be confirmed. Thus the base-budget model is a special case of the fair-share model; but neither the fair-share nor the strict-incremental model necessarily presume that the level of change will preserve the same proportion of the base.

21. Potentially important exogenous variables include both local, configurative characteristics (e.g., demographic factors, the political system, the nature of the budgetary process) and also broad, system characteristics (e.g., the national political system, with its control of grants and its broad authority over service provision, and the national economic system, manifest in the rate of inflation and in changes in commodity and labor prices). A fully elaborated model of resource-allocation changes would need to specify all these sets of variables. Currently, most research takes a more limited perspective, attempting to examine a certain subset of the complex of variables that might provide plausible explanations. The demographic explanation have been examined in Chapter 4. For an attempt to specify macrolevel exogenous variables in the American context, see Davis, Dempster, and Wildavsky (1974), op. cit.

22. There seems no reason to suspect that the findings are unrepresentative of other county boroughs. The findings might be generalizable to other governmental budgeting contexts. But it is important to note that this research has not replicated the framework in most American-based studies because there is an important difference in the budgetary processes. In the American-style process, budget-making is factored into a distinct set of episodes with discrete, measurable, and public decisions, including the spending unit request, the pruning unit's revision, and the legislature's decision. In contrast, county-borough budgeting is better characterized as a flow of transactions through time rather than a discrete set of actions. Over a four-

month period, there is continual formal and informal bargaining between spenders and pruners at various levels. Negotiations with each spending unit are independent and all figures are strictly confidential. Only the final estimates presented to council, normally authorized without much revision, are reliable and appropriate data. Thus the multistage quantitative models used for American-style systems are not applicable to county boroughs. See Chapter 7. For use of the American-style system in a Norwegian municipality, see Cowart, Hansen, and Brofoss, op. cit.

23. For the regression analyses, the tables report the significance of the regression coefficient as measured by the F-score, given the appropriate degrees of freedom. Although the primary commitment of the research is to decide upon substantive significance, the following levels of statistical significance are appropriate:

p	$< .05$	$< .01$	$< .001$
F-score	4.75	9.33	18.64

For brevity, the tables do not report the F-score, standard error, or regression equation.

24. It might be that pooled data hide interesting year-to-year variations in the magnitude of allocation changes. To assess this, the data were disaggregated by borough and year for each category in Table 5.2. The time frame and number of services are too limited to support strong generalizations; but the figures did suggest some clusterings. For example, "relatively incremental" increases and decreases seemed to cluster in particular years. Interestingly, there were few similarities between boroughs in any year. The opposite finding would have suggested the impact of macropolitical or macroeconomic forces.

25. Wanat, op. cit., p. 1221.

26. Natchez and Bupp, op. cit., p. 963. Natchez and Bupp speculate that greater fluctuations might be expected in more specific expenditure categories. Analysis of the county-borough data revealed that fluctuations were substantially greater with each further breakdown of expenditure categories. This is not a meaningless, breaking-out of data in the county boroughs. In Brighton, for instance, the standing orders required that each line-item in the budget be separately calculated, authorized, and monitored. If any line-item (e.g., wages and salaries for home nurses within the home-nursing sector of the local health services) was overspent by more than a minimal amount, an entire reauthorization procedure was required for a supplementary allocation.

27. Due to amalgamations in Dudley and West Bromwich, the financial years 1965 to 1966 values for this model are treated as missing values in the analysis.

28. Crecine found some negative relationships in two of the three American municipalities but did not expand upon the finding. Crecine, op. cit., pp. 197-199. Applying Crecine's method (autocorrelation of $ALLO_t$) to the county-borough data, over half the correlation coefficients are statistically significant, many are quite high, and twenty-four (of twenty-eight) are negative.

29. The category of net total expenditure is not included in these figures because the strict-incremental model is the only applicable naive model.

Chapter 6

ORGANIZATION-LEVEL EXPLANATIONS

In this and the subsequent chapter, explanatory approaches are examined that focus explicitly upon the processes and the behavior of budget-making. The demographic explanation and the naive econometric models inferred process and behavior from data on outputs; but the approaches in Chapters 6 and 7 take process and behavior as the primary data and attempt to infer the shape of outputs. While there is a degree of overlap in the perspective of the process-based explanations, we shall separate them by means of an analytic distinction. Chapter 7 will examine those explanatory modes that treat the *individual* as the object unit of analysis (that is, the unit whose behavior is to be explicated). In this chapter, however, the focus is upon those explanations that take the organization as the object unit of analysis. First, the key antecedents to the budget-making process in the county boroughs are characterized. Then the normative model of budgeting is explicated. Third, the actual budget-making process for each of the four county boroughs is described briefly. And, fourth, the major portion of the chapter assesses the organizational-process approach as an explanation of the budgetary process in the four county boroughs. The primary data for these analyses of process in Chapters 6 and 7 are over 100 transcribed, open-end interviews with participants in the budgetary process of the four county boroughs and various public and confidential documents.

Antecedents to the Budgetary Process

In order to make research on the process manageable, the focal question of this analysis is: how is the problem of budget creation in Y_t solved?[1] This cross-sectional (as opposed to historical) perspective constitutes a conceptual simplification; but it does align with the perspective of budgetary decision makers, whose problem is to create a new budget, given certain important antecedents. While it is not possible to specify with precision the impact of these antecedents of the Y_t budget-making process, it is useful to characterize them in order to establish a sense of their effects.

There are four primary antecedents which act as constraints on the budgetary process.

(1) *The previous year's budget.* It is a commonplace that the Y_t budget solution is based on the Y_{t-1} pattern of allocations. Chapter 5 established that in longitudinal analysis for the four county boroughs, Base $ALLO_{t-1}$ estimated over 50% of the yearly variation in Base $ALLO_t$ in one-half the cases.[2] While the explanation of any year's allocation simply in terms of the previous year's allocation degenerates into an infinite-regress explanation, this analysis will be sensitive to the nature of the existing allocation level as a constraint on the change dynamic between $ALLO_{t-1}$ and $ALLO_t$.

(2) *The capital program.* New capital projects, which have been initiated several years before Y_t, have an impact on current expenditure through new operating costs and interest charges. In fact, there was a striking correspondence, in each of the four budget-making systems, between the process generating the revenue budget and the process creating the capital budget. Other than the fact that the capital budget concerns capital projects which require external loan sanction and the fact that commitments are made more-or-less

firmly over a five-year period, the basic procedures of initiation, vetting, and approval of capital expenditure can be viewed as comparable to those discussed for current expenditure in this chapter.[3]

(3) *Staffing decisions.* Prior to budget creation, an Establishment Committee determines which grading changes and alterations in staff size will be authorized.[4] While upgradings are automatically entered into the spending figures, the key decisions about whether to fill vacant and authorized positions are made during the budgetary process.

(4) *Policy decisions.* The constraining nature of policy commitments based on Council decisions, Parliamentary acts, or central department circulars is difficult to characterize. Chapter 2 noted that externally generated policies require a local response, but that the county borough normally has substantial latitude in the level of resources allocated. Internally generated policies move through authorization by the relevant Spending Committee and, where a specified minimum expenditure is involved, must also be considered by the Finance Committee.[5] The great majority of policy decisions are policy-serving—that is, they propose alterations or elaborations to existing schemes.[6] With few exceptions, a policy decision is not a guarantee of resource allocation; rather it is a force which strengthens the demand to consider funding the proposal and which increases the probability that allocators will fund it.

The Normative-Process Model

The normative description of the budget-making process is quite simple. It is normally the only available description of county-borough budgeting.[7] According to this view, each spending department begins to prepare its estimates in October-November. The department considers its allocations for the current year, how these relate to its actual spending trends (April through September), and any approved increases or modifications of existing service provision. The Y_t set of estimates are built up from these factors, with account being taken of changes in costs, salaries, and so forth. The estimates are presented to the Spending Committee, which examines and revises them on policy grounds, and then approves them. The Finance Committee, with the technical assistance of the Borough Treasurer's Department, compiles and evaluates the estimates for all Spending Committees. Finance Committee suggests revisions, normally reductions, in various estimates on the basis of financial considerations and the general perspective of available resources. If the Spending Committee accepts a revision, it becomes the estimate; if not, Council will be the final adjudicator. Finance Committee and the Treasurer also estimate the total available revenue from government grants, rents, charges, and so forth. On the basis of the difference between recommended expenditure and available revenue, Finance Committee recommends a level of rate-in-the-pound sufficient to balance the budget. Council, at its March meeting, debates the estimates and the rate, may revise them, and by a majority vote, authorizes resource allocations for the fiscal year.

Several important normative rules structure these procedures. All policy decisions affecting the budget should be settled, as far as possible, prior to the budget-making procedure.[8] The Spending Committee (and Department) must have the right to stake their claim for resources *before* the financial actors interfere.[9] They can continue to press for an estimate right up to the rate-approving session of Council. Council should delegate detailed scrutiny of the estimates to the Finance Committee, and should normally accept their recommendations.[10] But Council itself is the final arbiter in disputes about committee estimates and the rate.[11] Finally, the Borough Treasurer and his staff should assemble information, make technical calculations, point out possibilities and consequences; but the making of decisions must be left to the elected members of Council.[12] Beyond these general norms, detailed procedures vary, depending on local tradition, Standing Orders, or special circumstances.

Descriptions of the Four Budgeting Systems

While the normative-process model prescribes how budget-making ought to occur, none of the four budget-making systems examined conforms closely to this idealized version. This section is descriptive, attempting to characterize broadly the major aspects of each borough's approach to the recurrent problem of budget creation. In a subsequent section, the budgetary systems will be treated analytically, employing the conceptual approach of the organizational-process explanation.

SOUTHEND

Of the four county boroughs, Southend's budgetary process has the most correspondence to the normative-process model. Budget estimates (allocation requests) are prepared initially by senior administrative officers in each spending department. These estimates are built from the available information about the previous two years' expenditure, changing wage and cost conditions, and desired program expansion. In the subsequent three-month period, there is a series of independent reassessments of the department's estimates. Attention is focused upon each line-item and the fundamental question is: how is any increase from Y_{t-1} justified? The first assessment is between the Spending Department administrative officer and the Treasurer's accountant. The accountant then meets with each of the top officers in the Finance (Treasurer's) Department. In these meetings, the accountant justifies and evaluates the components of each requested increase under the scrutiny of his superiors. Next, the Chief Officer justifies his requests before the Spending Department Committee, under the probing/challenging of a senior Finance Officer. The Committee makes some reductions in the requests, and forewards the estimates to the Policy and Finance Committee (composed of all Spending Committee Chairmen). This body of elected representatives then delegates the analysis to a five-member Executive Board of professional chief officers.[13]

The Executive Board, given information about the rate implications of the aggregate requests, determines the amount of reductions necessary to achieve a rate level which is likely to be acceptable to the Majority Party Group on Council. With this amount of reductions as the constraint, the Executive Board meets individually with each Chief Officer. On the basis of a stylized debate between Chief Officer as spending advocate and Treasurer as pruning advocate, the Board "recommends" a figure for each line-item. The Policy and Finance Committee is forewarded the detailed budget and then conducts its own meetings with each Chief Officer. The Committee adjudicates appeals for reinstatement of requests that were pruned by the Executive Board and, if a lower rate is desired by the Party Group, effects further reductions with the informal advice from the Treasurer. With occasional exceptions, the budget recommended by the Executive Board closely resembles the one approved by the Policy and Finance Committee and then authorized by the Council.

BRIGHTON

In Brighton, like Southend, budget creation involves the building and pruning of line-item requests; but the process is not identical. The Spending Department Committee essentially approves the estimates generated by the department's top administrators (rather than serving as a "cutting committee," as in Southend). Then the "prebudget" meetings are held. In these informal but highly structured confrontations, the Chairman of Finance Committee has determined his goal, a target rate levy, based on information from the Treasurer about the possible range of rates, given varying degrees of "toughness" in cutting spending-department requests. The Treasurer provides the Chairman of Finance Committee and the Chief Officer with a list of those estimates that he thinks are pruneable, and how much each could be cut. The meeting is a debating-and-bargaining session between the Treasurer and Chief Officer concerning different judgments of "necessary" and "desirable" expenditure. The Chairman of the Finance Committee is the judge, operating under moderate pressure from his party colleague, the Spending Committee Chairman, who normally supports his Chief Officer's argument. Meeting separately with each spending department, the pruners attempt to reduce draft estimates sufficiently to reach the desired rate. Normally, the prebudget meetings produce about 85% of the reductions in draft estimates. The remaining changes occur when Finance Committee meets to consider what their Chairman has done. Finally, the Council authorizes the budget proposed to them by Finance Committee.

DUDLEY

The budget-making processes in Dudley and in West Bromwich vary substantially from those in Southend and Brighton and from the normative-process model. These systems were instituted in the mid-1960s to replace the process of detailed, marginal adjustment with one stressing both corporate planning and professionalism.[14] There is broad decision-making by top managers, but discretion on detailed allocations is left to departmental officers. In Dudley, there is an explicit attempt to apply the guidelines set by the Government concerning desired rates of growth for each service area. A special unit within the Treasurer's Department, the Foreward Planning Section, creates two sets of estimates. One set strictly translates the published Government guidelines into increased expenditure levels for each specific spending area. The second set are "lowest feasible cost" figures, which sum $ALLO_{t-1}$ plus inflation plus wage increases plus new approved projects (usually new capital projects entailing expenditure). The Foreward Planning Officer then "marries" these two sets of figures—that is, the Government-guidelines figures are adjusted (both up and down) to account for special circumstances revealed in the lowest-feasible-cost figures.

This schedule of total proposed expenditure for each spending unit is transmitted to the Treasurer, who assesses the assumptions and calculations of the Foreward Planning Officer. When the Treasurer is satisfied, each department is notified of its "rate target." The Chief Officer is theoretically free, within this total expenditure figure, to allocate resources among all aspects of the services the department provides. The Chief Officer is expected to honor (broadly) the policy decisions of his Spending Committee and is required to base expenditure commitments on their implications for a full fiscal year.[15]

WEST BROMWICH

The allocation process in West Bromwich is anchored in a sixteen-category schedule developed by the Finance Department. The schedule specifies sixteen types of expenditure increases, each of which corresponds to a generalized priority ranking from 1 to 16. Examples are:

#1   Precepts and pooled expenditure contributions.

#3   Running costs of newly completed assets.

#4   Additional demand where Council has no discretion.

#7   Increased provision for services operating below an acceptable standard.

#11 Provision to implement Council policy which has been agreed "in principle."

#14 Other desirable developments.

Each Spending Department submits estimates for Y_t. A single Senior Finance Officer, using information from his accountants and the spending department officers, determines the location of each increase between $ALLO_{t-1}$ and $ALLO_t$ in one of the sixteen categories. The figures are treated (unlike the other three boroughs) in constant Y_{t-1} prices, in order to "kill" inflation. The Finance Officer then compiles an aggregate schedule which reflects the spending implications of all proposed increases, in Y_t prices. The schedule shows the tax rate for the borough if all departments are granted all increases categorized in #1, in #1-2, in #1-3, and so on. If necessary, certain categories for existing programs could also be developed in order to generate a schedule for the reduction of real spending. The Chairman of Council's Finance Committee is then able to examine this schedule and, moving from #0 toward #16, to determine the rate levy and, as a consequence, the amount of new expenditure granted to each department. Each Chief Officer is notified of his "ration" of funds for Y_t, which he allocates, given the broad restrictions of established programs and policies.

Conceptualization of the Organizational-Process Approach

The organizational-process approach is another conceptual approach which attempts to explain how budget-making occurs. It is distinguished from the normative-process model since its focus is primarily empirical rather than prescriptive. And it is distinguished from the descriptive characterizations of budgeting presented above since it attempts to generalize about the processes of budgeting in an analytical and comparative framework. The organizational-process approach treats the organization as the object unit of analysis. In this approach, budget-making is conceptualized as a recurring problem which the organizational unit—the local government—solves by regularized decision routines. It is assumed that the method by which the organization locates and selects solutions can be explicated by reference to certain key analytic concepts. According to this approach, the nature of the process and the content of the solution can be understood in terms of the particular mix of problem-solving techniques employed.[16]

The most important theoretical work for this approach is *A Behavioral Theory of the Firm* by Richard Cyert and James March.[17] Four key concepts underlie their theory of organizational choice and control:

(1) Quasi-resolution of conflict, including goals as independent constraints, local rationality, acceptable-level decision rules, and sequential attention to alternatives;

(2) Uncertainty avoidance, involving negotiated environments and reaction to feedback;

(3) Problemistic search, which is motivated, simpleminded, and biased;

(4) Organizational learning by means of adaptation of goals, attention rules, and search rules.[18]

In general, the Cyert-March theory argues that certain *standard operating procedures* (SOPs) dominate the making and implementation of choices in the short-run. These SOPs include task-performance rules (which transmit past learning and make behavior predictable), records and reports (whose form can be an important determinant of decisions and behavior), information-handling rules (which establish either who communicates with whom about what, or what kinds of biases are built into the information flow), and plans and planning rules (including time goals, subunit goals, and the use of existing decisions as precedents).[19] Since the notion of SOP can become extremely comprehensive, the concept will be employed here only for those procedures which are best understood as a property of the organization as the object unit of analysis rather than as the contribution of a specific participant.[20]

Given an interest in the process of budget-making, the organizational-process approach stimulates a series of analytic questions:

(1) What are the major goals of budget-making?

(2) How is uncertainty avoided?

(3) What is the strategy of search for solutions?

(4) What is the nature of the search for information?

(5) How are acceptable-level decisions identified?

(6) What are the crucial standard operating procedures of budget-making?

(7) Is there evidence of organizational learning?

One appropriate test of the Cyert-March approach is a computer model. The most rigorous application of the approach to resource-allocation behavior is Crecine's simulation model for municipal budgeting in three large American cities.[21] In addition to the absence of basic empirical research upon which to ground a simulation model of county-borough budgeting, there are two other reasons why such an application is not, at this stage, realizable. First, county-borough budgeting involves interdependent solutions to the problems of level-of-spending and level-of-taxation. In Crecine's municipalities, the level of available revenue is a given for the budget-making model.[22] Second, in county boroughs like Brighton and Southend, each specific category within each particular service within each spending department requires a separate and accurate allocation during the budgetary process.[23] In contrast to this requirement to make more than 1,500 distinct allocation decisions, central budgeters in the municipalities in Crecine's study make only about five major expenditure decisions per department. Given these kinds of differences, a simulation model which does correspond to the process of budget-making in the county boroughs would be extremely complex. While it would be possible to develop a highly simplified simulation, such a model would be quite unrelated to the actual process and would be less illuminating at this point than a nonquantitative appraisal of the validity of organizational-process-approach concepts for explaining county-borough budgeting.[24]

Crecine's conclusions represent the most complete set of propositions about local-level budgeting from the organizational-process perspective. Those which seem most suggestive for this analysis of county-borough budgeting are:[25]

(1) The key problem is to *balance* the budget, not to allocate resources optimally. (p. 217)

(2) Guidelines for the allocation of total resources to departments consist of historical level and trend data, not cues from the environment. (p. 192)

(3) Extragovernmental inputs including environmental forces or needs and political or interest-group pressure are not received and translated into allocations; rather they are perceived as relatively constant in the short-run. (pp. 190-194)

(4) Subunit (interdepartmental) conflict is not an important feature of the budgetary problem-solving process. (p. 198)

(5) The problems are solved by arbitrary rules that maintain the relative positions of coalition members (departments). (p. 198)

(6) Accounts within a department are independent of one another. (p. 175)

(7) Within constraints on totals, departments are free to allocate as they see fit; community influence appears an important consideration at this point. (p. 192)

(8) Allocations are based on dollar amounts and only later transformed into personnel and materials. (p. 194)

(9) Adaptation of attention rules is not a key part of the budgetary decision-making process in the period studied. (p. 202)

Application of the Organizational-Process Approach

In describing the four budget-making systems above, it was evident that there were differences in the manner in which the process operated. However, it might be that the explication of the budgeting systems by means of the concepts of the organizational-process approach will identify analytic similarities. Hence this section aims to specify the critical variables or components for each of the seven analytic questions generated from the Cyert-March theory.

WHAT ARE THE MAJOR GOALS OF BUDGET-MAKING?

In all the county boroughs, budget-making behavior is motivated by the statutory requirement that there are sufficient revenues to cover expenditure. Thus the primary goal, viewed as a constraint, is to create a balanced budget—a plan in which all expenditure will be offset by revenue from income, governmental grants, and the rate. The operational goal is to develop, before April 1, a distribution of financial resources and of tax burdens which will purchase a mix of public goods and services for citizens that is acceptable to the Council majority. Budgeters do not even consider meaningful the notion of an "optimal" allocation.[26] If one were to speak of ultimate goals in budget-making, these would concern a distribution of rewards sufficient for the government to maintain support both from the citizenry and from the members of the government-organization-as-coalition.[27]

HOW IS UNCERTAINTY AVOIDED?

A fundamental method to reduce the uncertainty of choice-making is to limit severely the set of alternatives considered. This is effected in budget-making by the pervasive reliance on one standard operating procedure—*the use of existing decisions as precedents*. In particular, the previous year's budget is treated as the basic structure for decision. It is a commonplace that the Y_t budget solution is dominated by the Y_{t-1} pattern of allocation.[28] As in other budgeting contexts, quantitative analysis of longitudinal county-borough data in Chapter 5 has established that for most budget categories $ALLO_{t-1}$ estimates over 90% of the yearly variation in $ALLO_t$. The antecedent decisions discussed above regarding capital projects, staffing, and policy commitments also have some effect in defining the range of expanded spending alternatives.

According to the Cyert-March theory, organizational actors also reduce uncertainty concerning their roles and behavior by negotiating (that is, by regulating) both the external and the internal environment. In the four county boroughs, there is a variety of methods commonly employed to *negotiate the external environment*. Councillors articulate a Burkean view of representation regarding budgeting—that they must judge the best interests of the borough rather than yield to special interests. They classify as illegimate many of the groups and demands that they do not favor.[29] Low levels of community support for and negative reactions to their decisions are rationalized by the view that citizens have insufficient information to understand the complex decisions regarding resource allocation.[30] While some Chief Officers occasionally attempt to organize citizen advocacy groups (especially on divisible-benefit services), most Chief Officers prefer to remain insulated from direct citizen demands. Field personnel can interpret public response to service provision and the Council can buffer the Chief Officer from local pressures. A Borough Engineer remarked:

> People here make their complaints heard to Councillors, not officers. Frankly, I'm damn glad that the people do go to the Council, as it keeps them off our backs. The Council are our public relations men, and we can get on with the job.

The implication of these perspectives is that the budgeters are not particularly responsive or receptive to citizen inputs regarding budgetary allocations. These barriers, plus the sheer complexity of the budget problem, result in minimal direct involvement or participation by those external to the local government. Given the potential volatility of the allocation situation if many interested groups were to be mobilized, these techniques which muffle inputs and depress feedback tend to enhance the certainty and stability of the system.[31] The only external actors with whom the budgeters have a continuing linkage are the officials of the various central departments. In this case, the primary drive is to cultivate friendly relationships, since the Ministry can be an important source of support and resources.[32]

The *negotiation of the internal environment* is primarily a matter of reducing the uncertainty among budgetary actors. In particular, the routinization of standard operating procedures provides all actors with a relatively clear understanding of their own role—that is, their rights and responsibilities—and the roles of other relevant actors. There are several broad characteristics of this system that are important. Although the allocation process can be viewed as the struggle among spending units for scarce resources, procedures are systematically structured so that direct interdepartmental conflict rarely occurs.[33] Advocates of expenditure in different departments are insulated from contact with or information about the requests of other departments. With the exception of the Executive Board in Southend (whose members must operate as both spending advocates and pruners), spending advocates of different services are always handled in isolated deliberations.

There is an even broader kind of insulation—*the use of privacy and confidentiality* in the budget-making process. Spending Committee meetings and also any sessions between spending advocates and those pruning requests are private and confidential. All documents during budget-making are confidential and have limited, specific circulation. The Majority Party Group meets privately to resolve conflicts of value and strategy concerning allocations, and the Group practices a sort of "democratic centralism" in public. Only a handful of finance officers and leaders in the majority party are aware of the full set of budgetary allocations prior to the presentation of the budget at Council—a time when the allocations have become virtually a fait accompli. Thus the system localizes conflict and facilitates situations where budgeting participants can formulate agreements and compromises with minimal pressure from others.

WHAT IS THE STRATEGY OF SEARCH FOR SOLUTIONS?

In terms of the Cyert-March theory, the manner in which the organization searches for budget solutions is characterized by three features. Search is *motivated* by the statutory requirements that make the yearly budget-creation process a necessity and by the fact that changing social and economic conditions prevent the exact duplication of the previous year's solution. Search is *simpleminded* in the sense that it attempts to locate a solution that is extremely similar to the previous year's solution rather than a substantially different solution. Finally, search is *biased* by the dominance of the Finance Department orientation among those who structure the available choices.

While these generalizations are true for all four county boroughs, the particular search strategies vary importantly. In Brighton and Southend, the search is structured to evaluate each line-item of expenditure. For each line-item, a distinction is made, most explicitly in Southend, between expenditure to maintain existing levels of service and expenditure to expand provision. In these budgeting systems, the solution involves reducing the total cost of requests for new expenditure to reach some acceptable aggregate level of spending. West Bromwich's search for solutions might be understood as a comprehensive elaboration of this mode. Rather than treating all requests for expansion as a single category, the system further classifies these requests into one of the sixteen different categories, each with its own relative priority. In West Bromwich, however, all requests for expansion are considered simultaneously rather than on a department by department and item by item basis. Dudley also distinguishes the new from the ongoing expenditure requests. But the problem is viewed as the determination of the size of the total resource share to be allocated to each chief officer, and the solution for the problem is located in an extrapolation from the Government's guidelines on desirable growth rates for each department. Thus, in Brighton and Southend the search for solutions is shared by advocates and pruners down to the detail of each line-item; but in Dudley and West Bromwich, only the aggregate-level solution is shared and detailed solutions are delegated to the relevant chief officer, who has the right to employ local rationality.[34]

WHAT IS THE NATURE OF
THE SEARCH FOR INFORMATION?

The problem-solving routines of the four county boroughs are relatively similar with respect to the generation and use of information during budgeting. As the discussion concerning negotiation of the external environment suggested, certain information from external sources does filter into the network of information among the budgeters. However, apart from technical data and directives from central departments, most of the information for budget-making is generated, processed, and transmitted by two units. On the one side, the Chief Officer and his staff translate both the existing level of provision and the feasible and/or desirable expansions of service into financial terms. On the other side, the Borough Treasurer's staff predicts available revenue and analyzes the revenue implications of the spending department's requests. Budgetary decisions emerge from some mix of these two sets of data. Each source is professional and the quality of information is high. But each source also contains a systematic bias. The information from the department is structured to promote the largest expansion of expenditure for which the Chief Officer judges there is a convincing case. Information from the Treasurer's Department is grounded in the financial criterion of economies. In particular, the Treasurer's staff provides data on the minimum cost for maintaining existing service levels and prepares a critical financial analysis of requested increases. Although each source takes account of the other's perspective, this information is clearly biased in opposing ways: expansion versus fiscal economies.[35]

HOW ARE ACCEPTABLE-LEVEL DECISIONS IDENTIFIED?

The pivotal decision for which an acceptable solution must be determined is the level of the tax rate. The *level-of-the-rate decision* is essentially a political one, made by the leaders in the Majority Group on Council. As one Borough Treasurer observed:

> The real decision-making comes at that point where the Finance Committee Chairman knows, either by political instinct or by consulting his majority colleagues, what the rate increase limit is. The senior and/or influential members of the majority party have a quiet natter and decide what they will accept. . . . Inherent in every town is this testing of the wind by the senior members of the majority party.

It should be stressed that this rate-setting activity is of fundamental importance. Most local politicians are extremely sensitive to the issue of rate increases and they treat this as the one aspect of the budgetary process that might have high political costs, provoking the displeasure of the rate-payers. Thus the setting of the total rate is the point where the attitudes of the citizens are most carefully assessed and where the politicians do significantly shape the allocation process.

In each system there is a critical determination by a top leader in the majority party of "what will go," expressed as both a maximum acceptable rate increase and as a desired rate target. In Brighton this decision is made by the Finance Committee Chairman immediately prior to the "prebudget" meetings. In West Bromwich, it is made at the end of the cycle, when the Finance Committee Chairman draws the line somewhere along the sixteen category schedule. In Dudley it is made more-or-less mechanically by the Foreward Planning Officer in the marriage of Government guidelines and lowest-feasible-cost budgets, although the Finance Chairman can redefine acceptability. There is least clarity about the acceptable rate level in Southend, where the Treasurer, the Executive Board, and even the leader of the majority party operate on the basis of assessments of what rate will ultimately be acceptable.[36]

There are two other aspects of the identification of acceptable-level decisions. Normally, the base level is to *maintain the existing standard of service provision*. This minimum is most explicit in the notion of lowest feasible cost in Dudley; but in all four systems the procedures are structured to focus attention on that expenditure which is regarded as an expansion of the current standard of provision. Given this base level, the Chief Officer in Brighton and Southend must bargain on each line-item, and the nature of an "acceptable-level" is a function of the many factors which might be invoked in this bargaining. The substantial discretion of the Chief Officer to distribute his rate ration in Dudley and West Bromwich means that the criteria of acceptability in these systems will be contingent upon somewhat more individualized decisions.[37] The second base level is to *resist a tax reduction*. Most politicians realize that while this has short-term appeal, the favorable impacts will be outweighed by the inevitable need for a tax increase. Elected officials and financial officers share the preference to carry over a surplus in contingencies rather than to reduce the rate.

WHAT ARE THE CRUCIAL STANDARD
OPERATING PROCEDURES OF BUDGET-MAKING?

It has been noted above that the concept of SOP tends to become a broad, residual category for important behavioral or structural properties of the organization. Some of the major task-performance rules, information-handling rules, and planning rules have been identified in the responses to other analytic questions in this section. There are certain other SOPs which merit attention.

As in other organizational domains, *the use of slack resources* is an important task-performance rule which counterbalances some of the inflexibilities in the budget-making systems.[38] The solutions to resource allocation in both Dudley and West Bromwich are relatively arbitrary and chief officers might develop a sense of futility regarding their capacity to influence the size of their allocation share. In Dudley, however, the Rate Support Grant level is usually readjusted upward three or four times during the year. These additional resources, plus certain consciously created excess, are treated by the Borough Treasurer as extra resources. It is clearly understood that the Treasurer, in consultation with the Chairman of the Policy and Finance Committee, will allocate these resources to those chief officers and services that have been particularly disadvantaged or insufficiently supported by the initial rate rations.

In West Bromwich, the mechanistic nature of the solution concerning the selection of projects for expanded funding is countered by an SOP providing for substitution. After the rate share has been set, the Chief Officer has a general prerogative to replace the authorized additional expenditures from the priority matrix with his own preferred schemes. Clearly, extensive use of this SOP would undermine the apparent priority-setting rationale for the sixteen-category schedule.

In Southend, the arbitrariness of the twelve-month cycle of resource allocation and spending is minimized by an SOP which allows many kinds of allocations that are unencumbered at the end of the fiscal year to be carried over as a credit into the next year (rather than returned to contingencies). Moreover, the spending department has substantial latitude to transfer funds from one line-item to a related one. And there are "special items" categories which provide a spending department with discretionary funds for desired items that can be classified as "nonrecurring." Thus in at least three of the four county boroughs, there are SOPs which function to provide organizational slack in a process that has certain inherent rigidities.

An interesting SOP in Brighton is *the transmission of a plan for new expenditure.* At the beginning of the budget-making cycle the Treasurer sends a letter to each Chief Officer, communicating the Treasurer's reading of the fiscal climate for various kinds of allocation requests. Since the norms do not allow the Treasurer to make policy, the wording is circumspect: "Given conditions a, b, and c, the Finance Committee will probably look hard at requests for d, e, and f. . . . For reasons g, h, and i, increases are expected for k, l, and m." Given the power of the Treasurer in budget-making, the chief officer takes this as the most important signal about the requests that are likely to succeed and those that might damage his credibility. While the other three budgeting systems also transmit an early plan for spending, including the circulation of the Government's guidelines in Dudley, none have information content or significance comparable to the Treasurer's letter in Brighton.

The form in which the budget estimates are broken down for analysis might also be considered an important SOP.[39] In West Bromwich, of course, all increases must be classified as one of the sixteen categories. In Brighton and Southend, each line-item is broken into two parts: (1) expenditure to maintain the same level of service; and (2) additional expenditure proposed. In Southend, moreover, the working budget sheets include a column in which the pruners' questions regarding the item are written. This set of questions is transcribed on to the subsequent year's working budget sheets, exacerbating the tendency to do both horizontal (that is, comparing allocations on the same item from year to year) and history-dependent analyses. Only Dudley does not explicitly format the allocations to draw particular attention to the horizontal difference for each expenditure line-item.

A final SOP of significance is a task-performance rule—the use of highly *stylized confrontations between advocates and pruners.*[40] In brighton's prebudget meetings, the adjudicator is the Chairman of Finance Committee. In West Bromwich, the Executive Board of Chief Officers evaluates the arguments of each department's chief officer. In Southend, there is a series of such assessments, during which the judgments are made by various Finance Department managers, by a board of chief officers, and by a committee of powerful Councillors.

IS THERE EVIDENCE OF ORGANIZATIONAL LEARNING?

It is important to note that, at least, the budget-making systems were not stable during the decade. Southend substantially reorganized the top leadership structure on both the Council and the chief officer side, and these changes led to alterations in the organizational process of budget creation. Both Dudley and West Bromwich totally restructured the budgetary process, creating systems based on the allocation of rate shares to each operating department. Only Brighton maintained a stable system of budgeting throughout the decade; but in the early 1970s, even Brighton was well-advanced in planning the implementation of a system of rate rationing.

In the short period of research, it is difficult to assess whether learning and adaptation (of search and attention rules) were occurring. In the more stabilized systems (Brighton and Southend) there were no obvious examples of adaptation. It did appear that some actors were adapting their behavior to the altered systems of Dudley and West Bromwich. In West Bromwich, some of the more perceptive Chief Officers were experimenting with behavior to manipulate the system. In particular, a few were attempting to "load" their requests with items which seemed likely to receive high priority classifications and then to substitute preferred schemes.[41]

Even in fluid environments, however, most actors seemed to

rely upon well established behaviors. In the mid-1960s, Dudley and West Bromwich were disrupted by the amalgamations of each borough with adjoining local authorities. When budgeters were asked about the impact of the amalgamation upon their budgeting behavior, most commented that there had been a rise in uncertainty about the appropriate manner of establishing estimates. But nearly every budgeter observed that the process had been less difficult and less error prone than they had anticipated, primarily because their standard behavioral repertoires had been effective. A senior finance officer reflected the common view:

> We found, to our great surprise, that developing estimates was not so very much different. Mind you, there were a lot of guess-estimates and it did take additional time. But the procedures for building the estimates were the same as we had always done them. Most surprising to me was that few of the figures were very far off and these showed up quickly when the Chief Officer began to shout.

EVALUATION OF THE ORGANIZATIONAL-PROCESS APPROACH

According to the organizational-process approach, budget-making can be explained by specifying the nature of and linkages among critical variables which characterize the organization's problem-solving technique. The analytic level of analysis is the organization, and the critical variables include the goals of the process, the methods of searching for and selecting acceptable solutions, the key standard operating procedures, and the adaptation mechanisms.

This chapter has been a nonquantitative application of the organizational-process approach to county-borough budget creation.[42] The analysis in this chapter validates the notion that budget-making is a recurrent task of the organization and can be understood in terms of regularized problem-solving routines and a decision-making structure. In the four county boroughs examined, there are certain major analytic correspondences in process. Given the basic goal-constraint of producing a balanced budget, each system operates to provide an acceptable (rather than an optimal) level of financial support for all approved services, while achieving a rate level that is politically feasible. In each budgeting system, this central problem is broken into sets of subproblems, organized as allocation decisions for more detailed budget categories. Moreover, the sources of information in each system are the professional officers in the spending departments and in the finance department.

Could these four county-borough budget-making systems be characterized by a single organizational-process model? Although the central analytic concepts do identify some correspondences in process, there are important structural differences in the configuration of these conceptual variables. In particular, the problem-solving processes of the various budgeting systems differ in the manner in which subproblems are defined, in the strategy of search for acceptable solutions, and in the nature of involvement by political actors.

In two of the systems, the dominant modality is a *fluid bargaining process,* with a series of discrete episodes involving interaction between pruning actors and particular spending advocates. While these episodes are institutionalized and routinized, budgetary decisions are somewhat contingent upon the personal styles of and the interplay between specific individuals. Thus the budget solution can be viewed, rather like a decision explained by means of Norton Long's "ecology of games" metaphor, as the overlapping and somewhat accidental outcomes from relatively independent sets of interactions.[43] In the other two budgeting systems, the dominant modality is a rather *structured problem-solving process.* Budget creation is anchored in the application, by a limited number of technical specialists, of somewhat mechanical procedures. In these systems, the budget solution is best understood as the consequences of the organization's problem-solving routines, and the impact of individual behavior and personalities is secondary.

In the fluid bargaining systems, the influence of the political actors tends to be more pervasive. Each allocation decision is made under some scrutiny from the leading representatives of the majority party in Council and is open to evaluation by the criterion of political acceptability. In the structured problem-solving systems, however, the primary involvement of partisan actors is limited to broad, policy-setting decisions, typically either the level of the rate or the general rate of growth for functional areas. In general, the departmental chief officer is likely to have more influence over the total size of his allocation share under the fluid bargaining system; but he is likely to be less constrained in allocation decisions regarding specific aspects of his function in the structured problem-solving system.

The nature of conflict over decisions also tends to vary across the two modalities.[44] The structured problem-solving process might seem less conflictual, since disputes should be limited to technical questions regarding the correct application of decision procedures. And the fluid bargaining systems might seem more exposed to pressures and disputes from partisans and spending advocates. In fact, the situation is more complex. The cost of visible and regularized decision principles is that many participants can observe the process, can evaluate the "fairness" of the allocation decisions, and can dispute unequal treatment. Such oversight is unlikely in the bargaining systems, since these systems have no clear and consistent decision principles, deal independently with each spending advocate, and can more easily utilize slack resources as side-payments. Thus the possibility of substantial conflict exists, in theory, for either modality. In fact, despite the compelling imagery of budgeting as a struggle over scarce resources and the insistence by some scholars on the pervasiveness of intraorganizational conflict,[45] there was little evidence of serious conflict in any of the four budgeting systems. In an era of limited (but not shrinking) resources, both the structure of the allocation systems and the rules of the game tended to contain and depress conflict.

A related issue in assessing the organizational-process approach is whether specification of the particular problem-solving routines generates accurate predictions about decisional outputs. Process-based approaches should enable one to infer/ predict/explain these allocation decisions on the basis of the insights they provide about problem-solving and decision principles. For example, Dudley's use of Government guidelines for growth rates as an acceptable-level decision rule leads to the expectation that there will be a reasonably close correspondence between these guidelines and the actual rates of growth in departmental allocations. Table 6.1 examines the relationship between these two sets of figures for a representative set of fiscal years. While the aggregate growth rate in Dudley was quite similar to the level recommended by the Government, only about one-half of the spending areas (and, from further analyses, different spending areas from year to year) had increases that were relatively similar to those recommended by the Government. In fact, the Foreward Planning Section uses the guidelines artfully rather than "importing" a solution. As the Foreward Planning Officer observed:

> My section produces the target figures for each committee. We use the Government's directions. We accept that we are not a typical authority; but we find if we go to the members and say: if we take

Table 6.1: Dudley: Relationship Between Rate Target and Government Guidelines, 1971-1972 to 1972-1973[a]

Spending Area:	Percentage Increase $ALLO_{t-1}$ to $ALLO_{t-1}$		
	A. Rate Support Grant Order, H.C. 72	B. Recommended Rate Target	Ratio of B to A
Education	4.2	4.4	1.05
Finance	1.3	1.1	.85
Fire service	2.9	0.4	.14
Highways	6.8	12.4	1.82
Libraries	3.4	3.1	.91
Local health services	3.9	3.5	.90
Parks	3.3	0.9	.27
Planning	3.5	1.3	.37
Public health services	5.5	1.1	.20
Social services	9.3	15.8	1.70

a. Source: Figures supplied by Foreward Planning Section.

the figures that the Government has given us, this is the totals we come out with—then they are quite happy to accept them. You've still got to get to a figure for your total. But as far as the rationing, they will accept a formula based on the Government's percentages far more easily than another rationing that comes from one member of one department of the Corporation. There isn't any better way of doing it at the present time.

Thus in Dudley it seems less that solutions are imported than that "the system," rather than any individual, is attributed responsibility for the decisions which are generated.

Similarly, despite the notion of an acceptable-level decision constraint of "feasibility" for increases in the rate-in-the-pound, this criterion is clearly both time- and situation-specific. Table 6.2 displays changes in the rate for the four budgeting systems. In a broad comparative sense, the magnitude of change is never large, but the average rate of increase in Brighton is nearly twice that of Dudley and Southend. Decreases in the rate do not occur, but there is no systematic pattern in the rate-level changes. One might hypothesize that the fluid bargaining systems would have the highest level of rate instability since solutions are the result of a more fragmented decision system. And Brighton does in fact have the highest mean change rate and also the highest variability in changes (as indicated by the standard deviation). However it is the structured problem-solving system in West Bromwich, not Southend, that has rate increases and rate instability nearly equal to those in Brighton. Again, these actual allocation decisions do not correspond to those that seem reasonably inferred from differences in organizational processes.

A broader assessment of predictive adequacy is to consider the characterizations of the organizational processes in light of existing empirical data. Earlier chapters produced some findings about the nature of resource-allocation decisions in the four county boroughs. Chapter 3 data located a borough's allocation levels relative to the mean level for all county boroughs. The naive econometric models provided some evidence of consistent

Table 6.2: Rate-in-the-Pound for the Four County Boroughs

| | | | County Borough | | | | | |
| | Brighton | | Dudley | | Southend | | West Bromwich | |
Year	Rate	% Change[a]	Rate	% Change[a]	Rate	% Change[a]	Rate	% Change[a]
1960-1961	178		258		222		258	
1961-1962	201	13%	276	7%	240	7%	258	0%
1962-1963	226	12	294	7	240	0	280	9
1963-1964	90	b	116	b	122	b	120	b
1964-1965	93	4	122	5	122	0	128	7
1965-1966	104	12	130	7	133	7	138	8
1966-1967	110	6	134	3	140	7	148	7
1967-1968	115	5	139	4	145	4	156	5
1968-1969	120	4	140	1	150	3	160	3
1969-1970	127	6	145	4	157	5	177	11
Mean		7.75		4.15		4.1		6.25
Standard Deviation		3.9		2.2		2.9		3.5

a. This column records the percentage change from the previous year in the rate measured in (old) pence. From 1967-1968, the **domestic** rate was reduced by a government grant, the Domestic Element of the Rate Support Grant. This would reduce the figures in the table for the domestic rate of 5 pence in 1967-1968, 10 pence in 1968-1969, and 15 pence in 1969-1970.

b. In 1963-1964, all property was revalued, making comparison of change from 1962-1963 to 1963-1964 misleading.

longitudinal patterns for certain services. And there are some instances (displayed in Table 6.3) where the predictive power of a regression equation from the demographic explanation is sufficiently high to allow comparison of expected and actual outputs.

Thus it is possible as a loose test of adequacy, to determine whether the organizational-process approach would have been suggestive of certain characteristic features of allocations in the four county boroughs. Would the discussion in this chapter have led to the expectation: (1) that local health-service spending is well below average in Southend?; (2) that spending on the local health services has been increasing rapidly in Brighton?; (3) that there are favorable pupil-teacher ratios in Dudley?; (4) that total net spending is above that predicted by the regression equation for West Bromwich and below that for Dudley?; (5) that an up-down yearly change pattern exists for many services in Brighton?; (6) that rates of change in highways spending tend to be quite erratic?; (7) that "fair share" allocations seem the rule in West Bromwich?; and (8) that Southend allocation levels tend toward both the high and low extremes relative to other county boroughs?

In general, it does not seem that the organizational-process approach, as presented in this chapter, would have led to inferences/predictions of these phenomena. It is true that when a simulation based on the organizational-process approach and incorporating historical-trend data is employed, most of these patterns would be identified. But such identification is somewhat contingent upon capturing in the data base the very factors which one is attempting to explain. At least, it seems that the explanation of, rather than the identification of, the unique budgetary outputs in the four county boroughs will require sensitivity to more configurative characteristics of the budgeting systems.

The quantitative applications of the organizational-process approach to budget-making, particularly Crecine's important study, do blend the conceptual model of process with historical-trend data and with certain parameters which are based on the

Table 6.3: Comparison of Actual Expenditure with Predicted Expenditure on the Basis of Regression Equations, 1968-1969

Provision Measure:	Total Expenditure	Rates Per Head	Total Education	Secondary Education	Housing Provision	Children's Service
BRIGHTON						
a. actual	1193	670	26,711	8523	12.0	1109
b. estimated	1217	752	26,315	8742	11.2	908
c. a-b	−24	−82	+394	−119	+.8	+201
a-b stnd.error	−.52	−1.78	.25	−.17	.22	.87
DUDLEY						
a. actual	1046	485	27,711	9234	24.4	703
b. estimated	1062	552	28,288	9577	26.9	890
c. a-b	−16	−67	−518	−343	−2.5	−187
a-b stnd.error	−.35	−1.46	−.33	−.48	−.69	−.81
SOUTHEND						
a. actual	1101	597	27,155	9536	8.0	724
b. estimated	1042	543	27,729	9252	10.0	930
c. a-b	+59	+54	−574	+284	−2.0	−206
a-b stnd.error	1.30	1.17	−.36	.50	−.56	−.89
WEST BROMWICH						
a. actual	1182	586	31,960	11,140	28.6	660
b. estimated	1140	632	30,992	10,974	24.9	981
c. a-b	+42	−46	+972	+166	+3.7	−321
a-b stnd.error	.92	−1.00	.62	.23	1.03	−1.39

inputs of specific actors in key roles. It can be argued that the conceptual domain of the organizational-process approach, strictly interpreted, does not include these historical-trend data and configurative data. This seems too stringent a criterion. A strength of the organizational-process approach is that it provides a conceptual framework which facilitates the combination of variables representing both the process and the outputs of budgeting. This combination does make it more problematic, however, to determine whether the predictive adequacy of the model derives from the trend data or from the operationalization of process characteristics.[46]

On balance, these data and observations suggest that *a single organizational-process model could not adequately characterize the four county-borough budgeting systems.* Nonetheless, the organizational-process approach does guide research and analysis within the structure of a valid and useful set of concepts. Analysis of search routines, SOPs, information processing, and so on, of an organization as a problem-solving system is a sensitive and illuminating method of explicating budget creation. While these concepts are not yet linked into a theory (they are linked operationally in the Cyert-March and the Crecine applications), they do seem capable of integration. This approach could achieve Verba's "disciplined configurative approach," in which relevant factors vary in their configuration (the unique aspects of the actual case) but not in their analytic nature (the variables which are generalized across cases).[47]

NOTES

1. For grammatical flow, discussions of the budgeting processes in the county boroughs are in the present tense.

2. See Chapter 5. It was also shown that the incremental-trend model typically explained over 90% of the year-to-year variance in allocations. However, statistical problems were noted that undercut seriously the explanatory appeal of this model.

3. Some scholars have argued that capital-expenditure decisions have had an increasing impact on revenue expenditure during the 1970s, given the tighter budgetary conditions and the more stringent control of some capital grants by the central government. See, for example, Judge, op. cit., Chapter 4. For a detailed discussion of

decision-making regarding the capital budget in the four county boroughs, see Danziger (1974), op. cit., pp. 320-338. A thorough analysis, which compared the shifts in capital and revenue expenditure in a longitudinal frame (allowing for lags), provided no evidence that shifts in revenue expenditure were more responsive to capital-expenditure shifts than to other decisions. See Danziger, Ibid., pp. 288-293.

3. Prior "approval in principle" is necessary from the relevant Spending Committee.

5. The minimum in Brighton, for example is £1000. Finance Committee is supposed to judge the merits of the proposal from a strictly financial standpoint and its opinion is merely a footnote to the proposal when presented at Council. In fact, however, Finance Committee's position is in most cases only loosely financial and represents the evaluation by influential members of the majority party about the relative desirability of a new proposal.

6. For example, an analysis of three Brighton Council agendas revealed that there was not a single critical departure in policy among the 92 items upon which Finance Committee gave an opinion. Only 11 of these items might influence allocations in the short-run: 7 authorizations to increase staff and 4 proposals to finance slightly augmented service provision.

7. See, for example, A. H. Marshall, *Financial Administration in Local Government* (London: Allen & Unwin, 1961); Kitching, op. cit.

8. Marshall, op. cit., p. 264.

9. Ibid., p. 278.

10. *Budgeting in Public Authorities,* Study Group of the Royal Institute of Public Administration (London: Allen & Unwin, 1959), p. 96; Marshall, op. cit., p. 291.

11. Marshall, op. cit., p. 278.

12. Ibid., p. 285.

13. The membership includes the Town Clerk and Treasurer, by virtue of their offices, and three others. In 1971, these were the Borough Architect, Borough Engineer, and Chief Education Officer. The method of selection is not clear. It seems that selection of the three other officers emerges from discussion among the Chief Officers and needs approval of the Policy and Finance Committee.

14. On the role of corporate planning, see Greenwood and Stewart, op. cit. See also Royston Greenwood, C. R. Hinings, and S. Ranson, "The Politics of the Budgetary Process in English Local Government," *Political Studies,* XXV (March 1977), 25-47.

15. Financial officers often asserted that if spending officers were given a free hand to allocate a lump sum of resources, the spending officers would manipulate their allocations to overextend the necessary spending in Y_{t+1}. For example, if there was provision for 8 new staff positions for the last six months of Y_t, it would necessitate twice as much money to continue to fill these positions in the full twelve months of Y_{t+1}. The monitoring by the Finance Department of decisions about resource allocation within each service was often justified in terms of such "financial control."

16. Among the other approaches which take the organization as the basic unit of analysis, an important framework for analyzing English local-authority budgeting is being developed by Greenwood, Hinings, and Ranson. Their conceptualization centers upon the intraorganizational configuration of organization attributes (partic-

ularly measures of values, interests, and power) and also incorporates certain environmental contingencies. Their contingency approach specifies key variables for the cross-unit correlational analysis of linkages among process and output indicators. In contrast, the organizational-process approach is oriented primarily to specifying the regularized routines for solving problems encountered by the organization and for predicting/explaining decisions in terms of these routines. See Greenwood, et al. (1977), op. cit.

17. Cyert and March, op. cit.

18. See Ibid., pp. 114-147 for a summary of the theory, incorporating these concepts. At other points they list organizational goals, expectations, and choice as the basic concepts.

19. Ibid., pp. 103-112.

20. The concern is with the organization as the object unit of analysis. Data may be taken from (that is, the subject unit of analysis might be) the organization, a group, or an individual. But where a parameter appears to be the unique contribution of a particular individual, the data are more appropriately the domain of the individual-level approaches in Chapter 7.

21. Crecine, op. cit. Also see Gerwin (1969a), op. cit., whose application of the approach resembles the one here.

22. Ibid., p. 68.

23. One of the county boroughs is a clear example of the level to which allocation decisions are broken down in the budget-creation process. Each detail head is separately authorized. The level of specificity is: Service = Local Health Services; Division of Service = Care of Mothers and Young Children; Subdivision of Service = Clinics; Detail Head = Salaries and Wages. Each detail head must be accurate, since only a minimal overspending is allowed without a supplementary authorization procedure.

24. Crecine argues strongly that the basic value of such a model is its correspondence to process. Crecine, op. cit., pp. 143-144. The next stage, if the organizational-process approach seems an accurate and economic model of county-borough budgeting, would be the development of a highly simplified simulation.

25. These propositions, which are more or less validated by the empirical analysis itself, are extracted from Crecine, op. cit., at the noted page.

26. This is consistent with Crecine's first proposition that the key concern is to balance the budget, not to allocate resources optimally.

27. On the organization-as-coalition, see Cyert and March, op. cit., pp. 27-32.

28. The seminal work underlying this observation is Wildavsky (1964), op. cit.

29. For further evidence see the notion of "unfavored groups" in Dearlove, op. cit.; and Kenneth Newton and D. S. Morris, "British Interest Group Theory Reexamined," *Comparative Politics,* 7 (July 1975), pp. 591-594.

30. This point is corroborated in a study of the opinions of senior Labour councillors in Reading shortly after they lost control of Council. See Gregory, op. cit., pp. 37-47. These findings of insulation by the budget makers are in line with the observations of Crecine, op. cit., pp. 190-194, 218-219. Crecine does not, however, explicitly discuss the use of rationalization techniques which we have found, nor does he note the attempt to manipulate the external environment. Also see Kenneth Newton, "Role Orientations and Their Sources Among Elected Representatives in English Local Politics," *Journal of Politics,* 36 (August 1974), p. 619.

31. The notion of barriers to citizen inputs is ably presented in Peter Bachrach and Morton Baratz, *Power and Poverty* (New York: Oxford Univ. Press, 1970), esp. Chapter 1. Stability is maintained without careful attention to feedback (short of extremely strong inputs) because these are systems which, with respect to resource allocation, are akin to Meltsner's "sleepy political systems." Arnold Meltsner, *The Politics of City Revenue* (Berkeley: Univ. of California Press, 1971), p. 49. The research literature on British local government does note that citizen interest groups contact elected representatives and departments. See, for example, Newton and Morris, op. cit.; Dearlove, op. cit.; and Paul Peterson, "British Interest Group Theory Re-examined: The Politics of Comprehensive Education in Three British Cities," *Comparative Politics*, 3 (April 1971), pp. 381-402. It is not clear, however, that such contacts importantly influence the outcomes on routine decisions. With respect to budgetary decisions in the four county boroughs, citizen groups rarely exercise direct influence; rather, the most significant impacts involve what Dahl characterizes as "indirect influence." See Dahl, op. cit., pp. 163-165.

32. The role of the government departments has some comparability to the role attributed to the federal government in Crecine, op. cit., p. 164. However, the Ministry is both *more* involved in finances, due to the power of loan sanction, and *less* involved in the actual linkage between policy shifts and expenditure changes, due to the absence of earmarked grants or control over county-borough revenue by the specific central departments.

33. This aligns with proposition 4 in the list derived from Crecine's study. The absence of manifest interdepartmental conflict is contrary, however, to the model articulated in Greenwood, et al., op. cit., and in C. R. Hinings, R. Greenwood, and S. Ranson, "Contingency Theory and the Organization of Local Authorities: Part II Contingencies and Structures," *Public Administration*, 53 (Summer 1975), pp. 169-170.

34. Thus the situation in Brighton and Southend contradicts Crecine's proposition (number 7) that, within constraints on totals, the departments are free to allocate as they see fit. Crecine, op. cit., p. 192. In the four county boroughs, there is considerable variation in the discretion of the spending department to establish its specific allocations.

35. Cyert and March observe: "in the long run, the organization learns to provide counter biases for each bias." Cyert and March, op. cit., p. 110. See also pp. 81-82.

36. It is true, however, that particular decisions are only occasionally perceived as having high political content. This supports Crecine's assertion that most of the relevant constraints for the problem solver on a particular item are nonpolitical. See Crecine, op. cit., p. 219.

37. Crecine found that there were cutting priorities across spending departments and across broad expenditure categories (e.g., salaries, equipment) within departments. It is clear from data in Chapter 5, such as the "prosperity-change scores," that some spending areas are doing better or worse than others. Budgeters, by means of a form of self-anchoring scale, did attribute variable levels of "budget success" and of "cuttability" to different services. But analyzed ordinally, there were rather low correlations in the rankings of budgeters within three of the four systems. It seems that it might be easier to estimate such parameters than to explain their source in the budgeting system. There was strong agreement in all four boroughs about the priorities for broad expenditure categories. In about one-half the cases examined,

correlations of rates of change of component services within a department confirmed Crecine's conclusion (proposition 6) that accounts change independently; but in the other cases, the data were ambiguous or reflected departments where the changes in accounts are associated.

38. For a discussion of slack resources within the organization, see Cyert and March, op. cit., pp. 36-38.

39. Cyert and March observe that the form of records "determine in large part what aspects of the environment will be observed and what alternatives of action will be considered." Cyert and March, op. cit., p. 106. The dominant role of the physical form of budget sheets is also stressed by Crecine, op. cit., p. 218.

40. The Cyert-March theory does not clearly distinguish task-performance rules from the type of information-handling rules called routing rules, which establish who communicates with whom about what. This SOP could be viewed as either of these.

41. This supports the notion of Cyert and March that there will be organizational learning over time. See Cyert and March, op. cit., pp. 99-101, 124-125. Crecine, on the other hand, found no evidence of such adaptation in the short period of his study. See Crecine, op. cit., p. 202. Several Chief Officers or their senior administrators stated that they were budgeting "less honestly" under the new system. It was clear that some of these actors were altering their strategies more quickly than other actors in order to maximize their ability to receive desirable outputs. The differential occurrence of adaptation is the clearest support for its existence. Certain spending departments were explicitly persisting in the same budget-creation behavior that they had utilized before the new system, while other departments were consciously altering their behavior. A senior Finance Department officer noted: "All the Chief Officers have received a great deal of information about the changes in the manner of budgeting. But a number of them have, it seems to me, either ignored the changes or have decided that nothing has changed. I can't agree with either notion."

42. Cyert and March are explicit that the theory they present is meant to be operationalized as a computer model. Given our decision not to use a simulation, we can only do a partial evaluation of the approach, on the basis of the explanatory adequacy of the concepts and propositions.

43. Norton Long, "The Local Community as an Ecology of Games," *American Journal of Sociology,* 64 (November 1958), pp. 251-261.

44. This discussion is developed more fully in James N. Danziger, "A Comment on 'The Politics of the Budgetary Process in English Local Government'," *Political Studies,* XXVI (March 1978). See also Wildavsky (1975), op. cit., esp. pp. 329-330, 380.

45. Greenwood, et al. (1975), op. cit.

46. Crecine's strongest argument for the model-process linkage is that the major predictive failures of the model are at the points of non-normal allocation. Crecine, op. cit., p. 144. But it seems likely that the naive models, particularly the base-budget model, would err at the same point without any claim to be reflecting decision processes.

47. Sidney Verba, "Some Dilemmas in Comparative Research," *World Politics,* XX (October 1967), pp. 111-127.

Chapter 7

INDIVIDUAL-LEVEL-PROCESS

APPROACHES

The purpose of this chapter is to examine certain aspects of the budget-making process that capture phenomena relating to individuals or roles. In particular, one perspective will encompass an array of behaviors that are a function of the cognitive limitations of the individual budgeter, and a second perspective will concern instances from the four case-studies where the behavior or style of a particular individual appeared to have major consequences for the budgetary process.

While the focus is on the individual budget maker, the perspective can overlap with that of the organizational-process approach.[1] As the decision rules or role behavior of individual participants become routinized, there is diminishing variability in the input of a particular role-actor.[2] From the view of an individual-level-process approach, this represents a stabilized role; but the organizational-process approach might treat this regularized behavior as a standard operating procedure for the organization as a whole, particularly when these stabilities are generalized across a number of budgetary actors.

Certain phenomena seem appropriately conceptualized at either the individual or the organizational level, depending upon the theoretical interests of the analyst.[3] This does require, however, careful specification regarding shifts in the level of analysis. In general, the analytic (and somewhat arbitrary) distinction between process phenomena in this chapter and in the preceding chapter is to focus here upon significant individual-level behavior in the budget-making process. There is a particular attempt to identify points at which behavior seems driven by the cognitive limits of the individual and points at which there are "nonstandard" contributions to the determination of resource allocations. Nonstandard is meant to signify behavior, especially decisions, which seem contingent upon the particular person taking a role. At least, this might provide insight into the "deviant" allocations in each county borough. More broadly, the analysis should suggest the extent to which an adequate explanation of the budget-making process can be grounded solely in individual-level behavior.

The Cognitive-Limits Approach

It was argued in Chapter 5 that incremental theory is normally understood as an explication of a decision-making style rather than as a theory predicting the content of decisions. This theory, as articulated by Lindblom, Simon, Downs, and others,[4] characterizes the relationship between the cognitive limitations of the decision maker, the potential complexity of his task, and his behavioral responses. The budgetary decision-maker is faced with a classic case of the kind of problem complexity that surpasses his cognitive capacity. Limited by his capacity to process information, by time pressures, by the availability and quality of information, by the costs of analysis, by the mix of incommensurable goals, and by the sheer complexity of the budget as a problem, the budgeter responds with a series of decision shortcuts.

Studies of budgeters by Barber, Wildavsky, Fenno, and others have yielded a series of propositions about the simplifying and uncertainty-reducing techniques that budgeters employ:[5]

(1) The previous year's levels of expenditure are taken as prima facie valid.

(2) Attention focuses horizontally—on changes in specific items between Y_{t-1} and Y_t (rather than vertically among different items in Y_t).

(3) Analysis centers on concrete detail rather than on policy alternatives or value choices.

(4) Budget allocations are seen as amounts of money rather than translated into levels of service.

(5) Many items are defined as "uncontrollable," which means that they are desirable/essential and need not be reevaluated (rather than that it is impossible to cut them).

(6) Well-established role relationships among participants stabilize and regulate the process.

(7) Manifest conflict is undesirable and there is a drive to resolve disputes by compromise.

(8) Spending units present the "best case" to justify their expenditure requests.

The objective in this section is to approach budget creation from the cognitive-limits perspective. The individual budgeter is the object unit of analysis. The central concern is to identify those strategies which the budgeter employs to reduce the cognitive complexity of his task.

COGNITIVE SHORTCUTS—THE DATA

It is axiomatic in the cognitive-limits approach that the budgeter uses techniques which redefine and simplify the data that he must comprehend. First, there is a clear propensity among county-borough budgeters to direct attention to the most specific and *concrete aspects* of choice. A senior Councillor in Southend quipped that his spending committee spends 45 minutes debating the cost and style of carpeting work costing £50, and 5 minutes on the remainder of the committee's budget, involving £150,000. A related technique is to evaluate value conflicts by translating them into decisions on *specific policies*. For example, the discussion of the Council's responsibility to the rate-payers would always be shifted immediately to a concrete problem, such as the decision regarding weekly versus biweekly collection of refuse.

Second, it has usually been claimed that budgeters think in terms of *amounts of money* rather than levels of service. It is true that budget-making requires the translation of all services into the common dimension of money and that this translation facilitates between-service comparisons. But the generalization about thinking-in-money is only a partial truth. In every county borough, the major budgeters—the Treasurer, the Chief Officers, the Finance Chairman—perceive budgetary choices in both financial and programmatic fashion. For example, discussions regarding the pruning of requests typically begin with the determination of a subgoal in money terms—cutting £X. But given this constraint, attention centers on locating units of provision that are pruneable—can N staff positions be left vacant for Service A?; can the repainting of buildings B, C, and D be put off for a year?; can the street-miles for which resurfacing is "essential" be reduced? The secondary consideration is to translate these service reductions into cost savings. Thus these top budgeters do, in fact, shift constantly between the cost dimension and the service dimension in their deliberations.[6]

A third data-simplification technique might be termed the *"on-paper"* phenomenon. Several senior finance officers observed that once an estimate was given an actual figure in a circulating document, most participants were reluctant to alter it. At least, the figure was taken as the valid working estimate, regardless of its genesis. The cognitive-limits approach might suggest that the written figure is infused with value because it eliminates the stressful task of generating the figure.

COGNITIVE SHORTCUTS—THE PROBLEM

The basic strategy for simplifying the problem which must be solved is to rely on *horizontal evaluation*—the comparison of each specific $ALLO_t$ request with the comparable $ALLO_{t-1}$ rather than attempting to evaluate the relative merits of competing allocation requests in Y_t. Year-to-year comparison on each line-item of expenditure is extremely prevalent in Brighton and Southend. Each participant has a responsibility either to justify the expansion or to reduce the difference, at the line-item level, between $ALLO_{t-1}$ and $ALLO_t$.

> Most of the questions that would be raised about the requests are contained in these notes on the left-hand page. They break down the nature of the change from last year to this year. Moreover, most of these points are copied on from year to year—even where the query may no longer be relevant. Very few inquiries are raised each year that would add new notes to these existing ones.
>
> [A Senior Accountant, Southend]

> When looking over the figures I always have the previous two years' figures before me. . . . I say very often at the informal meeting: why has this item gone up £2000? I always mark any figures that show substantial increase over those of the last two years.
>
> [Finance Committee Chairman, Brighton]

In Dudley and West Bromwich, the situation is less clear. Although each system identifies the expansionary aspects of each request, neither problem-solving system focuses explicitly on the horizontal evaluation of individual items. Horizontal evaluation is undertaken only at the level of aggregate department expenditure. Some actors who deal with detailed figures (senior accountants and administrative officers) continue to do horizontal evaluation.

The single important example of a budgeter who consciously employed *vertical* evaluation is the Senior Finance Officer in West Bromwich. He articulated a systematic strategy of evaluating the relative priorities of each proposed increment against all others, from the same spending committee and from other committees. The array of proposed expenditure on the sixteen-category schedule which he prepared incorporates this vertical evaluation. Certain other budgeters (e.g., Dudley's Foreward Planning Officer, Southend's Executive Board) claim some commitment to vertical evaluation; but the evidence shows only minimal use of this technique.

About one-half of the Chief Officers in Dudley and West Bromwich, the budgeting systems where individual chief officers have reasonable latitude to allocate their aggregate total, did characterize their problem as the distribution of additional resources to high-priority areas.[7] But rates of change for component services of these chief officers did not differ systematically from those who did not articulate a vertical evaluation strategy. Moreover, the naive models revealed that Southend, where horizontal evaluation was the most pervasive, also had the largest proportion of extreme yearly changes in account categories. There are, of course, other constraints upon allocation choices; but the evidence suggests that horizontal evaluation is a dominant strategy among key budgeters in at least three of the four budget-making systems.

The fundamental characteristic that simplified budget-making for its participants is the pervasiveness of *stabilized role relationships*. Wildavsky, among others, has noted the critical importance of stabilized role relationships during the budgetary process. Various roles fit together, creating patterns of mutual expectations among participants. These patterns serve to reduce the burden of calculations for the actors, thus lending stability and clarity to the process.[8] The existence of regularized role relationships is particularly important in Brighton and Southend. As the number of contributions to the budget solution increases, there is a nearly exponential increase in the points where there might be conflict or confusion among the budgeters. In Dudley and West Bromwich, where allocations appear to be determined by rational-technical formulas, the points for interrole tension are reduced in number. But in these systems also, there is a fundamental need to be assured that behavior is predictable, that role rights and responsibilities are clear, and that allocation decisions will be comprehensible.

The explication of SOPs, strategies of search, and so on in

Chapter 6 revealed many aspects of these stabilized role relationships. The "pre-budget" meetings in Brighton are a clear
example of a highly stylized arena of conflict-and-cooperation
among key budgeters. The extent to which common expectations are negotiated is typified by the action of the Borough
Treasurer:

> It is my practice that I will not raise a query in the pre-budget meet-
> ings or to Finance Committee unless I have already told the Chief
> Officer exactly what will be involved. If I am going to challenge
> eighteen points in a committee's requests, several days before I ap-
> pear I will send a memo to the Chief Officer telling him exactly
> those eighteen points and the figures I will suggest.

In another example, the Chief Officer in Dudley knows that,
although he will not have a major impact on the absolute size
of his rate share, he will be given a relatively free hand by the
financial people in the allocation of those resources among his
component services. Similarly, the West Bromwich Chief Officer knows that if he can generate a reasonable justification,
the finance officers will at least tacitly support his request to
substitute a new scheme he prefers for a scheme that was included in the priority schedule.

Initially, the absence of formal contact between the Executive Board (of Chief Officers) and the Policy and Finance
Committee in Southend appears to diminish the coordination
between these pruning bodies. In fact, this is a consciously
structured separation that is meant to stabilize role relationships in the Executive Board (which is actually responsible
for cutting the estimates). The Chairman of the Policy and
Finance Committee explains why he eliminated the formal
linkage as a method of clarifying behavior:

> I decided the presence of an elected member at the Executive Board
> would be an inhibiting factor in any discussion. I believe that when
> the Chief Officers get together, they sometimes get quite nasty with
> each other—in a friendly way, of course. I hope they do; I am sure
> they wouldn't if I were there. We'd be likely to get the usual sort

of backscratching. No one would want to spit in his mate's eye. And elected representatives are notoriously unreliable, so the officers wouldn't want to fight in front of me.

Thus resources can be allocated in private sessions, by professional experts who speak a common language and who are insulated from direct political or public pressure.

A third method by which budgeters simplify the cognitive problem is to define most budget items as *"uncontrollable."* The core of the base-budget mentality is the view that most existing expenditure cannot be reduced. Chief Officers and Councillors talk of the "commitment" to a level of service. Actors on the financial side also speak of committed expenditure which, according to different estimates, composes 75% to 95% of total expenditure. But, as Barber suggests, the notion of commitment or uncontrollability usually signifies unwillingness to change rather than irrevocability. One Deputy Borough Treasurer stressed this:

> We find that it is very difficult to discontinue an existing local authority service. Very rarely will politicians agree to stop providing a service now operating, or even to substantially reduce one. The same can be said about Chief Officers. Fundamentally, we do not look critically at existing services. This despite a Finance Committee resolution that we should. But the hard fact is that once a service is funded, it is a necessity ever-after.

Occasionally there are items which are discontinued by conscious local choices. But these are usually trial programs or highly controversial ones which fail to sustain support beyond an initial funding. Controllability is seen to exist over the decisions about rates of expansion for existing services and about the timing and implementation of new programs. "Uncontrollability" is best understood as a preference for continuing on the basis of the existing configuration of allocations, rather than undertaking a search for a different one. The motivation, however, seems rather less a flight from cognitive complexity than the tug of political feasibility. Budgeters believe that reducing the funding for virtually any program will mobilize the forces of protest, not of approbation.

Configurative Individual-Level Behavior

The cognitive-limits approach seeks regularities in individual-level behavior that can be attributed to the attempt to avoid/reduce the cognitive complexity of budget-making as a problem. A broad tendency in individual-level analyses, particularly in the use of case-studies, is to identify the "special"—the unique impact of a particular characteristic or individual. The objective of analysis is to transform these configurative factors into analytic variables. In this section, the variations in impact that are a function of the specific holders of certain key budget-making roles are explored. In particular, critical dimensions of the spending department chief officer, of the top finance department officers, and of members of Council are assessed.

THE ENTREPRENEURIAL STYLE OF CHIEF OFFICERS

A factor which seems crucially important in explaining non-normal expenditure patterns might be termed the "entrepreneurial style" of each Chief Officer. With few exceptions, the spending departments whose expenditure pattern differed markedly from that expected also had a unique Chief Officer. An illuminating example is the local health services in Southend. Expenditure per head on this group of services and also on the individual services is extremely low in terms of both mean county-borough levels and also regression estimates. The explanation for the low levels is provided by a health-services officer in Southend:

> Bear in mind that much of our expenditure is on staff, on salaries. This authority has worked for many years on a shoestring budget. The present Medical Officer of Health (MOH) took over about four years ago from a regime that had been operating here since the early 1930s. We had a Medical Officer who came here as a Deputy and who had his close friend as his administrative officer. They ran the

department together for 30 years. The MOH was of the old school—
he would have viewed computerization and modern management
techniques as a load of old gunk. He and his chief admin' officer
took pride in the economical way that services were provided here.
They didn't stagnate—it was all done well. The MOH believed in
"the honest day's work" approach and it took a pretty persuasive
case to convince him of the need for an increase in staff. Our provision levels, in terms of staffing and especially in capital projects,
stem from the style of these men. This has tended to prolong itself
even since he has been gone. The new MOH sees many inadequacies;
but when he says that he thinks we should do this and that, every-
body asks: Why? we have been getting along. It will be a number
of years before the former MOH's ghost disappears.

An excellent contrast is the status of the same service in
Brighton. There, local health-services expenditure is extremely
high, both in the aggregate and on most specific services. Again,
the best explanation of the levels of spending is the Chief Officer's style. Brighton's MOH (for the past fifteen years) is
nationally recognized as a leader in local government health
services. He is a vigorous proponent of extensive use of the
community care services.[9] The characteristics of Brighton's
population, particularly the large proportion of elderly people,
provide the MOH with a reasonable need argument. He has
cultivated the support of his Spending Committee and has
maintained his credibility with the Council and the Finance
Department. His skillful use of these resources has resulted
in substantial growth in the local health-services budget (both
staff and capital projects) during the decade. Even in cases
where the Council has initially been reluctant, the MOH often
developed strategies which resulted in the acceptance of his
program as a fait accompli.

The contrast of these Medical Officers of Health is the most
dramatic example of the differential impact of Chief Officers.
The stress is upon an "entrepreneurial" nature of the style because it is not a corollary that he who asks most will receive
most. Southend's former MOH is an exception—most Chief
Officers attempt (or at least are perceived by other actors to

be attempting) to increase substantially their allocation and their scope of activity. But some Chief Officers are less effective in marshalling evidence of need, committee support, and the sympathy of the Treasurer and the Council. There are Chief Officers who are viewed as "overambitious," as "empire-builders," as "wanting the earth." When this opinion prevails among the more powerful budgetary decision makers, a Chief Officer is likely to experience little success in achieving his allocation goals.

One part of the entrepreneurial style relates to the Chief Officer's skill in manipulating information concerning local need and central-department policy. A second part is his ability to create a favorable climate of opinion in his Spending Committee and particularly in the Finance Department concerning the validity of his requests. A third crucial dimension is the Chief Officer's perception of his role. According to the normative theory, the chief officer is a professional servant of the elected members and his responsibility is to administer their will. There is great variation in the acceptance of this norm by chief officers. The range is indicated by the views of three Chief Officers:

My duty as a Chief Officer is to give expert advice to members. If they take it, all well and good. If they don't, what they decide becomes my policy. This means that periodically I become a sort of professional hypocrite. I advise them to spend more on our (service), and they don't take it. I do the best I can with what I've got.

You must give the service committee options. . . . We try to give them a choice; but it is, in many cases, a slanted one. You lean heavily on what you think is right. Our job as experts is to express preferences. You let the committee discuss all around and in the end it will come back to what you wanted in the first place. That may sound a bit cynical, but that is how it generally happens. . . . My generation of officers was brought up on the democratic notion that the committee decides. New officers are coming up with the notion of "direct action."

I think you can end up projecting your own shortcomings on the party make-up. I would be saying its really not my fault, it's the committee's fault. I believe that it is *my* fault if (Borough) doesn't get a particular service. It is my job to represent need and I ought to be a good enough public relations person to put over the situation clearly. . . . Some Chief Officers do hide behind the excuse of being blocked politically. If there isn't an adequate service, you ought not to look at the committee, you ought to look at the Chief Officer. If he is getting what in his opinion is a raw deal in financial or other terms, basically he is in a powerful position to make his views known.

In some cases, there is a unique historical factor which has resulted in a markedly non-normal level of allocations. But in the majority of cases for both divisible-benefit and indivisible-benefit services in the four county boroughs, these phenomena are best explained by the entrepreneurial style of the Chief Officer.

THE ROLE OF THE DOMINANT FINANCIAL OFFICER

In each of the four budgeting systems, there is one role that dominates the problem-solving system for budget-making. This role, which has primary responsibility for determining the broad implications of potential choices and also for evaluating the desirability of specific alternatives, is usually filled by a single Finance Department Officer. It might be the Borough Treasurer, as in Brighton and, to a lesser extent, in Southend, or it might be a budget officer, such as the Foreward Planning Officer in Dudley or an Assistant Borough Treasurer in West Bromwich. Since there is limited turnover in the occupants of these roles, assessment of the impact of the particular individual on the dimensions of the role are problematic. But it is possible to specify the contributions to the budget-making solution of this single role and also to suggest whether the specific role-actor has a distinguishable orientation.

The Foreward Planning Officer "marries" the lowest-feasible-cost budget and the Government guidelines on service growth into a set of recommended rate rations. As Table 6.1 revealed, there is no immediately apparent correspondence between the

Government's figures and the final allocations. The Officer notes that the final rate allocations are virtually identical to those she has proposed to the Treasurer. Thus it is evident that this Officer, guided by constraints defined in Chapter 6, determines the service-level solution to resource allocation. The current Forward Planning Officer does not interject her own subjective appraisal into the development of these sets of figures. She perceives her role in a technocratic fashion, aims to transform the various figures with objectivity, and limits the programmatic considerations in her activity. Of the four budgeting systems, this role and/or its current incumbent are least "dominant" as the key financial officer. Hence the role's contributions to budget creation are reasonably well explicated by the organizational-process approach.

The Finance Officer in West Bromwich contrasts sharply with the Foreward Planning Officer. The perception of this officer is dominated by the consideration of specific, alternative policy choices. In part, this might be attributed to his attempt to *classify* each increment into a particular category in the priority schedule. But essentially, this budgeter consciously attempts to bridge the gap between policy and financial criteria:

> Some local authorities allocate resources on the basis of national formulas. But we come back to a question of development: different services are developing in different ways. And different local authorities, because of the nature of the area they administer, have different demands on their committees and the services they provide. So you've got three factors to recognize: one is the Government policy and the Council's policy on the development of services; one is the social need of the area; and third is what the local people want. This may be entirely different from the other two and somehow we must recognize this in our allocations. It is my job, with the Chief Officers, to achieve the financial support for all these purposes.

This officer articulated a clear commitment to protect the share of resources for services with less political support:

> In allocating resources, we suffer the difficulty that certain committees like parks, libraries, and so on do not have a strong voice

based on policy decisions. So you act for these minority groups among the competing demands by other committees. We must make sure that these committees do get an adequate allocation for operation. You might say I make sure that they get a share of the resource pie.

Since no other actor in the borough expressed such an orientation, the correspondence of West Bromwich's allocation patterns to the "fair share" model in Chapter 5 must be attributed primarily to the policy agenda of this particular role-taker. While the role provides him with the opportunity to influence resource allocation, the exceptional competency and the clear commitment of the particular individual are critical to his impact.

The budget-creation process in Brighton and Southend is characterized by a dispersion of contributions. But the Borough Treasurer is, to a large extent, the dominant actor in the budget-making process of both Brighton and Southend. In Southend, the Treasurer "represents," on the Executive Board, the financial perspective developed by his staff. The Executive Board normally defers to his expertise on the revenue and expenditure implications of various requests and on the location of potential cuts. The Treasurer is also the source of technical financial information for the Chairman of Policy and Finance Committee.

The nature of individual-level differences for the financial Chief Officer is evident in contrasting the present (since 1968) and the previous Borough Treasurers in Southend. The present Treasurer relies upon delegation of responsibility within his department. Inputs to the budgetary solution are distributed broadly, with the Chief Accountant serving as the hub of coordination. The former Borough Treasurer, however, had an expansive view of his role and, according to budgetary actors, the budget mirrored his strong personal agenda regarding resource allocation. The responses of the Chief Officers to this question are striking: "Does the current Borough Treasurer, relative to the former Borough Treasurer, determine the size and distribution of your allocations?"

Substantially more	More	No change	Less	Substantially less
0	0	1	1	9

Characteristic of his style, the former Treasurer manipulated the rules of capital accumulation in order to finance locally the construction of a multimillion-pound, civic-center complex. More broadly, his aversion to borrowing helps explain Southend's extremely low level of net outstanding debt.

In Brighton, the Treasurer's role perception resembles that of Southend's former Treasurer. The Treasurer identifies the line-item reductions sufficient to achieve the acceptable-level rate and the Finance Chairman overrides him in the prebudget meetings only rarely, on political grounds. The Chief Officers in Brighton believe that the Treasurer is firmly in control of the budget-creation process. One Chief Officer observed:

> The Borough Treasurer is most insistent that these are *our* estimates, not his. If we insist we want to put in a certain estimate, he won't stop us. He may say that we'll never get it. . . . If the Treasurer has decided that an estimate is off, it will be cut. This fact is a given in all that occurs in budgeting.

While the Treasurer's personal impact is great, its specific substance varies from year to year, depending on his reading of the needs of Chief Officers, Council policy, Government policy, and financial constraints.

Clearly, it would be an oversimplification to state that the array of resource-allocation decisions in a budget can be attributed to any single individual. However, if the focus is only upon the marginal changes from the preceding year and if one allows that a single individual's impact might become cumulative and reinforcing over a number of years, the impact of several budgeters identified in this section is substantial. They are constrained by the spending history of the borough, by its financial and service needs, by the entrepreneurial style of chief officers, and by other factors; but the macrolevel configuration of resource allocations in several of the county boroughs has been powerfully influenced by the agenda of a particular financial officer.

THE ROLE OF THE ELECTED MEMBERS

There has been little explicit consideration of the elected members, in their roles as Councillors and as members of Council Committees. The data from the demographic-approach analysis revealed that there are few systematic relationships between party-political variables and quantitative measures of resource allocation. In the shorter-run, the impact of party control might be more evident in qualitative policy decisions rather than the history-dependent resource-allocation decisions. During the 1960s, there were only a few clear instances where changes in party control altered actual policy.[10] The Conservatives promoted the sale of Council houses while the Labour Party prevented it. The Conservative Party in West Bromwich altered, but did not demolish, the Labour-initiated comprehensivization of secondary education. The common situation was one party's acceptance, with modifications, of policies initiated when the other party was in control. For example, Southend's Lib-Lab coalition carried through Conservative plans to upgrade and remodel various entertainment facilities, despite their own opposition to the plans. In general, local factors, including what has been termed the county borough's "critical policy style," seem to have swamped the expected impact of local party differences on most issues.[11] While such major policy issues might be the expected location of local party-political impact, it is possible that the impact occurs more subtly, in the gradual alterations of particular resource allocations. It is difficult to determine this, since the pattern of party turnover seldom approximates an experimental design. The perceptions of actors is one source of evidence. Councillors and officers were asked: "If one party controlled the Council for about five years, and then the other party controlled it for the next five years, how would the budgets for each period differ? How would you distinguish them?" Virtually all respondents replied that in their particular county borough (excluding Brighton, where such a speculation is remote), there would be no evident differences in the budgets and that the two sets of allocations would be indistinguishable. Officers and even Councillors stated that changes in the majority party have relatively no effect on the changes in the pattern of allocations. Councillors observed that most decisions on service provision are nonpolitical and that local tradition dominates party considerations. Typical of the officers' viewpoint was this one:

> The way I prepare my estimates, what I request, what my allocation is—these are not at all related to which party is in power. You might think that the Socialists or the Conservatives would be sympathetic to certain types of requests. My experience in (Borough) is that it makes no difference. There might be minor differences in how I present my case, in the nature of my arguments; but local parties don't affect the size of my allocation or how I employ it.

A different aspect of the role of the elected members is the extent of their control over the various departments. Most Councillors assert that the Spending Committees firmly control departmental spending. In contrast, most officers view the Spending Committees as bodies that, with occasional exceptions, can be firmly "guided" to support the officer's position. The latter perception seems most accurate. Collectively, the elected members do have some effect on budget outcomes. They can take a strong policy stand, they can refuse to support a Chief Officer's program requests or budgetary needs. In most cases, however, the Spending Committee operates to support its Chief Officer. Only Finance Committee and, to a lesser extent, the Establishment (staffing) Committee stand as real obstacles composed of elected members. Yet even these committees are generally dominated by the professional and technical expertise of their chief officers (often the Establishment Officer is either the Treasurer or a senior Finance Officer). To a large extent, the impact of a spending committee is a function of the style of its chief officer. Sir William Harcourt's observation about Government Ministers at the national level might also be applied to Council committees: they exist to tell the civil servants what the people will not stand.

It is important, however, not to understate the cumulative impact on budget creation of the political actors. In the first place, the committees of Council have been involved in policy decisions which underpin the Chief Officer's decisions about how to structure his budgetary requests. Second, there is an important, if unmeasurable, effect on the decisions of officers by means of anticipated reactions concerning what is generally within the range of political acceptability to the political majority. And the single most important impact of the political actors upon the budgetary process is in the determination of the acceptable level for the rate. This decision, which is often taken by the Chairman of Finance Committee (who represents the opinion of the most powerful members of the Majority Party Group), is the basic determinant of the total resources available for allocation. In Dudley, for example, the low level of the rate and of spending on many services is best explained by a shared commitment among leading members of both political parties to limit public spending. Indeed, the public goal of key Conservatives was that Dudley should have the lowest rate in the country.

DELEGATION AND RESPONSIBILITY AVOIDANCE

The cognitive-limits approach explains the tendency to break decisions into smaller components and to distribute decision-making responsibility for resource allocation as methods to make complex problem-solving more manageable. It is important to distinguish between the capacity to make choices and the willingness to take responsibility for those choices. The capacity to make choices does seem a matter of cognitive limits—it can be viewed as a function of the actor's perception of the complexity of the task relative to his cognitive resources. Most elected members are unable to achieve the mastery over information and complicated tradeoffs involved in making broad resource-allocation decisions.[12] Hence their attention shifts downward toward simple, concrete decisions that ought to be administrative matters dealt with by departmental officers. It is the Chief Officers who have sufficient information and technical expertise, and thus the capacity to make the key choices among alternatives.

The bind is that the normative model gives the elected members rather than the appointed officials the responsibility for choice-making. At most, the norms of responsibility in budget-making imply that there is conscious selection among alternatives on the basis of policy preferences by elected members of Council. Minimally, responsibility means that the elected members are publicly accountable for resource-allocation decisions. A moderate and reasonable view of responsibility is the expectation that these decisions will be undertaken on criteria that are predominantly *policy oriented* and that those who take these decisions are *visible,* and, in that sense, publicly accountable.

It is evident that responsibility is delegated in each of the four budget-making systems. Council's authority to make significant choices is delegated to a Finance Committee, which grants most of this authority to its Chairman. In Dudley this authority is further transferred through the Treasurer to the Foreward Planning Officer. In Southend, the Executive Board is the locus of decision-making, with the Treasurer in a dominant role. In West Bromwich, responsibility is passed through a coordinating board of Chief Officers to the Treasurer, and on to a senior Finance Officer. Only in Brighton is the Finance Chairman actively involved in the full set of critical allocation decisions.

One important factor is the absence of a general policy-making group of elected officials in any of the four county boroughs. The ideology of corporate planning is invoked in all four county boroughs and each has instituted structural changes which appear to focus policy-making. But in each case, there is still no institutionalized group which establishes and implements a comprehensive set of priorities for resource allocations.[13] Most Chief Officers are quite unhappy with this situation. One observed:

There ought to be a policy-making committee who can look at all aspects of spending. Finance Committee cannot be a policy-making committee. They can say we've got so much money to spend. But it is not for the Finance Committee to say we will chop so much from Health, so much from Education, so much from Streets, because they really don't know what they are doing other than that they are keeping expenditure below a certain level. They don't know the effect of their decision. There should be a deliberate policy decision by a policy-making committee, advised by its Chief Officers.

Southend's Executive Board, which is composed of appointed rather than elected officials, is the only body which makes a relatively systematic attempt to set priorities across all spending categories. Even in Southend the system is, as a senior finance officer noted, "often extremely arbitrary." And the Board normally defers to the expertise of the Treasurer concerning the location and size of reductions. It is also the case that West Bromwich does have a system of "coordinators."[14] But, as one Chief Officer observed:

This is heresy, but the coordinators do not really coordinate among the important policy choices in the budget. The coordination system is a fantasy.

Chief Officers also complain that the individual Spending Committees have not fulfilled their policy-making role. As the Maud Commission corroborated, elected members fail to provide a framework of clear policy instructions and tend to meddle at a too-detailed level. In fact, Chief Officers do not desire *instructions* on policy, they desire *authorization* for their own policy decisions. Constrained by the normative rule that officers should not make policy, the officer wants an expansive range of administrative discretion that is shielded by broadly worded policy authorization. This ambivalence is reflected in the comment of a Medical Officer of Health:

I am much happier to make the decision of what is to be deleted rather than to leave it to my committee. But if they are to be policy-makers, they ought to fulfill this responsibility. In fact, the committee abdicates its responsibility as a policy-making body, leaving it to the Chief Officer and the Finance Committee to make these decisions about what estimates come out.

The most significant aspect of the situation is that most Chief Officers, in turn, are driven toward the position of evading responsibility. Because the elected members fail to establish broad, authorizing policy and because the norms preclude the officer from openly accepting responsibility for the decisive rejection (and selection) of particular programs, most chief officers prefer to let someone else make these choices. Thus it is the financial officers, by default, who do most of the difficult choice-making and pruning, invoking financial criteria as the ultima ratio.[15]

The situation described by a senior accountant fits Dudley, Southend and West Bromwich extremely well and fits Brighton to a lesser extent:

These schemes are cut back on grounds of financial expedience. If you have a situation where there are two schemes and you can only afford to do one of them, ideally you would do the most pressing one from the point of view of amenity. I would not like to say this is necessarily so. Certainly these things are not done without consultation; but it has been our experience that Chief Officers have pet schemes and they'll clamp to them. Someone has to come along and arbitrarily say which schemes have to be cut. In this authority, that person has been the Treasurer. I am sure the Treasurer would agree that he is not the most qualified person to choose among schemes on technical grounds. This is not perfect decision-making—for financial considerations are more important than planning ones. When a chop has to be made, it is made in the final analysis by the Treasurer and so it is made on financial, if impartial, grounds.[16]

The key factor is the response of the Chief Officer to proposed cuts. Even if the initial decisions on reductions were made on financial critieria, the chief officer and his spending department generally have the option to make substitute reductions on the basis of their own assessment of priorities.

In fact, this usually does not occur. The "on-paper" constraint might be part of this. But the best explanation is that the Chief Officer can, by not acting, transfer the responsibility for difficult choices. He knows that if he manages to reinstate a proposed cut, he must select reductions of an equivalent amount. In most cases, the Chief Officer prefers to accept the Treasurer's selections under protest and consequently to absolve himself from blame or criticism concerning the schemes which are and are not effected. The form of the Chief Officer's public protest is not that Scheme A *rather than* Scheme B has been financed; he simply claims that he has not been given resources to implement Scheme B. Thus even in those systems where the Chief Officer has latitude to redistribute his rate allocation to different programs, choices about levels of support for programs and exclusion of programs are usually based on the "financial, if impartial" decisions of finance officers.

The Treasurer's Department is in a particularly delicate position regarding the problem of responsibility. It is, like the Spending Departments, constrained by the norms prohibiting policy-making. Finance officers continually stress that they do not make policy decisions, that they are neutral, that they simply structure choices in terms of financial constraints. In a limited sense, this is true. Essential choices appear to be made by other actors. But the fact is that the Treasurer's staff locates most reductions (and consequently, establishes what will be allowed) in all four county boroughs. Moreover, the staff actually creates the budget in Dudley and West Bromwich. Yet all this is done under the fiction of providing "technical advice" and of "clarifying choices." One Chief Accountant, after talking of "guiding" Finance Committee and of "making realistic" the requests of Spending Committees, acknowledged:

> The budget, broadly speaking, is very much the Treasurer and myself. The budgetary process is predominantly a matter of the senior finance officers working out what can be done in terms of services relative to the cost the politicians are willing to support.

One might view the discontinuity between the legitimate foci of responsibility and the actual location of budget creation as a failure of public accountability. It is evident that most interest groups (and perhaps even most Councillors) are not aware of the points of effective access to influence resource allocations. There is no specific actor, except possibly the Chairman of Finance Committee, who appears to be publicly responsible for the entire pattern of resource allocations in a particular year. An alternative perspective is that the budget is an extremely complex, technical, and policy-serving document. Hence it is the legitimate domain of bureaucrats, who have expertise and are insulated from particularistic group pressures. While this latter view has merit, the critical point is that the county borough's budget *is* a policy-making document. Budget-making is the only point at which there are comprehensive policy decisions which involve explicit trade-offs among alternatives ("opportunity costs").

Thus the chain of delegations of authority filters control over budgetary allocations down to some distribution of actual influence among bureaucratic experts. Some of these decisions are made by the spending department top officers; but where there are manifest conflicts, it is typically the financial officers who make choices. Like Lowi's "new machines," these professionalized bureaucracies are not neutral, only independent— they are relatively irresponsible structures of power.[17] These groups are in no sense malevolent. But they are also not visible, barely accountable, and do not allocate resources on criteria that are primarily policy-oriented.

Evaluation of Individual-Level Approaches

This chapter has examined the process of budget-making from the perspective of both the cognitive-limits approach and of other individual-level phenomena. The cognitive-limits approach, unlike the organizational-process approach, views the individual role-actor as the object unit of analysis. It aims to

explain budgetary behavior and resource allocations as a function of the manner in which individuals respond to the complex
problem of budget creation. It specifies regularities in that behavior, particularly a set of strategies which reduce uncertainty
and complexity for the budgeter.

By organizing data collection and analysis at the level of the
individual role-actor, the cognitive-limits approach facilitates
the identification of characteristics which the approaches in
earlier chapters ignore. In particular, it sensitizes the analyst to
unique and significant inputs such as the entrepreneurial style
of certain Chief Officers or the commitment to fair shares of a
pivotal allocator. The most plausible explanations for many
cases of non-normal allocations in the four county boroughs
involve the kind of unique impacts that these individual-level
perspectives register. Thus a reasonable assumption is validated:
*a configurative approach is most effective in explaining deviant
cases of resource association.*

But this examination has also suggested the inadequacies
of configurative perspectives for systematic explanation and
theory-building. There are problems of both prediction and
generalizability. The cognitive-limits approach can specify certain behavioral traits that are likely to occur; but it cannot
specify the implications of this behavior for either the budgetary outputs or the budgetary process at the organizational
level. To the extent it generates any predictions concerning
outputs, the approach leads to the expectation that there
will be marginal alterations in the base; but this prediction is
handled more economically and precisely by the naive econometric models. Moreover, the analytic implications are not
made explicit. Why are some role-takers less constrained by
cognitive limits than others? What difference does it make if
decision makers think in units of money rather than units of
service? What is the effect on allocation outputs of stabilized
rather than protean role relationships?

The cognitive-limits approach explains why a certain decision
strategy is reasonable; but it fails to develop analytic linkages
which fuse components of role behavior into a systematic frame-

work of behavior or process. Ideally, the objective is to transform proper names into variables and to specify the relationships among these variables. For an institutionalized process like budget-making, a satisfactory analytic explanation seems less likely to be accomplished with approaches at the individual level of analysis than with approaches like the organizational-process explanation. Despite these shortcomings, configurative approaches at the individual level remain attractive because they provide a rich, descriptive data base from which to generate stories-as-explanations and because they capture more of the texture of politics than system-level or organization-level approaches.

NOTES

1. Crecine, for example, asserts that the propositions of the cognitive-limits approach can be viewed as a subset of those for the organizational-process approach. See Crecine, op. cit., pp. 205-206, footnote 45. While this seems reasonable, there is a tendency, with the organizational-process approach, to treat individual-level phenomena as though they are at the organization level of analysis. For example, the actual allocation of rate shares to each spending department in West Bromwich is contingent upon the unique problem-solving routines of the Senior Finance Officer, who classifies each request for increase on the basis of his own subjective appraisal. Such shifts in level of analysis tend to be insufficiently specified.

2. In this chapter, the object unit of analysis is normally a single "role-actor" or a set of actors with the interdependent roles. The role-theoretical literature defines a "role" as "a behavioral repetoire characteristic of a person or a position," in *Role Theory: Concepts and Research,* edited by Bruce Biddle and Edwin Thomas (New York: Wiley, 1966), pp. 28-31. Davis, Dempster, and Wildavsky define role as "the expectations of behavior attached to institutional positions," in Davis, et al., (1966), op. cit., p. 530. The notion of "actor" has been defined as "a person engaged in interactions with others" in *Role Theory,* op. cit., p. 24. Although it is not commonly used, we have combined the two concepts as "role-actor" in order to emphasize the fusion of a behavioral repetoire and the particular person performing that repetoire.

3. An important analytical statement concerning this problem by Heinz Eulau is taken as correct at this point. Eulau argues that the level of analysis is determined by the choice of the subject unit, and the choice of the subject unit is determined by the theoretical standpoint of the observer. See Eulau (1969) op. cit., esp. pp. 8-17.

4. See Charles Lindblom, *The Policy-Making Process* (Englewood Cliffs: Prentice-Hall, 1968); Anthony Downs, *Inside Bureaucracy* (Boston: Little, Brown, 1967), esp. pp. 3-4; Herbert Simon, *Administrative Behavior* (New York: Free Press, 1957).

5. Barber, op. cit., esp. pp. 37-44; Wildavsky, op. cit.; Fenno, op. cit.

6. It is quite evident that top budgeters do not assume a necessary correspondence between amount of money spent and quality of service. Amounts of money are understood, however, as indicative of levels of commitment to different services.

7. It is not clear whether priority decisions are equalized over time. An important aspect of the Cyert-March theory is that resources are allocated to maintain the relative position of coalition members. At the department level, such an output formula would result in a relatively incremental solution, with each specific service receiving a reasonable share of increases (that is, similar to the base-budget model). Cyert and March, op. cit., p. 270.

8. See Wildavsky (1974), op. cit., p. 136; Davis, et al. (1966) op. cit., p. 530.

9. These services, including home nursing, health visitors, and domestic helps, were all part of the local health services during the decade. Certain domiciliary-care services, domestic helps among them, were transferred to the Social Services Department from 1970.

10. Most of the generalizations here exclude Brighton, which had clear, uninterrupted rule by the Conservative Party throughout the 1960s. Southend had a dominant Conservative majority through most of the decade. However, the three-party system evolved into a period of both Lib-Lab coalition and no-majority years during the mid-1960s. Since then, the Conservatives have regained clear control of the Council. The old County Borough of Dudley had a moderate Conservative majority prior to the West Midlands Act; but most of the other areas incorporated into the expanded county borough had Labour majorities. Since amalgamation, the Labour Party has usually been the majority party on the Council. In West Bromwich, there has been persistent but unpatterned turnover of party control since 1960, with the Labour Party having a slight advantage.

11. One area which might be affected is the *nature* of projects; however, actors, including elected members, did not feel that this was often the case, even among the social services. The rate of expansion in the capital budget is a more likely point of difference, with the Conservatives tending to restrain the rate of effecting new projects. Given the unsettled nature of government fiscal policy and the inconsistent role of the central departments regarding loan sanction and the approval of project designs, it was not possible to assess this adequately.

12. One Borough Treasurer observed:

I don't feel that most Councillors really have a clue about the process. If you asked them what the decision-making process over the budget entailed, they couldn't tell you. The Councillor only knows that he goes along to the meetings of Finance or a Spending Committee and to the Council, and he votes his party's position. He is just a dot in the middle of his committee. Some of the more perceptive and cynical councillors would probably just say that the Chief Officers make the decisions.

13. There is some evidence that corporate planning is becoming a more significant factor in local authorities. See, for example, Judge, op. cit., and Greenwood and Stewart, op. cit. In the four county boroughs during the period of study, however, there was little *real* impact from these techniques. Like other administrative innovations (for example, PPB), it might be quite difficult to distinguish empirically between image and substance.

14. The "coordinators" are a body of chief officers who resemble the Executive Board in Southend. Each coordinator is responsible for a certain range of services. With regard to budget decisions, the coordinators serve, relative to the Executive Board in Southend, to give effect to the allocations of the Finance Department, rather than to establish the allocation levels.

15. In the context of budget-making, the "policy" bodies of chief officers in several of the county boroughs can be understood as adjuncts to the finance officer and his perspective.

16. A senior finance officer in another borough made a similar point:

In determining cuts, it was a partnership exercise. But if there was a difficulty in getting to the level of expenditure which we had set, I took the decision. I said: we will put this up on financial grounds and say that it can't be done and must be deferred. The officers accept this choice. The Chief Officer knows that if he is over the target, we put something up to achieve it and we'll be supported by the coordinators and the Finance Committee.

17. Theodore Lowi, "Machine Politics: Old and New," *The Public Interest* (Fall 1967), pp. 83-92.

Chapter 8

EXPLANATORY APPROACHES

TO BUDGET-MAKING

This book has been comparative in several important senses. In the first place, there has been a comparative analysis of the systematic relationship between resource allocations and the social, economic, and political characteristics of the British county boroughs. Second, the patterns of resource allocation for a broad range of services in four selected county boroughs have been established. Third, the processes of budgetary decision and creation in the four county boroughs have been compared. Fourth, and underpinning the other three modes, there has been a comparison and evaluation of several major approaches to explaining budgetary decision-making. In this chapter, the findings regarding the first three research concerns will be reiterated briefly. The major focus of this concluding chapter is to assess the relative adequacy of each approach in explaining budget-making.

The Budgetary Discretion of the County Boroughs

Having established the county borough as the level of anal-ysis, the initial concern was whether the county borough's discretion in resource allocation was adequate to make it an interesting research site. The county borough was a creation of Parliament and its range of activities was established by parliamentary acts. The county borough was an "all-purpose" local authority, providing a broad range of important govern-mental goods and services to its citizens. Parliament required that certain functions be performed and authorized many other functions, at the discretion of the borough's Council.

While Parliament had general control over the nature of county-borough activities, the most powerful external con-straint was the departments of the central government. Certain powers of the central department, including the setting of minimum standards of provision, the explication of responsi-bilities under obligatory legislation, and the inspection of service provision, were insufficiently precise to operate as more than vague constraints. The department's most effective device for manipulating county-borough behavior was its con-trol over capital projects by means of loan sanction and review of plans. This device could limit the rate of expansion of a service and, by means of the anticipated reactions of the county borough, might influence other aspects of service provision. In general, the central department-county borough department relationships were a mixture of cooperation and control. The central department enforced minimal levels of provision for many services; but within broad limitations, the county bor-ough had relative autonomy in its decisions concerning the funding of services.

Certain other constraints on the county borough's resource allocation decisions have been identified. The impact on the budget of inflation and of nationally determined wage and salary scales were relatively uncontrollable for local budgeters. At a general level, the central government's fiscal and monetary policies affected local expenditure decisions in indirect (and often indeterminant) ways. Overall, the county borough, as a resource allocator, operated within a complex environment which constrained its autonomy to some extent. But neither legal-institutional constraint nor macrolevel forces were so powerful as to limit severely the county borough's capacity to make important allocation decisions.

This study next examined whether the county boroughs appear to have exercised this decision-making potential. The critical test has been to compare the actual pattern of resource allocations in the county boroughs. For this purpose, various measures of expenditure per head, expenditure per unit of service, and other indicators of provision have been compiled for all county boroughs. Statistical representations of average levels, ranges of distribution, and central tendency have revealed a wide interborough diversity in outputs. In the four county boroughs selected for intensive study, analyses further corroborated the finding that both the actual levels of resources allocated and the levels of service provision varied substantially among the county boroughs. These aspects of the research were suggestive that each county borough had developed, over time, its own "critical policy style." The critical question has been whether certain explanations of budget-making account for these local-level differences.

Evaluating the Explanatory Approaches

The basic concern of this book has been to evaluate the adequacy of various approaches which explain financial resource allocation. Among the approaches examined, five have been examined in some detail: (1) the demographic approach; (2) the naive econometric models; (3) the organizational-process approach; (4) the cognitive-limits approach; and (5) the configurative, individual-level perspective. Other approaches, such as the normative-process model, and the rational-choice model have been considered briefly.

Most of these explanatory modes have been characterized as "approaches" rather than as "paradigms," "conceptual frameworks," or "models." There is much discussion among philosophers of science and of social science about the distinction between these kinds of concepts.[1] The notion of approach in this study is similar to Merton's concept of "general orientation." An approach consists of a set of empirical generalizations that possess a common focus and it identifies sets of interrelated variables. But an approach does not fully specify the dynamic relationships among variables, and there is no necessary structural correspondence between relationships among variables and among real-world phenomena.[2]

The notion of "explanation" also requires clarification. While social scientists disagree on what it means to explain social phenomena,[3] most would accept Mayer's observation that an explanation:

> Seeks to answer the question, "why did that event or state of affairs occur rather than another? . . . (The) "why" question about a social or political "fact" is answered by subsuming or integrating that fact in a more general proposition, by relating the fact, in other words, to another fact or concept. The more general proposition (or covering law as Hempel calls it) entails the fact to be explained.[4]

In a "complete" explanation, all antecedent causes which are necessary and sufficient conditions for the occurrence of y (the fact) are specified under a general law.[5] Most social-scientific research fails to achieve even "incomplete explanation," which:

> Implies a precise statement of the empirical implications of the premises or covering laws. . . . When the observable expectations deduced from a covering law cannot be precisely specified (generally due to the use of imprecisely defined concepts in the covering law), the proposition generates explanatory appeal but not explanatory power.[6]

It is apparent that the approaches examined in the attempt to explain budgetary allocations are at the level of explanatory appeal. The imprecision of both covering laws and empirical indicators has been evident in every approach considered. Consequently, there are no rigorous or clear-cut criteria for assessing the "adequacy of explanation" of the approaches to budgetary allocations. These explanatory sketches are ex post facto, probabilistic, identify only a few key variables, and are based on extremely vague covering laws. Thus adequacy is necessarily determined subjectively. One can ask whether an approach is particularly helpful in establishing regularities and uniform patterns among the phenomena being studied.

One basic issue in assessing the five approaches is whether they share a common theoretical perspective. In examining resource allocation decisions, there are two central theoretical questions: (1) how is the existing pattern of allocations explained; and (2) how is the creation of the new budget explained? The first question is about the particular *levels* of resource allocations; the second question concerns the process by which the allocations *change* (that is, "the budgetary process"). It is reasonable to expect that the factors which might explain allocation levels will be relatively static and history-dependent in the shorter run, and that those which might explain allocation change will be relatively dynamic and current.

A second issue is the distinction between explanations in terms of causes and in terms of reasons.[7] On the one hand, an approach which explains resource allocations in terms of *causes* specifies certain conditions or events which seem to produce budgetary *outputs*. The explanation is based on the co-relation (in its broadest sense) between the causes and the outputs. On the other hand, an explanation in terms of *reasons* attempts to make the *process* of budget-making intelligible. The objective is to provide Popper's "logic of the situation" for behavioral phenomena, which are viewed as purposive and rule-following.

Most research on resource allocations has focused either on allocation levels or on allocation changes; but the distinction between the explanatory modes of causes and of reasons has seldom been made explicit. Virtually all explanations of change, for example, typically posit causes or reasons that would lead to the expectation of incremental changes. Since most changes are, in fact, relatively incremental, it appears that a predicted linkage (and hence the particular explanation) has been verified. But the covering laws are imprecise and there is rarely a critical test to distinguish between competing explanations. Thus it is not evident that the particular causes or reasons utilized in a given study to explain allocation changes are necessarily a more valid explanation than untested rival hypotheses. Moreover, most studies of allocation changes have operated as if an explanation of process is also an explanation of output, and vice versa. Until theory progresses beyond explanation sketches, the process-output linkage will be another source of conceptual confusion.

These distinctions between levels and changes, and between causes and reasons suggest that it is useful to conceptualize a contingency table like that in Table 8.1. The five major explanatory approaches applied in this study can be classified with differing degrees of tidiness. The demographic approach is clearly an explanation of the antecedent causes which produce certain levels of allocative outputs.[8] The naive econometric models attempt to identify simple, abstract decision rules which produce systematic patterns of change in allocations.

While the configurative approach is most usefully applied to the issue of how certain levels of allocation occurred, the

Table 8.1: Conceptual Foci of the Explanatory Approaches

| | Explanation of: | |
	Allocation Levels	Allocation Changes
Causes (of Outputs)	Demographic Approach	Naive Econometric Models
Reasons (for Process)	Configurative, Individual-Level Perspective	Organizational-Process Approach Cognitive-Limits Approach

Explanation in terms of:

cognitive-limits and organizational-process approaches are primarily concerned with the question of how the changes in allocations occur. And, by incorporating historical-trend data into its perspective, the organizational-process approach also takes on characteristics of a cause explanation of allocation changes. The use of a PPB-version of the rational-choice is not included in the table because none of the four boroughs employed techniques which even vaguely resemble PPB or its variants. Given the classifications in Table 8.1, it is useful to reiterate briefly the strengths and deficiencies of each of the explanatory approaches for government resource allocation.

EXPLAINING ALLOCATION LEVELS

The *demographic approach* is most successful in estimating the general configuration of expenditure levels across all the county boroughs. With a limited set of social, economic, and political variables, the approach yields equations which estimate most of the interborough variation on levels of total expenditure per head, rates levied per head, extensiveness of housing provision, burden of housing rent, and total spending on the major education services. This study has provided solid evidence that the resource base and the political disposition of the county borough are powerful constraints on the aggregate spending level of a county borough. But in contrast with most studies of American states and municipalities, there were few systematic and significant linkages between demographic variables and most indicators of resource allocations, measured as either money spent or level of provision. Thus the approach produced satisfactory explanations in terms of causes for a few major expenditure categories; but the demographic approach does not have general explanatory appeal for resource allocation levels in the county boroughs.

The configurative perspective identified important individual-level characteristics in each budgeting system. It has virtually no covering laws and does not meet even the minimal criteria to qualify as an "approach." It is, however, a useful explanation in terms of reasons for certain allocation levels in particular county boroughs. Specifically, in those cases where a borough's allocation level for a spending category was distinctive (that is, somehow non-normal), a configurative, individual-level factor usually provided the most plausible explanation of that distinctiveness. These factors typically involved the entrepreneurial style or political agenda of a key budgetary role-actor in an appointive or elective position. While such configurative explanations seem compelling in deviant case analysis, they are not well-suited to explain most allocations and they are difficult to operationalize in a generalizable, analytic fashion. At this point, such configurative explanations are best understood as a residual category with explanatory appeal only in instances where decisions are atypical or unexpected.

EXPLAINING ALLOCATION CHANGES

The *naive econometric models* specify several different dynamics which might correspond to the configuration of year-to-year changes in allocations. Each dynamic is simple and bases its explanation on the distillation of one or more incrementalist "imperatives" into a single causal force—for example, the allocation of a certain rate of increase to all accounts or the maintenance of the relative share of each account. One of the models, which bases its predictions on the absolute size of the allocation figure, has extraordinary predictive power; but we have argued that this is rather more a statistical artifact than an illuminating explanation. None of the three naive models operationalized in terms of rates of change or proportions of total allocation has a striking level of predictive power (as an indicator of explanatory adequacy) for the four county boroughs' allocation changes. But this generalization is insensitive to the wide variability in explanatory appeal across boroughs and across services. The model which predicts that a spending category will maintain its share of the total (the base-budget model) is particularly successful in several boroughs and on certain services, including spending on parks and on primary education (among the services selected for analysis). The strict-incremental model revealed that there are a considerable number of cases where rates of change alternated somewhat systematically between substantial increase and low/no increase years. And one county borough showed moderate support for a model (the fair-share model) positing that all services are granted allocation increases comparable to the increase in total spending. In sum, the naive economic models do provide adequate levels of explanation for the longitudinal changes in the allocations to certain services in certain county boroughs. And the explanatory appeal of these models is considerably enhanced by their parsimony and generalizability. More extensive empirical research in a variety of contexts is required to specify more fully the conditions under which each model is most adequate.

The *organizational-process approach* is grounded in an analytic representation of the process by which the government-as-problem-solving-system does budget-making. In specifying and linking behavioral repetoires, standard operating procedures, and decision constraints, the approach can make understandable the process by which the allocations change. In the four county boroughs, there seem to be two different organizational processes for budget-making. One modality is more fluid and is more contingent upon the variable contributions and interactions of particular role-actors; the other modality is quite structured, with a generalized problem-solving routine and reasonably stable decision parameters. It is the latter modality, evident in Dudley and West Bromwich, for which the organizational-process approach provides a substantial level of explanatory appeal. The conceptual elements of the approach are rather less useful for transforming configurative factors into analytic variables in the two more fluid, budgeting systems. There is an additional dimension of combinatorial richness in the organizational-process approach, because it can be integrated with an approach based on historical-trend data (like the naive models). Crecine accomplished this fusion in his important simulation models of budget-making in three American municipalities. Although the budget-making solution in the county boroughs is substantially more complex and less amenable to such a model, a simulation is feasible, particularly for the more structured budgeting systems. In this sense, the organizational-process approach is the most promising of the explanatory approaches examined. It is the fullest of the explanatory sketches, has less rudimentary covering laws than the other approaches, and, most importantly, it has the potential to provide an explanation of both reasons and causes for allocative changes.

The *cognitive-limits approach* also attempts to make behavior understandable by identifying generalized techniques which role-actors employ to simplify and to make more manageable the complicated problem of budget-making. But the approach does not seem capable of specifying the differential impact of these techniques upon the behavioral process. More importantly, the explanation seems limited to the prototypical role-actor. While the approach explains the "logic of the situation" for the individual budgeter, it fails to provide insight about uncommon actors, about systems of roles, or about decision parameters. And the most significant propositions of this approach seem to be subsumed under the more comprehensive perspective of the organizational-process approach.

THE APPROACHES AS ALTERNATIVE EXPLANATIONS

This research suggests that there are environmental determinants which constrain the level of resources allocated to certain services, that there are systematic patterns of longitudinal change in allocations for some services, and that there are significant regularities in the problem-solving process by which a new budget is created (that is, there is a decision-making structure as defined in Chapter 1). None of the approaches examined in this book deals explicitly with all three types of phenomena. Normally, one or even two of these concerns are treated as relatively constant, while the approach provides an explanatory sketch for the other aspect.

It should be clear from Table 8.1 and the subsequent discussion that *these approaches are, at most points, alternative rather than competing explanations.* Given the present stage of theory-building and empirical research, these approaches provide complementary rather than mutually exclusive explanations. To the extent that the approaches are appropriately classified in different cells of Table 8.1, there is either a difference in the resource allocation phenomena which each approach attempts to explain or a difference in the type of explanation which is generated. Only the cognitive-limits and organizational-process approaches are competing explanations, and even these approaches differ in the object level of analysis. A "complete" theoretical explanation would need to fulfill the requirements of explanatory adequacy for at least two of the four cells.

This implies that, in the short-run, the most appropriate research strategy is to continue to factor the analysis of budgetary processes into a set of individual research problems. The explanatory capacity of any approach is low and an attempt to fuse the strengths of various approaches seems premature. It does seem desirable, however, that individual research designs employ the approaches in a framework that is comparative in two senses. First, budgetary research should deal with more than one object unit of analysis. Only demographic-approach studies have typically dealt with more than one budgeting system. This study of the county boroughs reveals that there can be considerable variation both in the nature of the budget-making process and in the configurations of budgetary outputs. The validity of generalizations based on any single system seem particularly problematic. Secondly, research ought to compare alternative explanatory approaches. A meaningful assessment of the explanatory/predictive capacity of an approach should be, at least in part, contingent upon comparing it to plausible rival hypotheses. Moreover, such a comparative framework would make it more difficult to "smuggle in" hypotheses and data that are based on a variety of approaches without specifying the assumptions, the perspective, and the theoretical consistency between these approaches and the apparent explanatory mode. Thus the desideratum for theory-building is a series of studies, each of which utilizes alternative approaches and multiple types of data within a set of comparable research settings.

Budgetary Decision-Making in Different Cultural Contexts

It is important to consider whether the process of budgetary decision-making in local-level governments is culture-bound. Most behavioral research on budget-making has dealt with Anglo-American examples. Wildavsky's recent work provides the strongest evidence for the assumption that at least some budgetary processes are comparable cross-culturally, for both national-level and local-level systems.[9] One might particularly expect such comparability among those English-speaking societies influenced by the Westminster model of government. The present research, in the context of British urban government, provides data on this point. The findings on county-borough budget-making suggest that the behavior and outputs correspond substantially with those described in various studies of American municipalities. In each setting, the budget is essentially an incremental solution based on marginal adjustments of the existing configuration of allocations. The same decision short-cuts characterize most participants in budgeting. And the problem-solving routines in the county boroughs are not unlike those established in American cities.[10]

While this research supports the broad generalization of comparability between American and British municipalities, there are important divergences. The general failure, in the county-borough context, of the demographic approach—whether the dimensions tapped are economic, or social, or political—is notable. In explaining this difference, the revenue-equalizing effect of the large transfer payments (in the form of unearmarked grants-in-aid) from the central government to the county borough and the cost-equalizing effect of national wage scales are crucial factors. It is also likely that the homogeneity of the county boroughs (relative to American states or municipalities) and the concentration of service jurisdictions at the county-borough level (relative to the overlapping areal division of functions in America) contribute to a large decrease in the correlation between allocation decisions and aggregate-level demographic differences.

Wildavsky has made an important attempt to generalize about the processes of local-level budgeting. His synthesis relies primarily upon several American examples. He identifies four central characteristics of these systems: (1) revenue behavior—resource allocation is constrained by the paucity of revenues and the requirements for a balanced budget; (2) the dominance of the chief executive in the budgetary process; (3) the acquiescence of the council in nonpartisan settings, but greater council involvement in partisan settings; and (4) the tendency of departments to make "utopian" requests for resources.[11]

In the county boroughs examined, only some of these generalizations are supported. The county boroughs clearly reflect revenue behavior, given the constraints on new resources and the obligation to balance the budget. However, there is no single executive role that dominates county-borough budgeting, possibly due to the absence of a functional equivalent to the American city manager or strong mayor. While the combined behavior of the Treasurer and Finance Committee Chairman in Brighton has some correspondence to the dominant executive, they are at least a dual executive and operate with independent agendas. Moreover, in budgeting systems like that in Dudley, there is no critical executive actor, and the most important single participant is a middle-level bureaucrat in the Finance Department. With respect to council's role, the councils in the four county boroughs are quite acquiescent *despite* the strong partisan nature of the ward-based representative system. Finally, most departments in the four county boroughs are modest rather than utopian in their initial budget requests. Although a few chief officers gain the reputation of "wanting the earth," most behave with restraint in order to maintain the credibility of the pruners. Only the unique "logic" of West Bromwich's budgeting system seems to have stimulated departments to be boldly expansive in their requests for new and upgraded services. Thus the variance between Wildavsky's generalizations and those most appropriate for the county boroughs amplifies the observation that there seem to be different organizational-process models of local budget-making.

Moreover, the local-level budget-making process is substantially more fluid in some of the county boroughs than in American municipalities. In American cities with a strong executive (strong mayor or manager), there tend to be clearly demarcated episodes in which departments formulate a package of requests, then the executive receives these requests and develops his own budget package, which is approved by the legislative body. This process is embodied in the Crecine model as a set of distinct, linear stages. In some of the county boroughs, however, there was constant interaction and mutual adjustment between spending units and pruning actors, and there was no integral set of estimates prior to those sent to Council. In these cases, the procedure was dominated by continual negotiations between professional administrators in the Finance Department and in the spending departments. Indicative of the dominance of professional officers is the fact that in three of the county boroughs, there was no specific episode where any elected member(s) performed a meaningful, comprehensive review of allocation requests.

The research supports the notion that the differences between budget creation in American and British municipalities are a consequence of variation in *structural variables*. That is, differences can be explained in terms of variation in such factors as the areal distribution of functions, the nature of the local executive, the system of finance, and the distribution of power and discretion between elected members and the professional bureaucracy. County-borough budget-making has been characterized by an extremely weak executive, by interborough equalization of resources, by a wide range of locally controlled functions, and by the large area of discretion available to the borough's officers, especially the Treasurer. It is not appropriate to draw cross-cultural comparisons too fully, since the present research was not formulated to generate such analysis. However, these points are suggestive of the structural variables underlying cross-cultural differences.[12] This type of Anglo-American comparison certainly merits further analysis. And, at a broader level, it appears that such research could incorporate certain other cultures. Although there are undoubtedly cultural variations,[13] bureaucratic problem-solving is an area of cross-cultural research in which there are likely to be substantial structural similarities.

Budgeting and Democratic Participation

In concluding this study, it is interesting to consider briefly the question of democratic participation in budgeting. The mainstream of normative budgeting theory is closely aligned with pluralist theory.[14] Stated oversimply, pluralist theory assumes that all groups have some political resources with which to influence public-policy decisions. In most cases, only a few groups utilize their resources. Other groups are generally satisfied and only become actively involved when there is an issue of great importance to them or when they are adversely affected by a decision. These inactive groups do continually influence the decisions undertaken, however, since the budgeters anticipate their demands and are constrained by them. Both the organizational-process approach and the cognitive-limits approach, especially the latter, rely strongly on such feedback in justifying the "democraticness" of budgetary decision-making.[15]

This analysis of the four boroughs has indicated that budget-making is characterized by extremely limited participation. In each case, a very small number of pivotal role-actors determine the nature of budgetary changes between Y_{t-1} and Y_t. This group, normally composed of certain chief officers and an elected councillor, translates diverse policy possibilities into an actual package of resource allocations. Clearly, there is, within each county borough, a budget-making "elite" which controls the crucial combination of resources: expertise and position.

This might reflect nothing more than the "necessity," on complex and rather technical decisions, for a few specialists to make decisions on behalf of the many. But the analysis of budgetary decision-making in Chapters 6 and 7 implies rather more than this. The findings provide little support for the view that the budget-making systems are generally open to citizen inputs, or that they are particularly responsive to community demands and feedback. Rather, the evidence has shown that the budget-making systems are structured to insulate important budgetary actors from public demands regarding resource allocation.

One aspect of this insulation is the internal procedures of the budgetary process itself. Organizational processes have been identified which physically insulate budgeters from both the public and from each other. All budgetary meetings prior to the Council's pro forma acceptance of the final budget are private and confidential. In the 4 to 6 months during which the estimates are developed, most relevant information is communicated through limited and closed channels controlled by the Borough Treasurer. The information available to most budgetary participants is fragmentary, limited to the specific substantive area with which they deal. Only the senior finance department officers and the Finance Committee Chairman (and executive officer boards in Dudley and Southend) have comprehensive information about total available resources and about the pattern and implications of competing requests for resources. Hence only a few individuals have access to sufficient information to consider the broad choices implicit in the resource allocation process.

Insulation is also assured by the manner in which the problems and subproblems of budget-making are defined. In all four county boroughs, the visible subproblems are defined at extreme levels of abstraction and/or specificity. In Brighton, for example, decision-making is fragmented into 1,600 separate "votes" and virtually everyone outside the budgetary elite has inadequate information and perspective to operate beyond the level of the individual line-item. In contrast, decision-making in

Dudley seems limited to the determination of the total rate share to each spending department on the basis of mechanical formulae. Moreover, there is a willingness among relevant actors in the four systems to define nearly all existing expenditure as "uncontrollable" and hence beyond the scope of current decision-making. The consequence of these kinds of factors is that the apparent decisions seem to be driven by technical criteria and the systems do not explicate basic value choices or opportunity costs, at least not in a manner that makes evaluation feasible for those outside the elite.

This physical insulation of budgeters is also revealed by the limited amount of feedback they perceive from interested publics. Few external groups are sufficiently informed and motivated to make concrete demands to budget-makers. Moreover, significant decision makers are separated from these publics by several levels of efficient gate-keepers, particularly the Councillors. And most of the messages which do reach the top budget makers are dealt with by devaluing the information or its source, since budgeters often define either the group, their demand, or the modes of expressing the demand as inappropriate. Specific demands are typically interpreted as manifestations of naive self-interest, since they do not consider the totality of needs, resources, and competing demands.

The Councillors are not very responsive to community demands for resources, apart from the generalized pressure to limit taxes. With occasional exceptions, Councillors do not believe that allocation decisions will enhance their constituency strength or their electoral support. The electorate retains the ultimate sanction of depriving the Councillors of their seats; but the actual linkage of this sanction with budgetary decisions is tenuous. Officers are even less sympathetic to such community inputs unless these can serve as evidence to support their own expenditure agenda. In fact, most budgeting feedback is in the form of "withinputs"[16] from field-level personnel in the spending departments. This information is transmitted up to the Chief Officer, who takes it into account when deliberating on his estimates. Some of these demands do originate at the service interface in the community; but they are, in most cases, demands created by staff "bright ideas" rather than generated directly by the citizenry. Indeed, the prevalent source of these ideas is not citizens but external reference groups, other local authorities, central departments, or the professional organizations of officers. Except as an extremely vague constraint, community feedback on county-borough budgetary decisions is minimal and seldom important.

A crucial substantive finding of this study is that the *essential nature of the resource allocation process insulates those with decision-making discretion, especially the officers, from public demands, from visibility, and even from public accountability.* To some extent, such insulation can be justified on the grounds of the technicality and the complexity of budget-making as a problem. However it is our conclusion that this system is sustained for another reason: key budgeters prefer and facilitate it. The mythology surrounding the process, the apparent fragmentation of decision-making, and the relative monopoly of most information are consciously maintained, since they serve to simplify the pressures of resource allocation on the major budgetary decision makers. The budgetary elite prefers an efficient, unencumbered problem-solving system to a system which facilitates participation and open communication. The four budgeting systems in this study clearly serve their preferences. It is evident that these systems are controlled by competent and benevolent technocrats; but the situation invites concern about the limits upon "democratic citizen involvement." These resource allocation systems seem fully congruent with Amery's observation that government in Britain is of and for the people, but not by the people.

NOTES

1. See, for example, Arthur Kalleberg, "The Logic of Comparison," *World Politics,* 19 (January 1966), p. 72 ff. on conceptual frameworks and approaches; May Brodbeck, "Models, Meaning and Theory" in *Symposium on Sociological Theory,* edited by Llewellyn Gross (New York: Harper & Row, 1959), pp. 373-403

on structural correspondence between a model and phenomena; the best known discussion of paradigm is Thomas Kuhn, *The Structure of Scientific Revolutions* (Chicago: Univ. Press, 1962). A more general discussion of these ideas is Lawrence Meyer, *Comparative Political Inquiry* (Homewood: Dorsey, 1972).

2. On "general orientation," see Robert Merton, *Social Theory and Social Structure* (New York: Free Press, 1957), p. 142. This also relates to Kaplan's "concatenated" theory. See Abraham Kaplan, *The Conduct of Inquiry* (San Francisco: Chandler, 1964), p. 298 ff.

3. See, for example, Vernon Van Dyke, *Political Science: A Philosophical Analysis* (Stanford: Univ. Press, 1960), esp. 22, 22-51; Eugene Meehan, *Contemporary Political Thought: A Critical Study* (Homewood: Dorsey Press, 1967), p. 96 ff; John Gunnell, "Deduction, Explanation, and Social Scientific Inquiry," *APSR*, 63, No. 4 (December 1969), pp. 1233-1246; Arthur Goldberg, "On the Need for Contextualist Criteria: A Reply to Professor Gunnell," *APSR*, 63, No. 4 (December 1969), pp. 1247-1250, and the subsequent notes by A. James Gregor and Gunnell.

4. Mayer, op. cit., pp. 20-21.

5. Ibid., p. 23. See also May Brodbeck, "Explanation, Prediction, and Imperfect Knowledge" in *Readings in the Philosophy of Social Science* (New York: Macmillan, 1968), p. 363 ff.

6. Mayer, op. cit., p. 25. The notion of "explanatory appeal" is found in Carl Hempel, *Aspects of Scientific Explanation and Other Essays in the Philosophy of Science* (New York: Free Press, 1965), pp. 22-33.

7. On the distinction made between explanations in terms of reasons and in terms of causes, see Van Dyke, op. cit., pp. 22-33.

8. A considerable body of recent work based on the demographic approach does use a dynamic-change framework rather than a static approach. Dependent and independent variables are typically measured as change ratios or as time-series data and loosely causal models of allocation change are applied to the data. See, for example, Barry Ames and Ed Goff, "Education and Defense Expenditures in Latin America: 1948-68," in *Comparative Public Policy: Issues, Theories and Methods,* eds. Craig Liske, William Loehr, and John McCamant (New York: Wiley-Halsted, 1975).

9. Wildavsky (1975), op. cit.

10. There is a general correspondence between these research findings and those in the American context at both state and local levels. Examples of that research include: Crecine, op. cit.; Barber, op. cit.; Thomas Anton, *The Politics of State Expenditure in Illinois* (Urbana: Univ. of Illinois Press, 1960); and Gerwin (1969b), op. cit. The same point holds for many national-level studies, including: Wildavsky (1964), op. cit.; and Ira Sharkansky, *The Routines of Politics* (New York: Van Nostrand Reinhold, 1970).

11. Wildavsky (1975), op. cit., Chapter 6, esp. pp. 128-131.

12. These kinds of observations accord with Przeworski and Teune's point that "the bridge between historical observations and general theory is the substitution of variables for proper names of social systems in the course of comparative research." Przeworski and Teune, op. cit., p. 25.

13. A classic example of cultural effects, in the context of bureaucratic behavior, is Michael Crozier, *The Bureaucratic Phenomenon* (Chicago: Univ. Press, 1964); in a non-Western context, see Lucien Pye, *Politics, Personality, and Nation-Building* (New Haven: Yale Univ. Press, 1961), esp. ch. 15 and 16.

14. The classic explication of pluralist theory is Dahl, op. cit., esp. Books IV-VI. For a discussion of group theory, see James Bill and Robert Hardgrave, *Comparative Politics: The Quest for Theory* (Columbus: Merrill, 1973), ch. 4. David Ricci, *Community Power and Democratic Theory* (New York: Random House, 1971) contains an interesting discussion of both group and pluralist theory in local-level politics.

15. See, for example, Braybrooke and Lindblom, op. cit.; also Aaron Wildavsky, "Political Implications of Budgetary Reform," *Public Administration Review,* XXI (Autumn 1961), pp. 183-190.

16. This concept, denoting demand inputs from within the political system, is from David Easton, *A Systems Analysis of Political Life* (New York: Wiley, 1965).

APPENDIX A

SELECTION AND CHARACTERISTICS OF
THE FOUR COUNTY BOROUGHS

I. Selected Characteristics

Chapter 1 discussed the method by which four county boroughs were selected for intensive study. A number of selection schemes, based on indices using objective measures of various local political, social, and economic characteristics were examined. These schemes produced groupings of county boroughs which were more or less arbitrary. As a consequence, less rigid selection criteria were utilized. The object was to identify units of analysis which were substantively interesting. Research economies were a secondary consideration. Hence the four county boroughs examined in the study should not be viewed as "modal" in any sense.

One research decision bearing on the selection of units has been to compromise the choice between the "most similar systems" and the "most dissimilar systems" analytic frameworks. All units of analysis were to be selected from a similar population-size grouping; but, on the basis of certain other characteristics, two subsets were to be distinguished. Units within each subset were to share these characteristics, which would generally contrast between the subsets. The primary criteria employed to differentiate the subsets of county boroughs were the class structure and the age structure of the population. There was also an attempt to achieve some comparability within each subset on other characteristics, including geographic location, financial resource base, and party-political composition on Council.

By means of these criteria, Brighton and Southend-on-Sea on the one hand ("Set I"), and Dudley and West Bromwich on the other ("Set II") were selected for analysis. The four county boroughs were closely matched

Table A.1

		Brighton	Southend	Dudley	West Bromwich
Class Structure					
1. % professional and managerial — Census Classes 1,2,3,4,13	(actual)	15.6	20.7	11.6	8.2
	(rank order)	69	78	38	10
2. % skilled working class — Census Classes 8,9,12,14	(actual)	38.4	32.5	49.9	49.6
	(rank order)	19	2	76.5	76.5
3. % unskilled laborers — Census Class 11	(actual)	7.9	5.8	9.6	10.3
	(rank order)	11	6	39	47
Age Structure					
4. % of population under age 15	(actual)	18.1	19.7	22.6	23.5
	(rank order)	6	8	29	49
5. % of population over age 65	(actual)	19.2	19.0	10.2	9.6
	(rank order)	77	76	8	6

on population, which ranged (1967-1968) from 162,000 to 178,000. Set-II county boroughs experienced substantial growth in population and area through amalgamations in the mid-1960s, while Set-I boroughs were stable. *Class structure* was measured objectively, by Census occupation categories. Relative to the entire set of county boroughs existing in 1968-1969 (N = 83), Brighton and Southend have a very high proportion of professional and managerial types, and a very low proportion of both skilled manual workers and unskilled laborers. Dudley and West Bromwich, in contrast, have a small professional-managerial class, a very large skilled working class, and median level of unskilled laborers. The *age structure* was examined at the extremes (that is, the proportion of the population aged under 15 and over 65), since these groups place particularly heavy demands on the governmental provision of goods and services. Set-I county boroughs have a very high proportion of elderly persons and a very low proportion of young persons. Table A.1 of this appendix presents the rank order and the actual values for the objective measures used to distinguish the two subsets on these criteria.

In geographic terms, Brighton and Southend are independent cities in southeast England, are near the coast, are bordered by rural areas, and are about one hour by commuter train from London. Dudley and West Bromwich are satellite cities (to Birmingham) in the West Midlands, an urbanized area. The Set-I county boroughs are commercial and resort towns, with extensive facilities and accommodations for holiday-makers. Set-II are primarily industrial towns in the heart of the Black Country, whose name was inspired by industrial pollution. Relative to the Set-I boroughs, Set-II boroughs have lower levels both of personal wealth (measured as value of domestic-property units) and of community wealth (measured as rateable value per head). The Councils of West Bromwich and, to a lesser degree, Dudley have reasonably strong Labour Party representation. In Brighton, the Conservatives clearly dominate Council. In Southend, the Conservatives are normally in control; but the Liberals fluctuate in strength, resulting in periods of a three-party system.

The Set-I and Set-II county boroughs should not be viewed as the extremes of some typology for all county boroughs. There are a number of characteristics upon which these subsets are either indistinguishable or group differently. Moreover, it is likely that other subsets could be identified by stipulating certain other criteria. There is a strong case, however, that the four county boroughs studied are substantively interesting both as similar-dissimilar units of analysis and as illuminating cases from among the entire group of county boroughs. Table A.2 displays the values of

Table A.2

		Brighton	Southend	Dudley	West Bromwich
RESOURCES					
1.	Rateable value per head (April 1, 1968)	£ 73.4	£ 51.4	£ 43.0	£ 48.3
2.	Standard product of the penny rate (1968)	£31,756	£32,024	£34,616	£33,235
3.	Product of the penny rate per local education-authority pupil (1968) in pence	530	342	267	258
4.	% of rateable value in domestic property (1968)	60.1	62.3	47.6	37.4
5.	% of domestic rateable value in units—value greater than £100	77.1	46.1	9.8	4.8
NEED-PERSONAL					
6.	Primary-school pupils per 1,000 population (1968)	80	85	101	107
7.	Secondary-school pupils per 1,000 population (1968)	52	60	59	68
8.	% of males over 25 whose terminal-education age was under 15 (1961)	67.6	64.1	79.6	79.9
9.	% of males over 25 whose terminal-education age was over 25 [includes continuing education group] (1961)	3.4	3.3	1.7	1.5
10.	"New commonwealth country" immigrants per 10,000 population (1966)	129	134	127	289
NEED-ENVIRONMENT					
11.	Population (1968)	162,160	165,760	177,760	172,650
12.	Population density per acre (1968)	11.3	16.2	12.0	14.7
13.	% of population living in accommodation with a density greater than 1.0 per room (1966)	10.9	7.6	11.2	17.4
14.	% of population living in accommodations with exclusive use of the four standard amenities [hot and cold water, WC, fixed bath] (1966)	70.3	76.9	79.7	78.9
15.	Number of within-county-borough migrations per 1,000 (1961-1966)	207	194	194	192
16.	Net county-borough-migration balance per 1,000 (1961-1966)	+6	+38	+34	−2
DISPOSITION					
17.	% of Council membership who are members of the Labour Party average for 1965-1966 to 1967-1968	28	30	51	50
18.	Index of interparty competition on Council—perfect competition: 1.0 (average for 1965-1966 to 1967-1968)	.58	.85	.89	.89
19.	% of total units of housing provided which were built by the local authority (1960-1965)	25	22	67	61
20.	Net outstanding debt per head (1968)	£ 269.3	£ 163.3	£ 250.2	£ 285.1

various objective measures which characterize aspects of Brighton, Dudley, Southend, and West Bromwich.

II. Data for the County Boroughs of Brighton, Dudley, Southend-on-Sea, and West Bromwich

A. QUANTITATIVE ALLOCATION DATA

One aspect of addressing the substantive questions in this research has been a more thorough analysis, for the four county boroughs, of variables from the large data set. There was also extensive gathering of further information from the four county boroughs. In particular, detailed expenditure data was compiled for each year between fiscal 1959-1960 and 1969-1970. Less detailed allocation figures for each county borough were recorded for alternate years since 1945-1946. And expenditure on the main service functions was also recorded for alternate years since the early 1920s, in order to examine long-term developments. The source of this data was the official General Revenue Account audits, which were kindly made available by each Finance Department. In order to minimize the interunit differences in account categories, a classification schedule was developed by the researcher. This organized the allocation data in a uniform way that enhances the comparability of the figures.

B. INTERVIEW DATA

All activities of the budget-creation process, except the meeting at which Council formally approves the rate and the budget, are held in private. Similarly, all documents circulated during the period in which estimates are developed, evaluated, and modified are strictly confidential. Consequently, the construction of an analytic description of the process was, of necessity, based primarily on the statements of participants. The researcher has attempted to assess the various and sometimes conflicting testimonies in order to construct what appears to me to be the most satisfactory explication.

The participants approached were generally very receptive and did their utmost to be helpful. A large number of confidential documents and communiques of relevance were shown or given to me. These were invaluable in grasping certain parts of the process; but they could not be detailed in this paper due to their confidential nature. Similarly, some actors, particularly officers, who are in a delicate position, discussed matters upon which they did not wish to be quoted. Where possible, their important answers have been used with sufficient anonymity to satisfy our agreement; where this was not possible, the points have been incorporated into the observations of the researcher.

Drastic simplification was necessary in many aspects of the methodology, a major one being the selection of interviewees. Prior to field work, choices were made, on the basis of the available literature, concerning the identity of key roles. Interviews with these people occasionally led the researcher to other role-actors who were found to be important participants. This use of "snowball sampling" was the technique for attempting to achieve adequate breadth among interviewees. There was not one suggestion that a member of the community other than a Councillor, past Councillor, or county-borough employee was an important contributor to the resource allocation process.

The "typicality" of some of those interviewed is, of course, a matter of judgment. It was quite impossible for the researcher to interview all Spending Committees, all Chief Officers and their senior staff, and so on. A research decision was made to focus intensively on a few selected spending departments and their corresponding spending committees. Specifically, research focused on the area of personal social services and local health services and on the area of public works (including highways provision and maintenance, sewers and sewerage, and so on). The financial officers interviewed were those whose duties related to these spending areas. Members of the Finance and Establishment Committees were also interviewed. The researcher is aware of the danger of generalizing from a limited and possibly biased sample. However, there were numerous cross-references in the comments of various actors and all spending committees were discussed in detail at some point. Moreover, the evidence suggests that the variations in process are not clearly linked to systematic differences across functional spending areas. In general, the researcher is convinced that the selection of departments and interviewees was adequate to support the reliability and validity of the analysis.

The form of the interviews varied with the person interviewed and the time available. Some interviews were quite open-ended: general questions were asked and then "guided" questioning was used during the course of the discussion. In short or in follow-up interviews, a rather tight interview schedule was often used. While such questions were framed to direct attention to a specific matter, they were meant to allow the interviewee a substantial range of response. With few exceptions, there was no "sought" answer inherent in the question. In any case, respondents were quite loquacious. Replies were seldom less than two minutes and, with follow-up queries, an average question would take about eight minutes. Interviewees were told at the outset that the questions were "suggestive" and that they should object to any question which they felt was inappropriately framed or missed the point. Normally, interviews were recorded on tape and transcribed afterwards. It is the researcher's opinion that in most interviews the rapport was very good and the responses were genuine and considered. In each of the four county boroughs, I was under the supervision and guidance of a senior officer in the Finance Department. These gentlemen not only arranged all interviews but also "legitimized" my research enterprise to those I was to meet.

The basic list of specific roles whose holders were interviewed varied among the county boroughs only to the extent necessitated by unfilled positions or illness. Normally, at least the following role-actors were interviewed:

(1) each Spending Department: Chief Officer, Senior Administrative Officer;

(2) each Spending Committee: Chairman, one other member;

(3) Finance Department: Borough Treasurer, one or more Senior Finance Officers (e.g., Deputy Borough Treasurer, Assistant Borough Treasurer, Foreward Planning Officer, and so forth), Chief Accountant, Senior Accountants;

(4) Finance Committee: Chairman, one other member.

In addition to this set of roles, other persons in the local authority structure or in the community were interviewed, where relevant. In cases where more than one political party had recently been the Council Majority (Dudley and West Bromwich), both past and present holders of certain key roles were interviewed. In each county borough, representatives of every political group on Council were interviewed. On average, 34 persons were interviewed at least once in each of the four county boroughs, and the average interview was about 90 minutes.

APPENDIX B

SOURCES OF DATA

The County-Borough Data (N=77)

SOURCES

A. Children's Service Statistics
   Education Service Statistics
   Fire Service Statistics
   Housing Statistics
   Library Service Statistics
   Local Health Services Statistics
   Police Service Statistics
   Welfare Services Statistics
   prepared by the Institute of Municipal Treasurers and Accountants (London: Lowes, Ltd., 1960-1961; 1964-1965; 1968-1969).

B. Return of the Rates, prepared by the Institute of Municipal Treasurers and Accountants (London: Lowes, Ltd., 1960-1961; 1964-1965; 1968-1969).

C. Census of England and Wales (including The County Reports; Migration Tables; Education Tables; Commonwealth Immigrant Tables), The General Register Office (London: H.M.S.O., 1961).

D. Sample Census of England and Wales (including The County Reports; Migration Tables; Commonwealth Immigrant Tables), The General Register Office (London: H.M.S.O., 1966).

E. Rates and Rateable Values in England and Wales. Ministry of Housing and Local Government (London: H.M.S.O., 1964; 1968).

F. The Municipal Yearbook (London: Longmans, yearly 1957-1970).

G. Housing Return for England and Wales, The Ministry of Housing and Local Government (London: H.M.S.O., 1960; 1965).

H. Statistical Review, The Registrar General (London: H.M.S.O., 1961; 1965; 1969).

VARIABLES (with Source)

1. Expenditure variables as expenditure per 1000: A.
2. Expenditure variables as rates levied per head: B.
3. Unit costs for individual services: A.
4. Percentage of service clients served (children in care, elderly in homes, pupils): A.
5. Rent as a proportion of Housing Revenue Account income: A.
6. Total net rate- and grant-born expenditure per head: B.
7. Total rate-born expenditure per head: B.
8. Units of local authority built housing as a proportion of total borough households: G, D.*
9. Population per police officer: A.
10. Population per fireman: A, K.
11. Product of the penny rate: A.
12. Net outstanding debt per head: A, K.
13. Rateable value per head: K.
14. Rate in the pound: K.
15. Population: K.
16. Density per acre: A.
17. Percentage of Labour Party seats on Council: K.*
18. Interparty competition on Council: K.*
19. Percentage of unopposed seats in the Council election: H.
20. Percentage of registered voters who voted for contested seats in the local election: H.
21. Percentage of population under age 15: C, D.
22. Percentage of population over age 65: C, D, A.
23. Net migration balance: C, D.*
24. Within-area migration: C, D.
25. Proportion of population with Commonwealth country birthplace: C, D.*
26. Socioeconomic status (based on occupation): C, D.*

---

*These variables involved certain mathematical computations on the published data.

27. Proportion of households with the four standard amenities: C, D.
28. Proportion of males over age 25 whose terminal-educational age was either under 15 or over 24: C.
29. Ratio of privately owned automobiles to total population: D.
30. Proportion of housing built in the county borough, 1960-1965, that was built by the local authority: G.
31. Percentage of total population in room density which is greater than 1.0 per room: D.
32. Percentage of total rateable value in domestic hereditaments: E.
33. Percentage of domestic rateable value in units whose value is greater than 100: E.

A SELECTED BIBLIOGRAPHY

A SELECTED BIBLIOGRAPHY

Analytical and General Works

ALLISON, G. "Conceptual Models and the Cuban Missile Crisis," *APSR,* 58 (September, 1969), pp. 689-718.

ALLISON, G. *The Essence of Decision.* Boston: Little, Brown, 1971.

ANDERSON, J. E. *Public Policy-Making.* New York: Praeger, 1975.

BARBER, J. *Power in Committees: An Experiment in the Governmental Process.* Chicago: Rand McNally, 1966.

BARTLETT, R. *Economic Foundations of Political Power.* New York: Free Press, 1973.

BIDDLE, B. and E. THOMAS, eds. *Role Theory: Concepts and Research.* New York: Wiley, 1966.

BLALOCK, H. "Correlated Independent Variables: The Problem of Multicollinearity," *Social Forces,* 42 (December 1963), pp. 233-237.

BLALOCK, H. *Causal Inferences in Non-Experimental Research.* Chapel Hill: Univ. of North Carolina Press, 1964.

BRAYBROOKE, D. and C. LINDBLOM. *A Strategy of Decision.* New York: Free Press, 1963.

COHEN, M., J. MARCH, and J. OLSEN. "A Garbage Can Model of Organizational Choice," *Administrative Science Quarterly,* 17 (March 1972), pp. 1-25.

CYERT, R. and J. MARCH. *A Behavioral Theory of the Firm.* New Jersey: Prentice-Hall, 1963.

DEUTSCH, K. *The Nerves of Government.* New York: Free Press, 1966.

DOWNS, A. *Inside Bureaucracy.* Boston: Little, Brown, 1967.

DRAPER, N. and R. SMITH. *Applied Regression Analysis.* New York: Wiley, 1966.

ETZIONI, A. *A Comparative Analysis of Complex Organization.* New York: Free Press, 1961.

EULAU, H. *Micro-Macro Political Analysis.* Chicago: Aldine, 1969.

HEMPEL, C. *Aspects of Scientific Explanation and Other Essays in the Philosophy of Science.* New York: Free Press, 1965.

JONES, C. O. *An Introduction to the Study of Public Policy.* Belmont, Ca.: Wadsworth, 1970.

KALLEBERG, A. "The Logic of Comparison," *World Politics,* 19 (January 1966), pp. 235-246.

KAPLAN, A. *The Conduct of Inquiry*. San Francisco: Chandler, 1964.

KATZ, D. and R. KAHN. *The Social Psychology of Organizations*. New York: Wiley, 1966.

LINDBLOM, C. "The Science of 'Muddling Through,'" *Public Administration Review*, 19 (Spring 1959), pp. 79-88.

LINDBLOM, C. *The Policy-Making Process*. Englewood Cliffs, N.J.: Prentice-Hall, 1968.

MARCH, J. and H. SIMON. *Organizations*. New York: Wiley, 1958.

MERTON, R. *Social Theory and Social Structure*. New York: Free Press, 1957.

MEYER, L. *Comparative Political Inquiry*. Homewood, Ill.: Dorsey, 1972.

MITCHELL, W. and J. *Political Analysis and Public Policy*. Chicago: Rand McNally, 1969.

PRZEWORSKI, A. and H. TEUNE. *The Logic of Comparative Social Inquiry*. New York: Wiley-Interscience, 1970.

SHARKANSKY, I. *The Routines of Politics*. New York: Van Nostrand Reinhold, 1970.

THIBAUT, J. and H. KELLEY. *The Social Psychology of Groups*. New York: Wiley, 1961.

THOMPSON, W. *A Preface to Urban Economics*. Baltimore: Johns Hopkins Univ. Press, 1965.

VAN DYKE, V. *Political Science: A Philosophical Analysis*. Stanford: Univ. Press, 1960.

VERBA, S. "Some Dilemmas in Comparative Research," *World Politics,* XX (October 1967), pp. 111-127.

WEBB, E., D. CAMPBELL, R. SCHWARTZ, and L. SECHREST. *Unobtrusive Measures: Non-reactive Research in the Social Sciences.* Chicago: Rand-McNally, 1966.

WILLIAMS, O. and C. ADRIAN. *Four Cities: A Study of Comparative Policy-Making.* Philadelphia: Univ. of Pennsylvania Press, 1963.

Works Related to British Central and Local Government

BEER, S. *British Politics in a Collectivist Age*. New York: Vintage, 1969.

BIRCH, A. H. *Small Town Politics*. London: Oxford Univ. Press, 1959.

BOADEN, N. "Innovation and Change in English Local Government." *Political Studies,* 19 (December 1971), pp. 416-429.

BOADEN, N. and R. ALFORD. "Sources of Diversity in English Local Government," *Public Administration,* 47 (Summer 1968), pp. 203-224.

BULPITT, J. G. *Party Politics in English Local Government*. London: Longmans, 1967.

CROSS, C. A. *Principles of Local Government Law*. London: Sweet and Maxwell, 1966.

DAVIES, B. *Social Needs and Resources in Local Services*. London: Joseph, 1968.

DEARLOVE, J. *The Politics of Policy in Local Government*. London: Cambridge Univ. Press, 1973.

ECKSTEIN, H. "The British Political System," in *Patterns of Government*. Edited by S. BEER, A. ULAM, and N. WAHL. New York: Random House, 1962.

FRIEND, J. K. and W. N. JESSOP. *Local Government and Strategic Choice*. London: Tavistock, 1969.

GREENWOOD, R., C. R. HININGS, and S. RANSOM. "Contingency Theory and the Organization of Local Authorities: Part 1. Differentiation and Integration; Part II. Contingencies and Structures," *Public Administration*, 53 (Spring 1975), pp. 1-23; (Summer 1975), pp. 169-190.

GREENWOOD, R. and J. D. STEWART, eds. *Corporate Planning in English Local Government: An Analysis with Readings, 1967-72*. London: Knight, 1975.

GREGORY, R. G. "Local Elections and the 'Role of Anticipated Reactions,'" *Political Studies*, XVII (March 1969), pp. 31-47.

GRIFFITH, J.A.G. *Central Departments and Local Authorities*. London: Allen and Unwin, 1966.

HAMPTON, W. *Democracy and Community*. London: Oxford Univ. Press, 1970.

JACKSON, R. M. *The Machinery of Local Government*. London: Macmillan, 1958.

JACKSON, W. E. *Local Government in England and Wales*. London: Penguin, 1966.

The Labour Party. *Local Government Handbook for England and Wales*. London: Victoria House, 1967.

MACKINTOSH, J. P. *The Devolution of Power: Local Democracy, Regionalism, and Nationalism*. London: Penguin, 1968.

MOSER, C. A. and W. SCOTT. *British Towns: A Statistical Study of Their Social and Economic Differences*. London: Oliver and Boyd, 1961.

NEWTON, K. *Second City Politics*. London: Oxford Univ. Press, 1976.

REES, W. and T. SMITH. *Town Councillors*. London: Acton Society Trust, 1964.

RHODES, G. *Town Government in South-east England*. London: London School of Economics and Political Science, 1968.

RICHARDS, P. G. *The New Local Government System*. London: Allen and Unwin, 1966.

ROSE, R. *Politics in England*. Boston: Little, Brown, 1964.

STANYER, J. *County Government in England and Wales*. London: Routledge and Kegan Paul, 1967.

WARREN, J. H. *The English Local Government System*. London: Allen and Unwin, 1962.

West Midland Study Group. *Local Government and Central Control*. London: Routledge, 1956.

WISEMAN, H. V. *Local Government at Work*. London: Routledge, 1967.

WISEMAN, H. V., ed. *Local Government in England 1958-69*. London: Routledge & Kegan Paul, 1970.

Works Related to Political Economy and Resource Allocation

GREAT BRITAIN

ALT, J. E. "Some Social and Political Correlates of County Borough Expenditures," *British Journal of Political Science*, 1 (1971), pp. 49-62.

ALT, J. E. "Politics and Expenditure Models," *Policy and Politics*, 5 (March 1977), pp. 83-92.

ASHFORD, D. E. "The Effects of Central Finance on the British Local Government System," *British Journal of Political Science*, 4 (July 1974), pp. 305-322.

ASHFORD, D. E. "Resources, Spending and Party Politics in British Local Government," *Administration and Society*, 6 (November 1975), pp. 286-311.

ASHFORD, D., R. BERNE, and R. SCHRAMM. "The Expenditure-Financing Decision in British Local Government," *Policy and Politics*, 5 (September 1976), pp. 5-24.

BOADEN, N. *Urban Policy-Making*. London: Cambridge Univ. Press, 1971.

Conservative Research Department. *The Finance of Local Government*, Crawley: Burridge, 1961.

DANZIGER, J. N. *Budgetary Decision-Making in a Local Authority*. Unpublished M.A. Thesis. Univ. of Sussex, 1968.

DANZIGER, J. N. *Budget-Making and Expenditure Variations in English County Boroughs*. Unpublished Ph.D. Dissertation. Stanford Univ., 1974.

DANZIGER, J. N. "Comparing Approaches to the Study of Financial Resource Allocation," in C. LISKE, W. LOEHR, and J. McCAMANT, eds., *Comparative Public Policy: Issues, Theories, and Methods*. New York: Wiley-Halsted, 1975, pp. 55-85.

DANZIGER, J. N. "Assessing Incrementalism in British Municipal Budgeting," *British Journal of Political Science*, 6 (July 1976), pp. 335-350.

DANZIGER, J. N. "Twenty-Six Outputs in Search of a Taxonomy," *Policy and Politics*, 5 (December 1976), pp. 201-212.

DANZIGER, J. N. "A Comment on 'The Politics of the Budgetary Process in English Local Government,'" *Political Studies*, XXVI (March 1978).

DAVIES, B. "Social Service Studies and the Explanation of Policy Outcomes," *Policy and Politics*, 5 (March 1977), pp. 41-59.

GREENWOOD, R., C. R. HININGS, and S. RANSOM. "The Politics of the Budgetary Process in English Local Government," *Political Studies*, XXV (March 1977), pp. 25-47.

HICKS, J. R. and U. K. *Standards of Local Expenditure*. London: Cambridge Univ. Press, 1943.

The Institute of Municipal Treasurers and Accountants. *Local Expenditure and Exchequer Grants*. A Research Study. London: MacKay, 1965.

JUDGE, K. *Rationing Social Services*. London: Heinemann, 1977.

KING, D. N. "Why do Local Authority Rate Poundages Differ?" *Public Administration*, 51 (Summer 1973), pp. 165-173.

KITCHING, W.A.C. *The Finance of Local Government*. London: Allen and Unwin, 1962.

MARSHALL, A. H. *Local Authorities: Internal Financial Control*. London: Institute of Public Administration, 1936.

MARSHALL, A. H. *Financial Administration in Local Government*. London: Allen and Unwin, 1962.

NEVITT, D. A. "The Burden of Domestic Rates," *Policy and Politics*, 2 (January 1973), pp. 1-25.

NEWTON, K. "Community Performance in Britain." *Current Sociology*, 22 (March 1976), pp. 49-86.

NEWTON, K. and L. J. SHARPE. "Local Outputs Research: Some Reflections and Proposals," *Policy and Politics*, 5 (March 1977), pp. 61-82.

NICHOLSON, R. J. and N. TOPHAM. "Investment Decisions and the Size of Local Authorities," *Policy and Politics,* 1 (September 1972), pp. 23-44.

OLIVER, F. R., and J. STANYER. "Some Aspects of the Financial Behaviour of the County Boroughs," *Public Administration,* 47 (Summer 1969), pp. 169-184.

PEACOCK, A. and J. WISEMAN. *The Growth of Public Expenditure in the United Kingdom.* Princeton: Princeton Univ. Press, 1961.

The Royal Institute of Public Administration, A Study Group. *Budgeting in Public Authorities.* London: Allen and Unwin, 1959.

STOREY, D. R. "Statistical Analysis of Educational Expenditure in County Councils," *Local Government Studies* (January 1975), pp. 39-57.

AMERICAN FEDERAL AND STATE

ANTON, T. *The Politics of State Expenditure in Illinois.* Urbana: Univ. of Illinois Press, 1960.

CNUDDE, C. and D. McCRONE. "Party Competition and Welfare Policies in the American States," *American Political Science Review,* 63 (September 1969), pp. 838-866.

DAVIS, O., M.A.H. DEMPSTER, and A. WILDAVSKY. "A Theory of the Budgetary Process," *American Political Science Review,* 60, No. 3 (September 1966), pp. 529-547.

DAVIS, O., M.A.H. DEMPSTER, and A. WILDAVSKY. "Towards a Predictive Theory of Government Expenditure: U.S. Domestic Appropriations," *British Journal of Political Science,* 4 (1975), pp. 419-452.

DAWSON, R. and J. ROBINSON. "Inter-Party Competition, Economic Variables, and Welfare Policies in the American States," *Journal of Politics,* 25, No. 2 (1963), pp. 265-289.

DYE, T. *Politics, Economics, and the Public.* Chicago: Rand McNally, 1966.

FENNO, R. *The Power of the Purse.* Boston: Little, Brown, 1966.

HOFFERBERT, R. "The Relationship between Public Policy and Some Structural and Environmental Variables in the American States," *American Political Science Review,* 60 (1966), pp. 73-82.

HOFFERBERT, R. and I. SHARKANSKY. "Dimensions of State Politics, Economics, and Public Policies," *American Political Science Review,* 63 (September 1969), pp. 867-879.

JACOB, H. and M. LIPSKY. "Outputs, Structure and Power: An Assessment of Changes in the Study of State and Local Politics," *Journal of Politics,* 30 (1969), pp. 510-538.

LYDEN, F. and E. MILLER. *Planning Programming Budgeting.* Chicago: Markham, 1972.

NOVICK, D., ed. *Program Budgeting.* Cambridge: Harvard Univ. Press, 1967.

PYHRR, P. "The Zero-Base Approach to Government Budgeting," *Public Administration Review,* 37 (January/February 1977), pp. 1-8.

RAKOFF, S. and G. SCHAFFER. "Politics, Policy and Political Science: Theoretical Alternatives," *Politics and Society,* 1 (1970), pp. 51-77.

SCHMITTER, P. "The Comparative Analysis of Public Policy: Outputs, Outcomes and Impacts." Paper presented at SSRC, Committee on Comparative Politics Planning, Conference on Comparative Analysis of Public Policy Performance, Princeton, N.J., 25-28 January 1972.

SHARKANSKY, I. "Four Agencies and an Appropriations Subcommittee: A Comparative Study of Budget Strategies," *Midwest Journal of Political Science,* 9, No. 3 (August 1965), pp. 254-281.

SHARKANSKY, I. "Government Expenditure and Public Service," *American Political Science Review,* 61 (December 1967), pp. 1066-1077.

SHARKANSKY, I. "Agency Requests, Gubernatorial Support, and Budget Success in State Legislatures," *American Political Science Review,* 62 (December 1968), pp. 1220-1231.

SHARKANSKY, I. *Spending in the American States.* Chicago: Rand McNally, 1968.

SHARKANSKY, I. *The Politics of Taxing and Spending.* New York: Bobbs-Merrill, 1969.

SHARKANSKY, I. "Economic Theories of Public Policy: Resource-Policy and Need-Policy Linkages between Income and Welfare Benefits," *Midwest Journal of Political Science,* 15, No. 4 (November 1971), pp. 722-740.

WILDAVSKY, A. "Political Implications of Budgetary Reform," *Public Administration Review,* XXI (Autumn 1961), pp. 183-190.

WILDAVSKY, A. *The Politics of the Budgetary Process.* Boston: Little, Brown, 1964.

WILDAVSKY, A. *Budgeting: A Comparative Theory of Budgetary Processes.* Boston: Little, Brown, 1975.

WILDAVSKY, A. and A. HAMMOND. "Comprehensive Versus Incremental Budgeting in the Department of Agriculture," *Administrative Science Quarterly,* 18 (1965-1966), pp. 321-346.

WINTERS, R. and B. FRY. "The Politics of Redistribution," *American Political Science Review,* 64 (June 1970), pp. 508-522.

AMERICAN MUNICIPAL

BAHL, R. and R. SAUNDERS. "Fabricant's Determinants After Twenty Years," *The American Economist,* 10 (Spring 1966), pp. 27-42.

BRAZER, H. *City Expenditures in the United States.* New York: National Bureau of Economic Research, 1959.

CAMPBELL, A. and S. SACHS. *Metropolitan America.* New York: Free Press, 1967.

CLARKE, J. "Environment, Process and Policy: A Reconsideration," *American Political Science Review,* 63 (December 1969), pp. 1172-1182.

CRECINE, J. *Governmental Problem-Solving: A Computer Simulation Model of Municipal Budgeting.* Chicago: Rand McNally, 1969.

DAVIS, O. and G. HAINES. "A Political Approach to a Theory of Public Expenditure: The Case of Municipalities," *National Tax Journal,* XIX (September 1966), pp. 259-275.

EYESTONE, R. *Political Economy: Politics and Policy Analysis.* Chicago: Markham, 1972.

FENTON, J. and D. CHAMBERLAYNE. "The Literature Dealing with the Relationships between Political Processes, Socio-economic Conditions and Public Policies in the American States: A Bibliographical Essay," *Polity,* I (1969), pp. 388-404.

FISHER, G. "Determinants of State and Local Government Expenditure," *National Tax Journal,* 14 (1961), pp. 349-355.

A Selected Bibliography

FRIED, R. C. "Comparative Urban Policy and Performance," in *The Handbook of Political Science*. Edited by F. I. GREENSTEIN and N. W. POLSBY. Reading, Mass.: Addison-Wesley, 1976.

GERWIN, D. "A Process Model of Budgeting in a Public School System," *Management Science,* 15, No. 7 (March 1969), pp. 33-46.

GERWIN, D. "Towards a Theory of Public Budgetary Decision-Making," *Administrative Science Quarterly,* 14, No. 1 (March 1969), pp. 33-46.

MARGOLIS, J., ed. *The Public Economy of Urban Communities*. Washington: Resources for the Future, 1965.

MASOTTI, L. and D. BOWEN. "Communities and Budgets: The Sociology of Municipal Expenditure," in *Community Politics: A Behavioral Approach*. Edited by BONJEAN, CLARK, and LINEBERRY. New York: Free Press, 1971.

MELTSNER, A. *The Politics of City Revenue*. Berkeley: Univ. of California Press, 1971.

MORSS, E. "Some Thoughts on the Determinants of State and Local Expenditure," *National Tax Journal,* XIX (March 1966), pp. 95-103.

PULSIPHER, A. and J. WEATHERBY. "Malapportionment, Party Competition, and the Functional Distribution of Governmental Expenditures," *American Political Science Review,* 62 (December 1968), pp. 1207-1219.

WILLIAMS, O., H. HERMAN, C. LIEBMAN, and T. DYE. *Suburban Differences and Metropolitan Policies: A Philadelphia Story*. Philadelphia: Univ. of Pennsylvania Press, 1965.

INDEX

INDEX

ABOUT THE AUTHOR

JAMES N. DANZIGER is Assistant Professor of Political Science in the School of Social Sciences at the University of California, Irvine. He is also a Research Political Scientist for the Public Policy Research Organization at U. C. Irvine. He was a Marshall Scholar at the University of Sussex 1966-1968, a Foreign Area Fellow to Western Europe 1970-1972, and a German Marshall Fund Fellow to the ECPR Berlin sessions in 1977. His published work has appeared in a variety of social science journals such as the *British Journal of Political Science, Public Administration Review, Policy and Politics, Political Studies,* and *Urban Systems.*